DUTY

A FATHER, HIS SON, AND THE MAN WHO WON THE WAR

DUTY

A FATHER, HIS SON, AND THE MAN WHO WON THE WAR

BOB GREENE

HarperLargePrint
An Imprint of HarperCollins*Publishers*

A hardcover edition of this book was published in 2000 by William Morrow, *An Imprint of* HarperCollins *Publishers*.

FIRST LARGE PRINT EDITION

The Library of Congress has catalogued the hardcover edition as follows:

ISBN 0-06-019755-2 Large Print

00 01 02 03 04 10 9 8 7 6 5 4 3 2 1

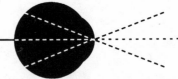

This Large Print Book carries the
Seal of Approval of N.A.V.H.

For Tim Greene

ONE

The morning after the last meal I ever ate with my father, I finally met the man who won the war.

It was from my father that I had first heard about the man. The event—the dropping of the atomic bomb on Hiroshima—I of course knew about; like all children of the post–World War II generation, my classmates and I had learned about it in elementary school.

But the fact that the man who dropped the bomb—the pilot who flew the *Enola Gay* to Japan, who carried out the single most violent act in the history of mankind and thus brought World War II to an end—the fact that he lived quietly in the same town where I had grown up . . . that piece of knowledge came from my father.

It was never stated in an especially dramatic way. My dad would come home from work—from downtown Columbus, in central Ohio—and say: "I was buying some shirts today, and Paul Tibbets was in the next aisle, buying ties."

They never met; my father never said a word to him. I sensed that my father might have been a little reluctant, maybe even a touch embarrassed; he had been a soldier with an infantry division, Tibbets had been a combat pilot, all these years had passed since the war and now here they both were, two all-but-anonymous businessmen in a sedate, landlocked town in a country at peace . . . what was my dad supposed to say? How was he supposed to begin the conversation?

Yet there was always a certain sound in his voice at the dinner table. "Paul Tibbets was in the next aisle buying ties. . . ." The sound in my dad's voice told me—as if I needed reminding—that the story of his life had reached its most indelible and meaningful moments in the years of the war, the years before I was born.

Those dinner-table conversations were long ago, though; they were in the years when my dad was still vital, in good health, in the prime of his adult years, not yet ready to leave the world. I had all but forgotten the conversations—at least the specifics of them, other than the occasional mentions of Tibbets.

Now my dad was dying. We had dinner in his bedroom—he would not, it would turn out, again be able to sit in a chair and eat after this night—and the next morning I told him that I had somewhere to go and that I would be back in a few hours, and I went to find Paul Tibbets. Something told me that it was important.

TWO

It wasn't the first time I had tried. In fact, I had been attempting on and off to talk with Paul Tibbets for more than twenty years.

I had left Columbus to become a newspaperman in Chicago when I was in my early twenties; as I became a reporter, and then a syndicated columnist, I traveled around the world in search of stories, and, as most reporters do, met any number of well-known people as I pursued those stories. As often as not, the people were only too willing to talk; celebrity is embraced by most upon whom it is bestowed, even those who protest that it is a bother. Whether a famous athlete or an ambitious politician or a movie star or a newsmaker just feeling the spotlight's heat for the first time, the people who get a taste of fame often seem to crave it in a way that can fairly be described as addictive. There can never be enough; when the light turns away for even a second or two, some of the most famous men and women in the world seem almost to panic. They need to feel it constantly.

Which is what made me so curious about Paul Tibbets. He had been the central figure in the most momentous event of the Twentieth Century; what he had done changed the world in ways so profound that philosophers and theologians will be discussing and debating it as long as mankind exists. "The man who won the war," of course, is shorthand—no one person accomplished that. But it is shorthand based on fact—Tibbets was the man put in charge of preparing a top-secret military unit to deliver the bomb, he was the person who assembled and trained that unit, and when the time came to do what had never in the history of mankind been done, to fly an atomic bomb over an enemy nation and then drop the bomb on a city below, Tibbets did not delegate. He climbed into the cockpit and flew the bomb to Japan.

But he was seldom spoken about; the war ended in 1945, and by the 1960s his was a name that few people seemed even to know. Part of this was doubtless because of the deep ambivalence many Americans felt about the end of the war. Yes, they were grateful that it had ended, and that the United States and the Allies had won. But the death and devastation from the bomb—the unprecedented human suffering caused by the unleashing of the nuclear fire—was something that people instinctively chose not to celebrate. Hiroshima was not the stuff of holidays.

So I would hear my father talk of seeing Paul Tibbets here and there in Columbus, and when I was a young reporter my journalistic instincts were to try to speak with him, to secure an interview. By this time—by the early 1970s—Tibbets was running a corporate-jet-for-hire service in central Ohio.

I wrote him letters, I left messages at his office—not just once, but periodically over the course of two decades I tried. I never received an answer. He didn't decline, he didn't explain, he didn't offer reasons. He simply didn't respond at all. Never. Not a word.

By the autumn of 1998, my father had been dying for several months. It was a word my family avoided—"dying" was not something we said in his presence, or very often in the presence of one another—but we all knew it, and I think he knew it best.

I was covering a court case in Wisconsin, and during a break I called my office in Chicago and the person who gave me the message was as careful as possible in how she told me: "Your mother called and said your father has been taken to the hospital, but she said to make sure to tell you it's nothing to panic about. She said they're just taking a close look at him."

Within days that had changed. My sister, who lived in Nevada, had flown to Columbus to help my mom. My father was home from the hospital, but he was not feeling strong enough to talk on the telephone. Another phone call from my sister: "Daddy wants you boys to come."

That day. Right away.

"I think he wants to say goodbye," my sister said.

My plane sat on the runway at O'Hare in Chicago for hours, its takeoff delayed due to some mechanical trouble or other. My brother was able to get to Ohio more quickly from Colorado than I was from Illinois. No working phones on the plane; no way to get word out, or to find out what was happening in my parents' home.

It was well after midnight when I landed at Port Columbus. I didn't call my parents' house—I didn't want to wake my father if he was asleep, and if the news was very bad, I wanted to hear it in person, not over the phone—so I just got in a cab and gave directions. The lights were all burning, at an hour when they never did.

My mom, my sister, my brother. All awake.

"Go on in and talk to him," my mom said.

Some moments, not a word is required. And my father and I had never talked all that easily anyway. I walked into the bedroom, seeing him smaller than I ever remembered him, gray and all but motionless in bed. My father had always been a man who led with a joke; he could make the soberest moment funny, especially when he needed to deflect matters of gravity.

Not tonight.

"Hello, Bob," he said. "Thanks for coming."

Too direct. Too unlike him.

"You've never seen your old man like this, have you?" he said.

I didn't ask him how he was doing. Having to

answer that one was not what he needed this night. *Thanks for coming.* That's how he was doing.

Back in July, just a few months earlier, if you looked closely enough you could see it in his eyes.

He wasn't saying anything out loud about feeling especially ill. He seldom did complain, during all the years that diabetes ruled his life. But at the reunion of our immediate family that we held at my parents' house in July, he would sit off by himself and sort of look into the distance. He was present—but for long spans, it seemed that he was barely there. There is a country song with the lyric: *I can't see a single storm cloud in the sky, but I sure can smell the rain. . . .*

The rain was somewhere behind his eyes. A dozen family members were in Columbus for the reunion, more than could fit into my parents' house, so some of us were staying at a motel next to the airport.

One summer morning, before it was time to go to the house, I noticed something across a two-lane access road that separated Port Columbus from our motel: a modest little museum in a converted hangar, a place with a sign saying that it was the Ohio History of Flight Museum. I walked over to take a look.

I was the only visitor. Three bucks to get in—

there were antique planes in the hangar, and air-plane engines, and photos of Ohio's relationship with air travel. Which is considerable. The Wright brothers came from Ohio, and John Glenn, and Neil Armstrong—from man's first successful powered venture off the ground and into the sky, to man's first step onto the surface of the moon, Ohio may be the state that has had the most significant influence on flying.

The man who had sold me my ticket was strolling around the empty place. I said to him: "Does Mr. Tibbets come around much?"

"Not that often," the man said. "Once in a while."

I supposed it figured. Paul Tibbets had been thirty years old when he flew the bomb to Japan. Now, if I was doing the calculations in my head correctly, he was eighty-three, the same age as my father. With all the renewed appreciation that the World War II generation was receiving, people were noticing something: The Americans who fought that war didn't go around telling stories about themselves. It made a certain sense that Tibbets would be a sporadic visitor here at best.

Outside the roadside air museum, it was a warm and beautiful summer morning in central Ohio. Land of the free. . . .

On October 20, my mother's seventy-ninth birthday, I was back in Columbus. She was determined to have her birthday dinner the same place she had eaten virtually every meal for the last two months: in the bedroom she shared with my father. If he couldn't leave to eat, then she wasn't going to either.

We ordered from a deliver-in place. My father, with some effort, had been moved from his bed into a nearby chair, and for about twenty minutes he was able to sit up and join us. He seemed almost ashamed of his halting, shaky motions; he had always been a physically strong man, and the fact that it was now a task for him to move a spoon from the plate to his mouth was something he was more than aware we were noticing.

My mother told him that his friend Bill Ehrman, who lived in Hawaii, had called that day to ask how he was doing. My dad smiled at that; Ehrman was a man with whom he had served in the war, and I never heard Ehrman's name mentioned without seeing a look of pleasure on my father's face. His friends from the war years seemed to occupy a place in his life that no other people did.

After dinner he fell asleep immediately. The meal had been the last time I would see him outside his bed.

I went into the room in my parents' house where they displayed the only visible artifact from World War II: an oil painting of my dad as a young soldier, painted, or so I had always been told, by a fellow American soldier in Italy who enjoyed doing portraits of his comrades. Growing up, when I had looked at the painting of my father, he had seemed so seasoned, so experienced. Now, looking at the portrait, I realized that he had been in his twenties when it was painted. On this night—as I looked at the portrait, with him sleeping not so many feet away—I was fifty-one. The man in uniform in the painting still seemed older than I was.

It was the next morning that I went to see Tibbets. I had written a column during the summer in which I mentioned my visit to the Ohio air museum. Soon after, I had received a call from a man named Gerry Newhouse, who said he was a friend of Tibbets. Someone in Texas had sent Newhouse a copy of the column from a paper down there, and Newhouse had showed it to Tibbets.

"He liked what you said about the World War II generation not going around bragging about themselves," Newhouse said.

I said that I had been trying to get a chance to meet Tibbets for the last twenty years.

"Well, I think he'd be happy to say hello to you," Newhouse said. "Do you ever get to Columbus these days?"

I said my dad hadn't been doing so well. I said I had a feeling that I'd be in town quite a bit.

• • •

When I was a teenager, all of my friends lived in houses, except for one: a boy named Allen Schulman, whose family lived in the only high-rise apartment building in Columbus at that time, a place called the Park Towers. It was big-time, for central Ohio; it actually had a doorman—a dapper young fellow by the name of Jesse Harrell. Jesse knew about everything we did, especially everything we did wrong.

Now, more than thirty years later, I arrived at the front door of the Park Towers. Gerry Newhouse had an office on the first floor; he and Tibbets were going to have lunch together that day, and they were going to meet at Newhouse's office before going to the restaurant. I had called Newhouse to say I was in town, and he had said to drop by.

At the front door was Jesse. I knew him before he knew me. Thirty years and more at that front door; the dapper young man was now sixty. "You ever see your friend Allen?" he said, and when I said that yes, sometimes I did, Jesse said, "He never comes back here. There's not a person in this building who was here when you all were kids."

He told me where Newhouse's office was, and I went back and introduced myself, and in a few minutes Tibbets arrived.

I'm not sure what I expected. He was a compact man with a full head of white hair, wearing a plaid shirt and well-used slacks. Hearing aids were in both of his ears; I sensed immediately that I would have to lean close to him in order to be heard. He could have been any of a thousand men in their eighties in the middle of Ohio. You wouldn't know him in a line at the grocery store.

I told him how pleased I was to meet him—and how long I had wanted to get the chance.

His answer offered a glimpse of the reasons behind his reticence.

"I've heard rumors about myself over the years," he said. "I've heard rumors that I had gone crazy, or that I was dead."

Evidently that is what people had assumed: that the man responsible for all that death must inevitably have gone out of his mind.

I didn't know where to take this—I didn't know whether it was an indication that he wasn't in the mood for conversation—so we just made some small talk for a short while, about Ohio and the Park Towers and the weather on the streets outside, and I told Tibbets that I knew he and his friend had lunch plans, and that I didn't want to hold them up.

"That's all right," Tibbets said. "I'm not that hungry yet. We can talk some."

THREE

Do people know my name?" Tibbets asked.
He was repeating the question I had just asked him.

A soft, private look crossed his face.

"They don't need to know my name," he said.

The deed he had carried out was one of the most famous the world has ever known; it will be talked about in terms of fear and awe forever. He, though, even here in the town where he lived, was not as famous as the local television weatherman.

"People knowing my name isn't important at all," he said. "It's more important—it was more important then, and it's more important now—that they know the name of my airplane. And that they understand the history of what happened.

"Although sometimes I think that no one really understands the history."

And so we started to talk. Neither of us knew it that day, but it would be the first of many conversations—about the war, about the men and women who lived through it, about their lives, and the lives of their sons and daughters: the lives of those of us who came after them, who inherited the world that they saved for us.

As I sat with Tibbets that first day—thinking of my father in his bed just a few miles away—it occurred to me that Eisenhower was dead, Patton was dead, Marshall was dead, MacArthur was dead. And here was Tibbets, telling me in the first person the story of how the great and terrible war came to an end.

On this day—the day I met Tibbets—all of his stories were war stories. That would change; gradually the stories would expand in context, would begin to explain to me certain things not just about this man, but about the generation of men and women who are leaving us now every day. It is a wrenching thing, to watch them go. As the men and women of the World War II generation die, it is for their children the most intensely personal experience imaginable—and at the same time a sweeping and historic one, being witnessed by tens of millions of sons and daughters, sons and daughters who feel helpless to stop the inevitable.

For me, as my father, day by day, slipped away, the overwhelming feeling was that a safety net was being removed—a safety net that had been there since the day I was born, a safety net I was often blithely unaware of. That's what the best safety nets do—they allow you to forget they're there. No generation has ever given its children a sturdier and more reliable safety net than the one our parents' generation gave to us.

The common experience that wove the net was

their war. And as I began to listen to Tibbets—to hear his stories, later to question him about the America that preceded and followed the war from which his stories came—I realized anew that so many of us only now, only at the very end, are beginning to truly know our fathers and mothers. It was as if constructing that safety net for their children was their full-time job, and that finally, as they leave us, we are beginning to understand the forces that made them the way they were.

Tibbets began to speak, and as I listened I thought I could hear a rustle of something behind the words—I thought I could hear the whisper of a generation saying goodbye to its children.

When I was very young, my father told me that he wanted me to come out to a local air base with him.

We went; by this time the war had been over for seven or eight years, he was not a soldier in uniform but a businessman in a suit of clothing. Which in a way, in the 1950s, made his garments just as uniform as what he had worn in the Army; he had automatically melded into the sea of men in suits who worked in the offices of the post-war United States.

That day, or so I recall, we went out to the air base, where it was stiflingly hot. The occasion was the unveiling of some sort of new fighter plane. A military honor guard stood surrounding the plane, which was covered in cloth prior to the unveiling. The young military men were perspiring heavily, unprotected from the sun.

There were some speeches from military officers, and some photo-taking with local elected officials, and on one side of the rope the honor guard stood at full attention, while on the other side those of us in the audience stood watching. Almost certainly the majority of the audience members were people very much like my father—men who had come back from World War II, who were civilians now, but who felt somehow obliged to be here to watch this ceremony. The introduction of a new plane that would protect America, and protect our hometown.

Suddenly, with no warning, one of the young soldiers who had been standing at attention fell face-first onto the hard runway. There had been no sign that he was about to lose consciousness; he had not swayed or called out for help. He just went straight down, his face making a sickening sound as it hit the cement.

"He remained at attention the whole time," I remember my father saying, with an admiring tone in his voice.

I recall being frightened for the young soldier; I recall thinking that he was dead. Only after medics had revived him and helped him to his feet, only after I could see for myself that he had fainted and was going to be all right, was I able to take my eyes off him.

But I can still see him falling. And I can still hear my father's voice, with something like pride in it, and a sense of identification:

The soldier had remained at attention.

As Paul Tibbets began to tell me his story, I sat as close to him as I could. It became evident within minutes that when I wanted to ask him a question, I would have to speak loudly, and with care about pronunciation. His hearing—there was no mistaking this—was all but gone. So I looked him in the eyes, and listened to every word, and did my best to make sure he didn't have to ask me to repeat my own words twice.

"Sometimes I think that no one really understands. . . ." he said.

And so it began.

FOUR

The airplane, he said, had been named in honor of his mother.

"She's the one who said it was all right for me to fly," he said. "My father didn't. He hated airplanes, and he didn't want me to go near one. In my father's mind, I was supposed to be a doctor. He sort of waved me off, and when he understood that I really wanted to be a flier, he said, 'If you want to kill yourself, go ahead.' But my mother understood. She encouraged me."

Thus, when he was preparing for the flight that would change the history of the world, the name he chose for the airplane—the name that was painted on the nose—was her name: his mother's first and middle names.

"I thought it was a good name for the plane, because it was a name no one had ever heard before," he said. "I could be pretty sure that no other B-29 would be named *Enola Gay*."

Some people, more than half a century later, still are appalled by what his government asked him to do. Some people are deeply proud and grateful. Others are ambivalent and, all these years later, confused. Tibbets himself is the only one who knows the whole story—and he has never talked much about it. His life—like the lives of so many of the men who served in the same war, and who unlike him will never be noticed by history—has been devoid of much publicity seeking or self-promotion.

Unlike the other men, though—men like my father, men whose names did not make the newspaper during their war—Tibbets was, indeed, asked to do something monumental. I told him that I was interested in the specifics of it—the things that preceded the politics and the controversy: the details. When the 9,700-pound bomb dropped out of the belly of his plane and began its descent onto the city of Hiroshima, what did the plane do—how did the B-29 react to all that weight suddenly being freed?

"The seat slapped me on the ass," Tibbets said.

A blunt and purposely inelegant phrase—and a rather mild one to describe what happened at that particular moment in the story of mankind.

"We'd been all through it," he said. "We knew that if everything went as planned, the bomb would explode forty-three seconds after we released it from the plane.

"In order to get away from there quickly enough that we would not be directly over the blast, I had to make a diving turn to the right, away from the area at an angle of 160 degrees. We were flying with quite a center of gravity—when you drop something that weighs almost 10,000 pounds out of your airplane in an instant, you know there's going to be an effect of the plane bucking up when the plane gets that much lighter all of a sudden.

"So my hand was on the yoke and my feet were on the rudders, and our bombardier, Tom Ferebee, released the bomb over the bridge in Hiroshima that we had selected as the target. The seat slapped me on the ass, and I was putting the plane into that severe diving right turn so that we could get away from the bomb by the time it exploded. . . ."

He was careful and precise as he said the words. It's not that the tone of his voice was without animation, and certainly not that it was devoid of feeling; what struck me was just that the voice of history does not have to sound historic, that history has usually been built by people with voices that sound not so much different from your neighbor's, or your eye doctor's. The words that Tibbets was saying to me would more appropriately have been intoned by Edward R. Murrow, or by George C. Scott in a widescreen war movie. The reality was that the words had the matter-of-fact quality of something out of any American barber shop.

I asked how he—out of all the men in the service—had been the one selected to do this. Not just to fly the atomic bomb to Japan, but to assemble the whole operation. Because that is what happened—General Uzal G. Ent had asked Tibbets, who was at the time only twenty-nine years old, a lieutenant colonel, to start a new unit from nothing. He had been given full responsibility for putting together the mission, with orders to be prepared to fly when the bomb was deemed ready to function the way it was designed.

"Why was I chosen to be the one to do this?" Tibbets said. "I don't know. I was told, 'This is your job,' and I saluted and said 'Yes, sir,' and that was it.

"I think I had a reputation in the Army Air Corps as an innovative individual. The only airplane capable of carrying that bomb to Japan was the B-29, and I knew the B-29 better than anyone else in the service.

"There wasn't much of an explanation when I was given the job. In those days, they didn't explain. You were given a job to do, and you didn't question it. My job was to organize and train a unit capable of dropping atomic weapons, a unit to be self-supporting in all regards."

He assembled an 1,800-man force—the 509th Composite Group—at a remote site in Wendover, Utah, operating in the strictest secrecy. The men on the base did not know why they were there—did not know the exact nature of their mission. And then, in August of 1945, when the bomb was ready, Tibbets and his eleven crewmen took off from the island of Tinian in the Pacific Ocean and flew toward Japan.

"It had been explained to me that the bomb would have the power of twenty thousand tons of TNT," Tibbets said. "Who could envision what that meant? Twenty thousand tons? I knew that it was going to be a big, big bang, but I couldn't think much beyond that.

"We were all pretty quiet on the flight to Hiroshima. It took about six hours. The T-shaped bridge came into view just like it was supposed to, and we dropped the bomb, and I went into that turn. . . .

"I was prepared for the power, but not for the devastation. From a B-29 you really can't see down below you from the pilot's seat at the moment the bomb is dropping. The tailgunner saw the whole show, but I didn't see it until we were flying back over it.

"I looked at that city—and there was no city, there was nothing but the fringes of where the city used to be. There had been a city when we were making our approach, but now there was no humanity there. It was just something that had been . . . scorched. That word doesn't seem sufficient to describe what had just happened, but that's the only word I have. I could never have imagined anything being scorched like that city was scorched."

No one really knows the exact number of people who died in the instant the bomb—creating a peak temperature calculated to be more than a half-million degrees Fahrenheit—exploded; some estimate 100,000, some say the number of dead was probably much higher. With the mushroom cloud billowing above Japan and shock waves rocking his plane and the world having no idea what had just taken place, Tibbets was already flying the *Enola Gay* back toward his island air base.

"I had a pretty good idea that the war was over," he said. "I could not imagine how any rational leader would choose to continue to fight us knowing that we had this kind of weapon in our possession. I have two memories of the flight back:

"The memory of being so tired.

"And of believing that the war was finally over."

When I had left my parents' house to meet Tibbets, I had made myself a bet.

He had said he would be at the Park Towers at 11:30 A.M. I made sure I was there by 11:15. I had a reason—the bet I had made myself.

I turned out to be right.

He didn't walk in at 11:29. He didn't walk in at 11:31.

He walked in at 11:30.

I knew he would. When Tibbets and his crew had flown the *Enola Gay* to Hiroshima, the plan called for the bomb to be released at 8:15 A.M. Hiroshima time.

There was no satellite navigation back then, no computers to guide the way. It was a six-hour, nearly 2,000-mile trip from the American air base on Tinian Island to Hiroshima. Tibbets and his crew made the trip by checking their watches and their flight plan.

He flew over the T-shaped bridge in Hiroshima and dropped the bomb at 8:15 A.M. plus seventeen seconds.

So I'd had a feeling that 11:30 it would be—and 11:30 it was. I found myself thinking about my dad, back in his bed, and about how he would have been just as prompt to keep an appointment—details mattered to him, details, it sometimes seemed, were everything to him. In a don't-sweat-the-small-stuff era, my father had always been a man who sweated the small stuff. And now I was sitting with the ultimate sweat-the-small-stuff aviator—the man who, on his 2,000-mile trip to try to end the war, had been late by all of seventeen seconds.

"We were off," Tibbets said to me now. "We weren't perfect."

I asked him about his precision.

"I think most people in the generation I come from are like me," he said. "I grew up being taught that there's only one way to do things—the right way."

But the task he had been asked to do by the United States government—the task of dropping the atomic bomb—yes, he had carried out that task virtually flawlessly, yet the ramifications of the request that had been made of him, the ramifications not only for the story of mankind, but for one man—for him, for Tibbets—personally . . .

"People thought that I should be weeping," he

said. "Weeping for the rest of my life. They don't understand.

"I'll meet people, and when they find out who I am—when they find out that I'm the one who flew the *Enola Gay* to Hiroshima so that we could drop the bomb—sometimes they ask me: 'Why didn't you just tell them that you didn't want to do it?'

"That's when I really know that they don't understand. It's usually younger people who say that to me. Because in those days—during World War II—you didn't tell your superiors that you didn't want to do something. That's reason number one.

"Reason number two is more important. The reason I didn't tell them that I didn't want to do it is that I *wanted* to do it."

He told me that he had never lost a night's sleep in all the years since his crew dropped the bomb— "I sleep just fine"—and if anything upsets him, it is that some people still consider the use of the atomic bomb as an unnecessarily barbaric act.

"The biggest misconception is that the war was going to end soon anyway," he said. "That what we did was not necessary.

"Do you have any idea how many American lives would have been lost had we launched a ground invasion of Japan, instead of dropping the bomb? And how many Japanese lives? I sleep so well because I know how many people got to live full lives because of what we did."

At the time, though—on the flight to Japan—was he full of anger? Did his fury at what the war had done fill him with the fuel of vengeance and vindictiveness en route to his assigned target?

No, he said; he had felt no anger at all as he flew the B-29 toward Japan.

"My mother was a very calm, pacific individual, and I learned from her to be the same way. You get a lot damn further by being calm when you're doing a job. Our crew did not do the bombing in anger. We did it because we were determined to stop the killing. I would have done anything to get to Japan and stop the killing."

I asked if he had returned to Hiroshima in the years since the end of the war.

"I have no interest in doing that," he said. "Why should I go back? I've been there. I didn't go there as a sightseer. There are other places in the world to go and visit. I think it would be wrong for me to go back."

He said that he was pleased by how well Japan has done for itself in the years since 1945: "The people aren't to blame for what their government did during the war." When I brought up the almost unimaginable number of people who were killed by the bomb he and his crew dropped that day, his voice stayed even and unagitated, but his eyes fastened on mine and did not look away as he spoke.

"Please try to understand this," Tibbets said. "It's not an easy thing to hear, but please listen. There is no morality in warfare. You kill children. You kill women. You kill old men. You don't seek them out, but they die. That's what happens in war.

"Think about this: What would have happened if they had come over here? Take Detroit, for instance—if they had attacked Detroit, do you think they would have made sure that the workers in the industrial plants were in one place, and that the women and children were in another place? No, they would not have. This was World War II."

And if the atomic bomb had been ready to use a little earlier—before Germany was out of the war?

"If I would have been asked to do it, I would have done it in a second," Tibbets said. "You're damn right—if the Germans had not surrendered, I would have flown the bomb over there. I would have taken some satisfaction in that—because they shot me up."

He was referring to the many combat raids he flew over Europe before being assigned the Hiroshima mission. As he told me about all of this, I somehow had an unexpected thought about all the presidents of the United States who routinely invite well-known actors, popular singers, championship football and basketball teams to the White House for congratulatory get-togethers in commemoration of their victories. What about Tibbets? Did he ever, as he grows older, get invited to come to the White House for dinners or ceremonies?

"I went as a tourist one time, because my wife

wanted to go," he said. "I stood in line with the other tour groups, just like anyone el e. No one knew who I was."

There was one exception, he said. Rignt after the war, Harry Truman invited him to stop by.

"We met in an irregular-shaped room," Tibbets said. "I suppose it was the Oval Office. It was short and quick. He offered me a cup of coffee.

"Truman asked me if anyone was giving me a hard time—saying unpleasant things to me because of the bomb.

"I said, 'Oh, once in a while.'

"Truman said, 'You tell them that if they have anything to say, they should call me.

" 'I'm the one who sent you.' "

It had all been done in such utter secrecy—the development of the bomb even as the war in Europe slogged agonizingly on, the assembling of Tibbets' unit on the salt flats in Utah, the preparation on the island of Tinian for the raid itself—that I found myself thinking about whether something like this could be pulled off today: a mission of this staggering importance, planned and carried out in total silence.

"Not a chance in the world," Tibbets said.

I asked him what made him so certain of that.

"There's no chance a secret like that could be kept today," he said. "It would get out—it would get out in the name of freedom of information. The reason we were able to do it is that the mission was considered a matter of life-or-death secrecy. It wouldn't work in today's world."

And what would have happened if Tibbets had failed—if, with the people of the world ignorant of what was taking place, he and his crew had taken off for Japan and never made it to the target? What did he think would have become of him then?

"If I had failed?" he said. "I would have been court-martialed and in prison. Nobody knew I existed—no one knew our unit existed."

I could tell he knew I thought he was exaggerating—that I thought he would not have been sent to prison had the mission somehow gone wrong.

That's when he told me about Don Young—the flight surgeon who, in the predawn blackness of August 6, 1945, handed Tibbets a small cardboard box containing twelve cyanide capsules.

"One for each member of the flight team," Tibbets said. "In case we had to make an emergency landing, and were on the verge of being captured."

That didn't happen, of course; they didn't fail, and they weren't captured, and within days of the Hiroshima bombing a second atomic bomb was dropped on Nagasaki, and the long war was over. And now, here in central Ohio, Tibbets could go, as I was told he often did, to have his lunch at the Bob Evans restaurant on East Main Street—the same Bob Evans where my father would go at least once a week until he got so sick—and the people in the restaurant, almost all of whom were younger than he, would walk past his booth without giving him a glance, as if failing to consider that this man in his eighties could possibly have any connection with their own lives.

"I get called 'old man' all the time," he said. "It's true, I suppose. Physically, I've slowed down quite a bit."

I asked him if there were days when the United States—whose uniform he wore, whose freedom he did so much to preserve—sometimes began to feel like a place he hardly recognizes.

"It's really not the same country, in many ways," he said. "Talk to a bunch of kids in school—try to teach them something. There are times when you get the impression that they don't like to pay attention to anyone or anything but themselves. I know I sound like an old person when I say this, but there is a certain price to be paid—a certain peril—that comes with the lack of being raised in a disciplined environment."

It could have been my father talking—the words were of the sort he often spoke, the sentiments could have been his. I told that to Tibbets, and he said:

"I cannot communicate with people who are less than sixty years old. It's as if all of us in this country know the same words, but we don't use the words the same way. We speak different languages."

There were even times, he said, when he began to half-believe that he and his contemporaries may have more in common with the Japanese soldiers, fliers and sailors they fought against than with some of their current-day American countrymen.

"Those of us on the American side were over there risking our butts to meet the obligations that were set forth by the leaders of our country," he said. "The other side was doing the same thing. There's a certain common thread there."

He said he didn't think there would be another day like the one when he was asked to do what he did—to fly an atomic bomb somewhere and drop it on a city below. "No one can afford to do it," he said. And the very nature of global politics, and of global conflict, had changed.

But if such a day were to come? And if someone were to turn back the clock that rules his body?

He said he would be first in line to fight one more time for his country.

"If you could fix me up so that I could do the same things in an airplane now that I could do in 1945?" he said.

"If you could do that, and this country was in trouble, I would jump in there to beat hell."

FIVE

Before I left Tibbets that day, I told him the story: the story of how I had first heard that he lived in the same town where I grew up, the story of my dad coming home from buying clothes for the office and saying that he had seen Paul Tibbets in the same store.

And I told him how poorly my dad was doing. I said I'd be going back to his house, and that I planned to tell my dad where I had spent the morning.

"Even though you were so important in the war and he wasn't. . . ." I began.

"Don't say that," Tibbets said.

"I don't mean it in a bad way," I said. "I just mean that as much as the Army meant to him, no one outside of his friends and his family really ever knew he was there."

"That was the whole point," Tibbets said. "That's what being in the Army meant."

"But everyone knew about you," I said.

"That doesn't matter," Tibbets said. "Who knew about who doesn't matter."

I said goodbye to him, and thanked him for the visit. He asked me what my father's rank had been, and I said that when he left the Army after the war had ended he had been an infantry major.

He took out a pen and signed something and handed it to me. "Give this to your dad when you get back to his house," Tibbets said.

I put it in my briefcase and thanked him again, and it wasn't until I was in the cab that I looked at it.

To Major Greene, a World War II warrior, with best wishes from Brig. Gen. Paul Tibbets, USAF (Ret.)

I got back to my parents' house; he was still in bed, just as I had left him. I showed the signature to my mother, who carried it over to the bed and handed it to him.

He moved it toward his face and looked at it. First I saw the smile. Then the glistening, the shining in his brown eyes.

One of my first memories of my father—one of my first memories of asking him for something—had to do with a song.

"Sing 'Army now.'"

That's what my mother tells me I said—she said that when I was two or three years old, I would beg my father to sing that song for me.

You're in the Army now, you're not behind a plow. . . .

Apparently that was his ritual, when he would come home from work. My mom and I would be waiting, and in his business suit he would drive up to the house, and—at my urging—he would sing to

me from the song. "You're in the Army now"—
every soldier knew the song, every civilian, it was
one of the last remnants of an era when not only did
composers write songs about life in the military, but
the songs became universally recognized.

So—I am told—"Sing 'Army now'" was my
every-evening request. Number One on my hit pa-
rade—I couldn't get enough of it.

There is a photograph—a snapshot—that, ac-
cording to the penciled notation on the back, was
taken in 1949. That means that I was two; that
means that my father was thirty-four. We had the
same names; he was Robert B. Greene Sr., I am
Robert B. Greene Jr. Both of us Bob Greene. He had
returned to America, to Ohio, at the end of the war,
less than five years before the picture was taken. In
the photo he is in a suit and tie, wearing a fedora, a
businessman supporting his family in a nation
newly at peace. In the photo I am so small that I am
barely visible. Bundled up against the cold, my face
tiny, I am standing in front of my dad. We are posing by the garage of our home.

He's reaching down toward me, his hands just
making it to the top of my head. He's smiling in the
cold. Two years before, I hadn't been born; four years
before, he was in Italy, in Africa, in uniform. So
much motion for him, so quickly; so many changes.

Who knew about who doesn't matter. That's what
Tibbets had said. All those soldiers, coming home
to the country they had saved, and all of a sudden

the country, and they, were on to the next page, the next chapter, moving forward, or trying to. What they had done in the war was yesterday. All those men. They had grown up in this country, and then gone away, and then they had been told that it was time to come home and start being someone new.

The hat on his head, the smile on his face, the tie around his neck. His son, in the picture, pressed against his knees. "Sing 'Army now,'" I would ask. And the businessman, home from a day at work, would comply.

You'll never get rich, by digging a ditch. . . .

There are shadows behind us in the picture, but from the front we are washed in winter sunshine.

That was before the walls went up. I suppose they always do—the walls between fathers and sons, the walls that separate one generation from the next. Fact is, from the time I was old enough to have any confidence in myself, I made it almost a point of pride never to ask my father for anything. Money, advice, perspective—I seemed to fear that it would be a sign of weakness to say that I needed him.

So I didn't. *Sing "Army now."* Who was that child who so unguardedly asked his dad to sing him that song every night? And who was the man who was only too pleased, even excited, to sing it to his son?

As he lay dying, I thought about that. Who was the man? *Who knew about who doesn't matter.* But now it did. I understood what Tibbets meant: Who knew about who didn't matter, they were all in the war, they were all doing the jobs they had been asked to do, they weren't doing it to become celebrated. They were doing it because nothing, at that point in the world's history, was more important.

Now, though, it did matter. The man dying in his bed, the man in the snapshot, home from the war, standing with his son—standing with me— who was he? He was fading in and out of lucidity as he died; who was this man, who had he been?

And then I remembered the tapes.

He and my mother had given us their life stories some seven or eight years before. My mom had written hers; my dad, who didn't like to write, had talked his into a tape recorder. They were gifts to my sister, my brother and me.

I had read my mom's story, had listened to my dad's, but I must confess that they didn't register quite so strongly at the time—my mother and father were both in good health then, they were both people I saw and spoke with all the time, and the life stories, while a wonderful keepsake, did not contain all that much urgency.

Now, though—my father's voice wispy and confused, his ability to maintain a cohesive narrative getting weaker by the day—I dug up the tapes.

There was his voice, strong and full. Telling the story of a life.

I was born on March 7, 1915, in Akron, Ohio. . . . Dad's parents were from very moderate circumstances, and from his very early days, Dad had to work. As a matter of fact, he sold newspapers on the streets of Akron. . . .

He was more or less self-educated; he did not go to college, but he did study law in a very prominent law office by the name of Vorys. He got his diploma by taking the Ohio State Bar exam and passing it with flying colors, which was quite an accomplishment for a poor boy with only a high school education.

I believe the earliest thing I remember was when our house on Casterton Avenue was being built, and we lived in the Portage Hotel. I also can think of the drugstore, which was off the main lobby in that hotel, and the wonderful hot chocolate they served, and whenever I smell hot chocolate I think of the treats we used to have going down to that drugstore and getting a cup of that steaming good stuff. I believe I was four or four and a half years old.

Another thing I can remember very clearly was looking out of the window in our room or rooms, it was in the middle of the night and the fire alarm rang. Not in the hotel, but out on the corner, and down East Market Street dashed a steam fire engine drawn by about six horses, it was spitting smoke and fire and clanging bells and that was a very, very thrilling moment for me. I can see those horses coming around the corner now, those sparks coming off their hooves as they hit the pavement. . . .

Sometimes I think no one really understands," Tibbets had said. He had been talking about himself—about the mission he had been asked to carry out for his country, about the ferocious storm of emotions that still, fifty years later, the mere mention of his mission tripped.

My father lay sleeping. My mother—I could see her across the bedroom—had reclined on the other bed, and now she had drifted off too. I sat in the room, and I looked at both of their faces.

The need to understand—the duty to understand—can come to you late. *Who knew about who doesn't matter.* Maybe not back then—maybe not when everyone was young. But whether you're a soldier the world never heard of, or the man who won the war, it matters in the end. In a way, it's all that does matter.

My father's breath and my mother's breath were the only sounds in the room.

SIX

The sole trip out of Columbus that my father and I ever took together—just the two of us—was when I was seventeen, and it was time for me to look at colleges. I had decided that I wanted to go to Northwestern University, if I could get in—it was said to have a good program in journalism—so one spring day in 1964 my dad and I got on a TWA plane at Port Columbus and flew to O'Hare International Airport in Chicago.

He had been making trips to Chicago all during his business career—not constantly, but enough that we in the family always assumed, without really thinking about it, that he knew the ropes, that Chicago was familiar territory to him—so I was a little surprised, when we got there, to sense that he was noticeably nervous.

This wasn't Ohio. This was big, intimidating, outsized. He rented a car at O'Hare, and we drove downtown—I could tell that the expressway traffic was much more daunting than what he was accustomed to in Columbus, he stared straight ahead as he drove and kept both hands on the steering wheel and occasionally registered startled disapproval as some Chicago driver would cut in front of him or speed past—and he didn't talk much. We got to a hotel called the Oxford House, on Wabash Avenue, and rode the elevator to our room and unpacked our bags.

It was so odd—his clothes in the drawers on one side of the dresser, my clothes on the other side, each of us sitting on one of the two beds, with no sounds of our family: no voices of my mother, my sister, my brother. He said that it was time to go down to dinner, so we ate in the hotel restaurant, and when we were finished it was still too early to turn in. He asked me if I would like to go to a movie.

We walked into the Loop—such an overpowering sensation, walking with my father through that burly, thick downtown, under elevated-train tracks and up crowded-even-at-night streets with famous names—State, Randolph, Washington—two guys from Ohio, one forty-nine, one seventeen, both feeling small and out of place, neither talking about it—and the lights from the marquees of all the movie theaters colored the night, and my father chose a marquee that was advertising *Seven Days in May*.

It was a military movie—actually, about a plot involving a military takeover of the United States—and many of the main characters were in Army uniforms, working at military installations. My father, sitting next to me in the theater in a coat and tie, almost twenty years removed from the military by this time, stared intently at the screen. When the movie was over we walked the famous streets again, back to the Oxford House. On the corners were newspaper boxes—all four Chicago dailies: the *Tribune*, the *Sun-Times*, the *Daily News*, the *American*.

That was quite a sight in itself—four newspapers, *four*, serving one town. To me it was almost intoxicating: the idea of a city with all that news, of there being so much news and so many people that four papers could exist and compete and, presumably, thrive. The main headline on each of the four papers on that night in 1964 said essentially the same thing, which was some variation of: MACARTHUR NEAR DEATH.

It caught my father's eye; we were walking past the news boxes, and he saw those big headlines, and he said, in a tone of soft surprise, as if speaking of an old friend, "Look at that. MacArthur's dying." I had only the vaguest idea of who General Douglas MacArthur was—a figure from the war, an eminent soldier—but I could not have told you much more than that. My dad bought a paper, and he started to read it as we stood on the sidewalk, and we went back into the hotel and up to our room and we got into our beds for the night.

He read his paper. He kept looking at the photo of MacArthur on the front page, and then he told me that we had to get up early in the morning to go up to Evanston and see Northwestern. He turned the lights off, and although he fell asleep right away, and started snoring, I had trouble sleeping. The

Chicago street noise from down below was wafting up to our windows, I had never had to try to go to sleep with big-city traffic in my ears, and with my dad lost to the world in the next bed I was far away from almost everything I was used to. I looked over at him in his pajamas, and at the newspaper on the nightstand with the big black-and-white photo of the dying soldier, and it was a long time before I finally drifted off.

Now more than thirty years had passed. Now my father was the one who was dying, older than old should ever seem as he lay in that bedroom of our home in Columbus, and for him of course there would be no headlines as he faced death; no one outside our family was even aware. Not even my parents' closest friends, really; he and my mother had decided not to tell them just how bad it was.

I would look at him in his bed during those last months, and on some of the longest days and nights of his dying it would be hard to remember that he was ever young, that he was ever full of life and health and his special spark. But there were those tapes I had found—there were those stories, in his own voice, stories of another time.

So jarring—the sight of him asleep and dying, and, later, when I was alone with the tapes in a room with the door closed, his voice:

. . . I remember my first two-wheeler bicycle . . . It was brown and it was not very fashionable, and I know that I was terribly disappointed that I didn't get the popular bike, which was called the America.

For a later birthday I did finally receive my America, which made me very proud. I remember that a fellow by the name of Bob McLaughlin wanted to ride my bicycle, and he said he would let me ride on the handlebars. So I let him drive me around, and by mistake my foot caught in the front wheel of the bicycle and broke some of the spokes. Well, I was scared stiff. I was afraid to tell my mother and father, and of course Bob McLaughlin would never tell them, but he lived way out on Portage Path. But I finally, I guess after a week or so, confessed this terrible sin of first letting somebody ride my bike, and secondly riding on the handlebars and thirdly causing damage to this beautiful thing.

To my great surprise, I didn't get hell. My mother and father simply had the front wheel fixed, and then off I went, never again to let anybody ride this bike. . . .

I would listen to my father's words on those tapes, talking about a boy I never knew—talking about himself. And meanwhile, as he lay dying and we saw him become terribly, heartbreakingly disoriented, there were times when entire days would go by when he did not say a single sentence that, in the world of the living, could be judged as making coherent sense.

On the last day I saw my father alive, my mother had a question for me.

"Have you said goodbye to him?" she asked.

She meant the real goodbye—the one that was going to have to last forever.

In those final months, my brother, my sister and I had been coming to Columbus, spelling each other as we sat with our parents. None of us could be there full-time, yet we knew that he wasn't going to get better—it wasn't a question of if the end was coming, but of when. So each time one of us left, we didn't know whether it was going to be the last time.

"Have you said goodbye to him?"

I hadn't, really; I had sat in the room with him, and listened as he talked, and when his disorientation was at its worst I had tried not to let him know just how far, in his dying, he had wandered from the person he used to be. There were certain hours—I think of one especially awful afternoon, when in an attempt to help him complete his bathroom functions, the four of us, my brother, my sister, my mother and I, had lifted him from the bed, and in the middle of this he had seemed to lose consciousness. . . .

I think of that now, and of how proud and self-sufficient he had always been, how confident of his strength, and it seems to me that we, all of us, were saying goodbye day after day, week after week, in ways more profound than words could convey. That by being there, by seeing him this way and looking his dying full in the face, we were saying the most complete and loving goodbye a family could possibly say.

But my mother meant something else. She meant: Have you sat next to him and told him what you think of him and let him know that this may be the last conversation the two of you ever have?

"I've been saying goodbye in my own way," I told her. She knew full well that my father and I were never any good at talking to each other about anything serious; I'm not proud of that and I'm not ashamed of it, it's just the way the two of us were, and I have a suspicion that we were far from the only fathers and sons in this world who were or are that way.

"Debby and Timmy have said goodbye," my mother said.

I knew that they had; I knew they had sat in the room with him and had done their best to have conversations that summed everything up. Whether he was comprehending what they said—and whether he remembered it even five minutes later—I am not certain.

"Go on in and say goodbye," my mother said.

I'd be leaving for the airport in half an hour. I went into the bedroom; outside those windows the trees had been deep green and full of leaves in the summer, when he had taken to his bed with this final illness, and during the months of his dying they had changed to the brown and orange trees of autumn, and now to the black bare branches of winter, all in the time he had been in the bed.

I looked at him and I knew he didn't want to be here for another spring.

We just sat. The door was closed, and no one else knew what was going on, and he clearly was in no mood for words and neither was I. I sat next to the bed and held his hand, and when he motioned that he was thirsty I held a glass of water to his lips, and there was ice on those branches outside the windows and I knew that this was the right way to do it, and I think he knew, too.

"You have to get on your airplane?" he said after a while.

"I do," I said.

I stood up and looked at him and I said, "I'll see you later."

He sort of smiled.

"You will?" he said.

"Of course," I said. "We'll be seeing each other."

He smiled again. He knew that I didn't mean in this world.

"That's good," he said. "I'll see you later, too."

• • •

My mother and sister were with him when he died. It happened on a Friday night in December; he fell asleep and he didn't wake up, and the after-midnight calls came to my brother and me. We were on the first planes we could get. The funeral was on a Monday.

During the months of his dying, I had been making notes about him—about his path toward death, and about the life he had lived, but mostly as I wrote things down I saw that they were questions. The world in which he had lived—the world that had existed prior to my birth—who had he been then, in that world? All of us know our parents as just that—as our mothers and fathers—but before we were born, they were someone else. Before they defined themselves as our parents, they were men and women whose universes had nothing at all to do with us.

And in my father's universe—the one closest to his soul—the central event, always, was the war in which he served. I sat at the funeral, looking at the casket, and I thought about the person he had been before I was even the remotest thought in his imagination.

I had found another passage on that tape he had made; it came early in his story, he was talking about a new elementary school in Akron that had been built when he was a young boy, and how when he was in the third grade all the students had been moved to that school—King School, it was called—and how handsome and sparkling it was in comparison to the forbidding, Gothic schoolhouse where they had gone before.

. . . One thing that I vividly remember about King School is that at the beginning of the school year we went to class despite the fact that the grounds were not completed as yet.

And in those days they didn't have bulldozers or any other backhoe type of heavy machinery to clear the ground. They had horses pulling great shovels. Well, one particular day, evidently the day was very hot, a poor horse died in harness and they let that poor horse stay in the schoolyard for days until it bloated up like a balloon. And I can still see that dead horse looking like it was ready to burst. Thankfully, they hauled it away one day, I guess to some burial place, long past due.

We must remember that this was in the early Twenties, shortly after the end of World War I. Even as a kid, I was fascinated with the war, and I always used to fantasize that I would be a soldier and I would return to Akron in triumph and one of the things that I would do would be to walk down the diagonal path that extended from Tallmadge Avenue to King School—I wanted to walk down that diagonal path to school as the conquering hero, coming home from the wars. . . .

I'll see you later," I had said to him.
All of a sudden, as I sat at the funeral, that seemed enormously important to me. "You will?" he had asked. "That's good. . . ."

I didn't know where or when. But when I got there, I wanted to have some stories to tell. Some stories that might make him know that I was doing my best, however belatedly, to understand.

SEVEN

With all the back-and-forth during the months of my father's dying, I did not write anything in the newspaper about my first visit with Paul Tibbets until a month after the funeral.

Back at work then, and, for the first time since summer, with the downturns of my father's health not on my mind—and with the new void left by his absence hitting me from all angles at unexpected moments—I went through the handwritten notes I had made during my hours with Tibbets. I thought that the story he had told me might make for reading that would interest people; I thought that, because of Tibbets' lifelong propensity for reticence and silence, there might be many people who literally had no idea who he was—and that those who did know might not even realize he was still alive.

And I was exhausted. The months of my father's leave-taking had affected me in ways that, as they had unfolded, I had been unaware. But—my father buried in Ohio, me back in Chicago, a job to do—I welcomed the chance to write something for which I had already done the reporting, something that, for a few days, did not require me to go out and talk to people. The way I was feeling, I did not want to listen to the voices of strangers, at least not quite yet.

The Tibbets notes were there—I had put them away after he and I had met, I had told virtually no one about our conversation—and as I looked at them, I decided to do a week's worth of columns about what he had told me. I shut myself in a room and wrote the stories—Tibbets' voice, as I had heard it.

The reaction staggered me.

It came from all over the world. The column is carried on the *Chicago Tribune*'s computer-version site, so I had known for a while that the readership was not limited by the geographic boundaries of the Chicago area, or of the towns where newspapers carry the column in syndication. Still, until the stories about Paul Tibbets began to appear, I had no idea of just how wide the reach of the new technology was.

Every day, my computer at work was jammed with electronic messages about the interview with Tibbets; regular mail also poured in, and phone calls. That one three-sentence thought of Tibbets'—"I cannot communicate with people who are less than sixty years old. It's as if all of us in this country know the same words, but we don't use the words the same way. We speak different languages."—seemed to affect people. Some were his age, some weren't, but all understood what he meant. And they wanted to say so.

The most overwhelming sentiment in so many of the letters concerned something I had not thought much about before I had met Tibbets. It was about the lives that were not lost when the bomb was dropped; it was about the American families that were allowed to be born and thrive and grow to adulthood because the soldiers and sailors had not been sent on a bloody and disastrous land invasion of Japan.

Voices:

"At the time of Colonel Paul Tibbets' mission, I was a young nineteen-year-old Marine," wrote a man named Robert A. Guth.

> We had just finished some intense training for the final push against the Japanese homeland. Although our exact invasion location was secret, we found out later that we would indeed be sent in.
>
> At that time we heard scuttlebutt that an invasion of Japan would be very costly in casualties. I would have liked to thank President Truman at that time for his decision to order the bombing—and I would like at this time to thank Paul Tibbets for his excellent mission.
>
> I thank Colonel Tibbets and his crew, my wife Mary thanks them, our five children and fifteen grandchildren thank them.

It was an expression of gratitude that I would read and hear over and over. The point was unmis-

takable—so many people, most of them of Tibbets'
and my father's generation, were absolutely convinced that untold numbers of American lives, including perhaps their own, would have soon been
lost had Tibbets and his crew not flown their mission in August of 1945. These correspondents did
not treat what happened in Hiroshima lightly; far
from it, they made it clear that they understood in
great detail the unfathomable extent of death and
carnage that resulted from the bomb being dropped.

But they also seemed to feel that the bomb—in a
complex and pervading sense—was their salvation,
and the salvation of family members not yet born
in 1945. A woman named Catherine E. Mitchell,
seventy-three years old, of Biloxi, Mississippi, put it
this way:

> I well remember that day when the bomb
> was dropped on Hiroshima. So often I have
> heard people saying that we should never have
> dropped that bomb. But those people were not
> living through the war.
>
> In early 1945, my husband was sent to the
> Pacific. The country was preparing for the in-
> vasion of Japan and we all knew it. Had the
> dropping of the bomb not happened, I know
> that my husband would not have returned
> home—so many American lives would have
> been lost.
>
> The younger generations cannot possibly un-

derstand what we went through and how we felt about our country being attacked [at Pearl Harbor]—you can't know until you live through it. My forty-six-year-old father was also in the Pacific with the Seabees then, and my twenty-year-old brother was finishing flight training.

I sincerely hope that the young people of today will never have to go through a war. I am glad that I did not have to make the decision to drop the bomb, but I am glad that it was done.

From a man named E. R. Klamm:

I was a naval communications officer, and we headed a large convoy of ships in Guam, Tinian and Saipan for the eventual invasion of Japan. We weathered three different typhoons.

In August, during a lull in the weather, I was playing badminton on deck (staying fit) when a staffman brought me a communication. I read it and then resumed playing our game. Then, like a bolt of lightning, I suddenly returned to the communication.

Its wording was technical and complex, but I interpreted that it involved the use of a mega-explosive in bombing Japan. It triggered in my mind that it could stop the invasion of Japan. Hallelujah! Hallelujah! Later aboard ship there was jubilation.

We never reached Japan. We did go to
Korea and China. I then returned to the U.S.
and the happiness of family life. I commend
Paul Tibbets and his crew. I congratulate him
for naming his B-29 the *Enola Gay*, in honor of
his mother. My mother, and my wife, were
happy on my return Thanksgiving Day, 1945.

From a twenty-five-year-old woman named
Chantal Foster Lindquist:

Paul Tibbets' voice is stern and serene. The
gravity of his act forces silence on the page.

I think most people my age don't understand the sacrifices our grandparents made
during wartime. I remember, in high school, I
wrote a paper about why we shouldn't have
dropped the bomb on Hiroshima. I was
adamant in my essay, but the moment I spoke
with my grandfather, a Navy Seabee, and listened to his account of the war, I changed my
mind.

His blue eyes flared when I said the bomb
was unnecessary, and he leaned across the table
to tell me how the bomb had saved his life.
How he was so grateful to go home and see his
family again. How he's pretty sure he would
have been killed otherwise. And so in a way I
realized I might not even be here if Paul
Tibbets hadn't done his job.

Some of the letters were filled with a perspective that could be born only of that war and that time. From a "septuagenarian ex-city editor" named Brad Bradford:

> You quite properly focus upon the *Enola Gay*'s pilot. His command responsibilities must have been enormous.
>
> But please bear with me. . . . To bring the *Enola Gay* over target within seventeen seconds of the planned time, navigator Theodore Van Kirk had to have been virtually perfect with no chance to relax even for a minute on that two-thousand-mile run to Hiroshima. His was simply an almost miraculous exhibition of technical expertise.
>
> I was a B-29 navigator in Stateside training that August. Training that summer at Smoky Hill Army Airfield in Kansas, I was slated to head for the Pacific and fly cover for a land invasion of Japan. The Air Corps shipped my footlocker to Okinawa, but thanks to the flight of the *Enola Gay*, the Army decided it didn't need me there after all and returned it to Smoky Hill. I left active duty that December a Stateside-safeside WWII veteran. And I still have that footlocker as a reminder of the debt I owe Paul Tibbets and his crew.

There it was, in almost every letter—a legacy of

the flight that was seldom spoken about publicly. One woman's words:

> My husband was with the 5th Marine Division and served on Iwo Jima. After the *Enola Gay* dropped the bomb on Hiroshima, my husband and the men he fought with did not have to invade the Japanese mainland. He came home to me instead.
>
> Ten years ago, my husband went into the bedroom to take a nap before dinner. When I went in to call him, he was dead. He was a wonderful husband and father, and our lives are very empty without him.
>
> I am writing to ask you if I could possibly have Mr. Tibbets' address. I would really love to write to him. I am aware {that he} remains out of the public eye. But maybe he would like to hear about the special man I shared my life with—because of the job he did.

Mixed in with my business mail, during that freezing January, were condolence notes—letters about my father's death, and about his life, from people who had known our family. Many had Columbus postmarks on the envelopes.

So each day, as I went through the volume of mail that inevitably comes in to someone who writes stories in newspapers, I kept an eye out for Columbus addresses. And one day, when I had found one such Columbus envelope and had put it aside, I opened it to find that it was not exactly what I had expected.

It was from Tibbets.

He had sat down at an old-fashioned typewriter to write the letter. For twenty years I had tried to meet him, with nary a word of response. Now, here was this. He had read what I wrote. This is what the quiet man who did so much to end World War II said:

"You made me think, after a word-by-word review, that maybe I am not too bad a guy. Thanks."

He wrote that he didn't know whether I would be coming back to Ohio any time soon, but that if I did, he would like me to let him know.

EIGHT

There's a General Something waiting for you in the lounge."

The clerk at the front desk of the hotel near Port Columbus barely looked up as she said the words. I had arrived at the airport and taken a cab to the hotel; this was my first trip back to Ohio since the funeral, a short visit to take my mother to dinner. The hotel is where Tibbets had said he would meet me before I went to my mom's house.

General Something. If he'd been the star of a network situation comedy, the desk clerk might have been able to work up a bit of interest in his presence in the hotel; if he'd been a football player or a singer, she might have known who he was, might have called her friends to excitedly tell them who she had just met.

But this old man—General Something—had stopped at the desk to tell her that someone might be looking for him, and to please refer the person to the hotel lounge, and evidently the name hadn't really stuck. I told her thanks; she said no problem.

Touch it?" Tibbets said. "No—I never touched it."

It was a little thing that had been on my mind

since the last time I had spoken with him. It was probably a meaningless point—but I kept finding myself thinking about whether Tibbets had ever touched the bomb. All that terrible power riding in the plane with him, all that nascent death—I tried to imagine the night he climbed into the *Enola Gay* for the flight to Hiroshima, and every time I thought about that, I had a picture in my mind of Tibbets stopping for a moment to touch the bomb he had been ordered to drop.

"I'm not sentimental or superstitious or anything else," he said. He was in the hotel lounge, just as the clerk had said he would be; he was finishing off a cup of soup. He's not a drinker, he told me; he doesn't mind being in bars, but he avoids alcohol.

"I could have touched it, when they wheeled it out," he said. "Tom Ferebee stopped and checked everything—he was the bombardier, that was his job. I had a team of professionals, and I trusted them. All I needed to know was: 'Will it work?' I trusted that it would."

I told Tibbets I had heard that some of the support team on Tinian in 1945 had written messages on the bomb before it was loaded onto the *Enola Gay*. The bomb was not fully armed until the plane was airborne; theoretically, there was no danger in approaching it and writing on it while it was on the ground. Still—walking up to the atomic bomb and fooling around with it. . . .

"I heard the same thing," Tibbets said. "That some of the guys had written something on it. 'To the emperor, with love'—I think that was it, something like that. It's probably true—they probably did write messages on the bomb. Didn't make any sense, really. Think about it—who the hell is going to read it?"

The otherworldliness of this was still sinking in on me. Here was Tibbets, who had turned eighty-four since I had seen him last, telling these stories while, on a TV set in the bar, an NBA game was on the color screen, and the handful of other patrons were staring at that game, following the action as if the outcome were a matter of life or death. A few feet away this elderly man whose identity was a complete mystery to the others in the bar narrated a tale almost beyond comprehension.

In the weeks since my father's death, when I had thought of Tibbets it wasn't only the flight to Japan about which I wanted to know more—the expertise of Tibbets and his crew was a matter of record, they got there and they got back and the war ended: They did their jobs. What puzzled me—what I also wanted to know more about—was how Tibbets was assigned to put together the unit at Wendover, Utah, that was responsible for the mission. He had, as far as I knew, at that time never run a business. Yet the Army—and the government—had told him, in the middle of a war, to in effect start a new

corporation. The corporation would have 1,800 employees—and Tibbets would be the chief executive
officer.

He was twenty-nine when he was instructed to do
that. Yes, he could fly a bomber with great skill. But
how do you learn to be the boss of 1,800 men when
you've never been a business executive? Where do
you get the knowledge and the confidence and the
leadership skills to do that?

"I went to military school when I was a boy," he
said. "I learned right away that I had to be good,
and I had to be right. I decided when I was very
young that I never wanted to do anything—any job
at all—until I had thought it out first.

"How's it going to work? That's the first ques-
tion I always asked myself about everything. And if
I didn't know the answer, the next question was:
How will I make it work?

"I have kind of an analytical mind. When I approach a problem, I'm thinking, what are the odds
that this will happen the way I want it to? How will
I make sure it will work? That's how I was thinking
when I was given the assignment to put our unit together.

"If I had to be the head of that unit, it was going
to be a question of commanding people—and I've
always been able to judge people pretty well. I can
judge who will succeed and who will fail. Yes, I was
twenty-nine when I was given the assignment. But
I was really thirty-five or forty. That's how I felt.

That was my nature—I always felt older than I actually was.

"And I am an orderly man. When I stay in a hotel room, I fold up the towels. I usually make the bed before I leave. I don't have to; I know that the housekeepers will do it if I don't. But I don't like the idea of other people doing something that I can do myself. A sense of order is very important to me."

So had he made it his business to know each of the 1,800 men at Wendover? Did he fine-tune his command duties to that extent?

"No," he said. "I probably only knew a hundred or so of the men by name. I saw faces. I was so busy going back and forth to Washington, and to Los Alamos, that I couldn't know every man. I knew every guy in command of a unit on the base, of course. But what you're asking is how I learned to run the whole operation when I had never done anything like that before.

"The answer is this: At twenty-nine I was so shot in the ass with confidence that it wasn't a question of could I do it—there wasn't anything I *couldn't* do. By the time I got the assignment to put together the atomic-bomb unit, I had worked my way through the war in Europe and North Africa, and I was completely convinced that I could do anything. I had succeeded as a combat pilot over there because once I got into the air, *I didn't have anyone who I had to ask what I had to do.* I just did it.

"Maybe it came from the house I grew up in. From my dad. The old man was a short fellow with a small-man complex. A cocky rooster. He would tell you once, and you'd better listen and get it right. That must have stuck, in some way."

He took such pride in the punctiliousness of his organizational skills, the double-checking and triple-checking of every detail; I told him that I had read something about the Hiroshima mission that seemed to fit in. When I had read it, I didn't know if it was true or an apocryphal tale. But now it seemed right.

"What's that?" he said.

"What was the last thing you did before you dropped the bomb?" I asked.

"I don't understand what you're getting at," Tibbets said.

"The last thing you said to your crew," I said.

"In the plane?" Tibbets said.

"Yes," I said.

"I suppose I asked everyone whether they agreed that it was Hiroshima down there," he said.

That's what I had read; on this monumental day in the history of the planet, with the T-shaped bridge coming into sight, Tibbets had polled his crew to see if each man thought they were approaching the right city. It hadn't occurred to me— that the men in the plane, never having seen Hiroshima before, might be a little uncertain about where they actually were about to drop the world's first atomic weapon.

"Do you remember what you said—the exact words?" I asked.

"Probably, 'Do we all agree that this is Hiroshima?' " Tibbets said.

"Amazing," I said, trying to comprehend the moment. Like guys on a car trip to a state where they'd never visited. Is this the right exit? Except that this was the most somber journey that any men had ever taken.

"I don't see why it's amazing," Tibbets said. "It's the same thing I'd do on any kind of a job. You check, just to make sure. That's not amazing. That's just good sense."

A cheer came from over at the bar. Someone on the television screen had just made a basket to beat the shot clock.

The apocalyptic destructiveness of nuclear weaponry notwithstanding, the Paul Tibbets who flew the *Enola Gay* to Japan in 1945 wouldn't even be allowed to be a passenger in a commercial jetliner half-a-century later had he not changed his ways. Just one more small example of how the world has evolved: Tibbets was a smoker back then. All the time. Including in airplanes.

Including the *Enola Gay*.

"I smoked everything," he said. "Pipes, cigars, cigarettes . . . I would smoke on every mission. Pipes, mostly—I was using Bond Street tobacco. I had a Zippo lighter that I carried with me constantly."

"So you were lighting your pipe with the atomic bomb right beneath you," I said.

"Sure," Tibbets said.

"That didn't make you a little nervous?" I said.

"Why should it?" he said. "The bomb was inert."

"I don't know," I said. "Just the thought of that—an atomic bomb in the belly of your plane, and you're smoking away . . ."

"A cigarette lighter's not going to set off the atomic bomb," Tibbets said. "It didn't work that way. I was smoking my pipe and probably lighting it up when they were loading the bomb into the plane."

Of course, he and he alone knew what the bomb was. The other crew members had not been told—they were not informed of the exact nature of the mission until they were well on their way to Hiroshima. All those months in Wendover and then on Tinian—and the secret had been kept. Even from the men under Tibbets' command.

Before he could tell the men on board, he had to get the plane into the air. Which was no simple job—the runway that had been carved out of the jungle-like conditions on Tinian was not long enough to easily handle the B-29 as it had been re-configured. With the heavy bomb underneath him, Tibbets knew that he would have to use virtually every foot of that runway before he lifted off.

"You had to take into consideration that airplane and all its problems," he said. "It was underpowered for what we had to do. If you were to lose an engine, you could not control that airplane.

"I know that some of the crew on the flight were getting very nervous as I kept the plane on the run-way so long as we were taking off. There was a cliff-like drop at the end of the runway, and some of them were thinking about that. But I knew what I was doing. I was building up every possible bit of power that I could before taking the plane up. Remember—this was before jet engines. If I lost an engine, and if we were to crash . . .

"I needed every inch. The co-pilot thought he knew more about the airplane than I did—he thought I should take it up sooner. It was all busi-ness in there—every man had his own responsibil-ity in the airplane to take care of. I wanted the men to know what was going on, but first we had to get up and off of Tinian.

"After we were up and the bomb had been armed, I decided it was time for no more secrets. I had to crawl through a twenty-six-inch circular tun-nel to talk to the men in the back of the plane. I told everyone: 'This is what it's all about. We're carrying a weapon that we've been working with.' Bob Caron, the tailgunner, said to me: 'Colonel, we wouldn't be playing with atoms, would we?' I said, 'Sure. That's it.' They weren't startled. I think a lot of them had guessed, but they had known not to ask."

The fact that Tibbets was flying the plane—was that a part of his duties? He had been assigned to assemble and command the unit that would prepare for the flight. But did that mean he was assigned to fly the mission, too?

"The order was for me to organize and train a unit to drop these weapons," he said. "When I was looking for a place to assemble the unit, and I flew over those mountains in Utah and saw Wendover, I thought it was the most beautiful and isolated place I had ever seen. I knew I didn't have to look any further—boy, this was the place for me. *So* isolated— the most isolated place I could ever imagine. I saw Wendover from the air, and I thought that this is a place where it's easier to keep a secret than anywhere else I had seen in my life.

"I went back to General Ent and I told him, 'I've seen Wendover, and I want it.' He said, 'It's yours.' "

"You were twenty-nine," I reminded him.

"I was twenty-nine," Tibbets said. "You were asking me if it was part of my orders to fly the mission. Yes, it was part of my orders—from *me*. I had the authority to do anything I wanted, and I knew that I could fly that damn thing better than anyone else.

"So, yes, I issued the order—I was going to be the pilot. If anyone was going to make a mistake on this mission, it was going to be me."

As he approached Hiroshima, and Tom Ferebee released the bomb and it detonated, as planned, some 1,800 feet above the city—the atomic bomb was not supposed to explode on impact, but well over the target—and the tumbling, rolling shock waves from the bomb reached the cockpit of the plane, Tibbets said he could taste it.

"It tasted like lead," he said. "It was like an electrical charge was running through the fillings in my teeth, and I could feel that electricity in my fillings and I had the taste of lead in my mouth. The feeling was like when cold ice cream touches one of your fillings, and the taste—the taste from that bomb is something I will never forget."

As he flew back toward Tinian, he was still smoking.

"No one asked me not to," he said.

He has stopped since. Doctor's orders. The atomic bombing of Hiroshima was the one most deadly act in the annals of man's time on Earth. But, in a twist the most inventive author could never have devised, in the years since World War II cigarettes have killed far more people than the bomb did that day—indeed, have killed far more people than all the military men who died in combat during World War II.

"Pilots smoked back then," Tibbets said. "Soldiers smoked back then. Everyone smoked back then. What did we know? The scientists hadn't told us yet."

Once in a while, as I talked with Tibbets, I half-forgot for a second that he didn't just suddenly materialize for the armed services when the atomic bomb project was being developed. The reason he was in the running for the job was because of his combat record in Europe. He flew twenty-five missions in B-17s, including being the lead pilot of the first-ever American daylight bombing raid against occupied Europe.

Still, occasionally he would drop a reference into our conversation that brought me up short. I had been asking him some technical question about the planes he flew in the war—I think this particular question was about the altitude at which the planes operated—and in trying to explain he said, "Well, when I was flying Ike to Gibraltar . . ."

"You knew Eisenhower?" I asked.

He gave me a look. "Yes," he said.

"Why were you flying him to Gibraltar?" I said.

"Because he had to get to the invasion of North Africa," Tibbets said.

"Oh," I said. Simple as that. Dwight D. Eisenhower had to get to the war, and Tibbets gave him a ride.

"How was he to fly with?" I asked.

"As nice a passenger as you'll ever find," Tibbets said.

Eisenhower, he said, was to be the overall commander of the operation, with Major General Mark Clark as his deputy. This was in November of 1942; Eisenhower was in England, the air was full of rain and fog, and there was much uncertainty about whether the planes could take off.

"We were standing on the runway," Tibbets said. "Eisenhower seemed like he wanted to get moving, but others were saying that the weather was just too bad. Eisenhower looked at me—were we going to take off or not?

"I said, 'General, if I didn't know the passenger who I'd be carrying on this trip, I'd make the decision to go.' Meaning if it was just me, I'd fly out of there.

"And Eisenhower said, 'I've got a war waiting on me. Let's go.'"

Tibbets said that a Jeep led his B-17 out onto the active runway, and that by the time he was airborne "I couldn't see three feet in front of me. I flew as low over the Channel as I possibly could—the last thing Eisenhower needed was for German radar to pick us up. I can't tell you exactly how low I was flying, because I don't know—but there was salt spray on the window of the plane."

And Eisenhower? "He was sitting on a two-by-four plank that we had put between my seat and the co-pilot's seat. He had told us that he wanted to watch what was going on. And he sat there with us and talked with us as if this was the most regular thing in the world—him sitting on a two-by-four and us flying him to run the war.

"He had a thermos jug of coffee with him—it's funny how you remember the little things, but I remember that Eisenhower shared his coffee with us. It was a 1,200-mile flight, and by the time we landed in Gibraltar the invasion had started—the paratroopers were dropping.

"He was all business. He just got out of the plane, thanked us, and he was gone. He was just as fine as anyone could be. He was wearing four stars when he was with us, but he was one of the boys. I was only—what?—twenty-seven, I think, at that point. You try not to show that you're feeling anything. But this was Ike.

"Made me feel good—that he trusted me to get him there. That moment at the airfield in England is one that stays in your mind. You're standing in the rain with Eisenhower, and he's looking at the sky and you tell him that you can do it and he says those words. 'I've got a war waiting on me.'

"And you go."

• • •

I hadn't told my mother that I was stopping off to see Tibbets on my way from the airport— for some reason, at this point the fact that he had invited me to continue our conversations was something I wanted to keep to myself—and as he and I talked I realized that I'd better be on my way.

"I'm going to go take my mom out to dinner," I said to Tibbets.

"You go to your mother's house," he said. "That's more important than talking to me."

I told him the place I was thinking about taking her—the Top, it was called, a steakhouse that has been around Columbus since the 1950s, a place where she and my dad used to go when they were a young married couple in the years after the war— and Tibbets said that he used to go to the Top all the time, too.

He asked me how late I planned on staying up. I said that my mom tended to go to bed on the early side.

"Well, if you're not tired and you feel like talking some more, I'll be happy to meet you back here," he said.

"Right here?" I said. "Same place?"

"If you feel like it," he said.

I said I did. He looked at his watch and said that we should set a time. I made sure to make it late enough that I was certain to be back from dinner and from my mother's house; whatever hour we chose, I knew he would be there promptly as promised, and I didn't want to keep him waiting. The lounge was nearly empty and he was the oldest man there.

NINE

The diploma was on the wall of the spare bedroom my father used as his office.

"I thought he didn't put that up," I said to my mother.

"He decided he wanted to," she said. "He hung it on the wall the week after you gave it to him."

"You mean it was up there all the time he was sick?" I asked.

"Yes," she said.

"I guess with everything going on, I didn't notice it," I said.

There it was: a diploma from Ohio State University, dated the previous June. It had his name on it—it said that Bob Greene had been awarded an honorary doctorate.

My father never graduated from college. It always made him feel insecure; I think one of the reasons he was so meticulous in his language, why he paid such attention to grammar and word choice, was that he knew he was operating in a society in which so many other people had college degrees. My mother had graduated from Wellesley and had been selected for Phi Beta Kappa; my father had never made it through the University of Akron.

He didn't say much to us about it, ever. But I found a reference to it in the tape he had made. It wasn't for lack of desire that he had left college:

I went to West High School. Akron was a working man's town, and West High School was the educational place for working people's children. There were a lot of the kids of rubber workers who attended, and this was right in the middle of the Depression, so it was kind of sad to see some of those kids come to school literally dressed in rags.

It was a hard time for all, especially high school kids who couldn't have the pluses that went with being a teenager in the big city. In other words, the last two years of high school, my junior and senior years, when usually there were class rings and pins and yearbooks and that sort of thing, the Depression caused all that stuff to be cut way back. So those were kind of grim years.

After high school, instead of being able to go away to school, I went to what was called a streetcar school. I would get on the 22 streetcar on West Market Street and ride it downtown and then walk up the hill behind Polsky's department store to go to Akron University, which was also a hardbitten working man's school. Some of my old bad habits started anew—I would start to skip classes. Oftentimes I had a Spanish class on the first floor of a real old building, and I would sit in the open window and when our Spanish teacher, Señor Maturo, would turn around I'd slip out of the window and was gone. I was out of there for the day . . .

My dad, as I told you, was an attorney. A self-made man, actually self-educated after high school, and I would say rather stern. He was always a beautiful dresser and known as Nick throughout the whole city . . . He certainly looked healthy enough as he walked down the street with his walking cane and his derby and his Chesterfield coat. But when he was about fifty years old he suffered some very serious illnesses, he had a gall bladder operation that was almost fatal. At that time I was a junior at Akron University, and I had to drop out of school in order to get a job and help my parents out. I never went back to college. . . .

A year before my dad got sick for the last time— a year before his dying began—I received one of the great honors of my life.

I was invited to deliver the commencement address at Ohio State University. For a boy who grew up in central Ohio, the idea of speaking in Ohio Stadium—the legendary gray football stadium where the Ohio State Buckeyes play—was overwhelming, thrilling almost beyond description.

Ohio Stadium—the massive gray horseshoe on the Olentangy River, the stadium inside of which Coach Woody Hayes walked the sidelines, inside of which generations of Ohioans have gathered on football Saturdays for most of the last century—is the single most famous place in Ohio. When you grow up in the middle of Ohio, your world at times feels small and constrained and quiet. And then, one Saturday, your parents bring you with them to Ohio Stadium.

On that day you walk through the dull and dingy concrete bowels of the stadium, up a short flight of stairs and into a tunnel and then into the sunlight—and all of a sudden your world changes. You are still in the middle of Ohio, but for the first time in your life you are in a place so huge, so filled with color and noise, so exciting, that you instinctively have new knowledge of life's possibilities. Of size, and scale, and potential, of infinite horizons about which you had previously scarcely dared to dream.

Ohio Stadium, to me, had always borne more symbolic weight than the White House, than Buckingham Palace. Ohio Stadium, to me, was the end of the rainbow. The perfect place.

To be invited to be commencement speaker there had a meaning I could not come close to articulating. Spring graduation at Ohio State is said to be the largest in the United States; fifty thousand people gather for the ceremonies.

But that is not why the June morning in Ohio Stadium was going to mean so much to me.

And that is not why, when what happened inside Ohio Stadium happened, it hurt so much.

My mother and father, for more than fifty years, went together to Ohio Stadium every football Saturday. Their marriage was one of the closest I have ever observed; they did virtually everything together. They had a date with each other every night, whether they left the house or not.

And—especially after my sister and brother and I moved away from Columbus—those Saturdays in Ohio Stadium were the cement that connected the weeks and months and years of their life in Ohio. Think about that: going to that stadium together for more than fifty years.

They finally had to stop. My father, even before his final illness, didn't get around so easily. Ohio Stadium on a football Saturday was just too hard.

But on that June morning, they made plans to come to the stadium one more time. They came to see me speak.

I had my own plan that day.

I had come up with it the night before—I had arrived in Columbus from Chicago, had gone up to the Ohio State campus, and had found an open gate on the exterior of the stadium. I had walked inside, and had looked around.

I knew that I had never been any good at telling my parents private things about how I felt about them—at least not out loud, at least not face-to-face. This was my failing, not theirs.

But on that night, in the empty stadium, I decided what I was going to do the next morning.

Without telling anyone about it beforehand, I was going to ask the people who had come for commencement exercises to do me a kindness. I was going to let them know about my parents, and about those fifty years of football Saturdays that were now over. And I was going to ask the crowd to rise and honor my father and mother with a standing ovation—a standing ovation in Ohio Stadium.

The next morning was one of the worst rainstorms anyone in central Ohio could remember. The fifty thousand people showed up and took their seats in the stadium. For more than an hour, they waited in the downpour for the ceremonies to begin.

Standing with the official procession underneath the stadium, I thought about my mom and dad sitting in that unrelenting rainstorm. I didn't know what to do. We finally marched in; the rain only intensified. I tried to find them in the crowd, but couldn't.

Minutes into the ceremony, it was called off. The weather was just too severe. Graduation would have to be canceled.

I found them beneath the stadium—soaked to the bone. Broke my heart. Made me want to cry. Fifty years into my own life, and here they were, sitting for an hour in a rainstorm for the chance to watch me do something. What else matters in life? The people you can count on like that—what else matters?

A year passed. I was invited to come back again to deliver the commencement address. It was to be the last commencement in Ohio Stadium for a while—repairs were scheduled to begin on the mammoth old place.

My parents were in the crowd again. The morning began with rain, but it stopped by the time we marched onto the football field.

I looked into the stands. More than fifty thousand people, stretching all the way to the sky, were there. Ohio Stadium, on a joyous and sunny June day.

I told the crowd about my parents. I explained about the year before.

And I asked the fifty thousand to do me the favor.

They did. In Ohio Stadium—the place where for so many years the crowds have risen to cheer for the football teams—on this day they rose to cheer for my mother and father.

The roar filled Ohio Stadium. It will sound in my heart forever.

My mother and I stood looking at the diploma on the wall of his office. This was the first time I had been back in the house since his death.

"Do you think I should take this with me now?"
I said.

"No," she said. "I think it should stay here."

I had meant for it to be a nice surprise—a gesture
he would like. As I had gotten ready for the reunion
weekend the summer he got sick—when all of us
came to Columbus—I had packed the diploma to
bring with me. Little more than a month had passed
since the morning in Ohio Stadium; the honorary
degree had been presented to me at the end of the
commencement speech, and my name—our name—
had been on it.

He had never had one of these. I was lucky
enough—because of the years of work he put in—to
be able to go to college; after that trip to Chicago
we had taken when I was in high school, I had been
admitted to Northwestern, and graduated from
there. He paid for it.

So on the last night of our family's reunion, as we
were all finishing dinner on the patio behind their
house, I had said that I had something I wanted to
give him. I handed him the package.

"What's this?" he had said.

"Open it," I had said.

He did.

"What am I supposed to do with this?" he said.

It wasn't exactly the reaction I had been hoping
for.

"It's yours," I said.

His expression was dismissive—even disdainful.

"Gee, just what I always wanted," he said, his voice full of sarcasm. At the time I thought that maybe he had had one too many drinks; later I concluded that the illness that changed his behavior toward the end had started to kick in.

Or maybe it just was what it was. Maybe he didn't want anyone else's diploma. Maybe I had made a big mistake by trying to give it to him. Especially in front of the rest of the family.

"Thanks," he had said, but had handed it back to me.

"I'm not taking it," I had said to him. "It belongs to you."

And now here we were—my mom and I, standing in the quiet house, the house from which he was gone. The diploma with his name on it—with our name on it—was on his wall.

"He put it up as soon as all of you left that weekend," she said.

I said that maybe we should head out to the Top for dinner.

How much has this place changed since you first came here?" I asked.

"Not at all, except for the prices," my mom said.

The Top, when it first opened in the Fifties, was—here is the only word for it—snazzy. A snazzy steakhouse, for all the young couples on the East Side of Columbus, back from the war and starting families. Forty years later the booths were the same, the decor was the same—I looked across the table, and I saw my mother, approaching eighty, and I tried to imagine her at thirty-five or thirty-six in this same booth, out for an evening with her husband. And I knew, as we sat there, that she wished I wasn't the person who was sitting across from her tonight.

"He still kept the 'Organize, Delegate, Supervise, Check' plaque next to his desk at home, I see," I said to her.

"Like he would ever forget the words," she said.

It was his credo—those four words, in that order, were, he said, what got him through his business career. Follow those words, he said, and you will be a success in your job.

Kind of a graduate business school for a guy who never had the good fortune to get to finish college. Four words. They seemed to have worked. They allowed him to do well enough at his job that he could send my brother and sister and me to good universities.

They were the first words in the eulogy at his funeral. We had made sure of that. Organize. Delegate. Supervise. Check.

The waitress came around, and my mom and I talked, and what I was hearing was his voice—his voice from those tapes he had given us. The part where he described going to work after he had to drop out of college to help his parents.

• • •

He had found a job at the most menial level at a scrap rubber company. He hoped to rise to something better, but he had to start somewhere:

I was an office boy, and a pretty poor one at that. . . . But the sales manager, a handsome Irishman by the name of Jack Costello, who never came to the office without a tremendous hangover but who despite all that operated at tremendous efficiency all the time, was a great help to me. He was about ten or fifteen years older than I, but he understood me and gave me an excellent grounding on how to conduct myself in business, whether in the office or on the road.

I shall never forget Jack Costello. One of the things he told me that I never forgot was, "Bob, when you're out on the road, which you will be, you're going to have an expense account and you can spend what you want on food and anything you need. But nobody ever got rich padding an expense account."

In the first place, I never knew what "padding" an expense account meant. I remember that he said to me, "Live well, but we do kind of frown on excesses like three dollar breakfasts and things like that." Well, up to that time I don't believe I had ever paid more than forty-five cents or fifty cents for breakfast, and so when I learned that three dollars for breakfast was a no-no, but that anything under that was acceptable, that, I believe, is when I started to gain weight. . . .

Suffice it to say that I mended my ways in the office and started acting like a grown-up, or almost, and then I was sent out onto the road. My travels consisted of driving into Pennsylvania, scouting the highways and byways and looking for junkyards where there might be huge piles of scrap tires. . . .

At the Top, my mom said that going out to dinner, even with her oldest friends, in these first months after his death was a chore at best—and painful at worst.

She looked over at the bar, and mentioned the name of a man they had known—a man who had a reputation for liking to spend time with women. She laughed.

"Daddy"—she was referring to my dad, not hers; often he was "Daddy" when she talked about him in front of my brother or sister or me, especially in the time after his death—"Daddy would say that if he ever wanted to find this particular man, he knew that all he would have to do is come to the bar at the Top."

But that was in the days after he was established in business, a homeowner in Columbus. He'd had to start somewhere. In this old restaurant on East Main Street I kept hearing his voice:

. . . One of the most important, yet devastating, things that ever happened as far as my work record occurred about this time. Suffice it to say that it involved a mistake that I made, which could have cost the company an awful lot of money, and it was purely because of carelessness on my part. I won't go into any details on it, but it was the beginning of the end. My services were no longer required.

I went to Cleveland looking for a job, to no avail. So I was kind of down in the dumps, but fortune smiled upon me, providentially. One day I walked into the Dime Savings and Loan Company where I ran into an old friend of mine by the name of Bill O'Neill. He said, "What are you doing?" and I said, "I'm not doing a damn thing, I got my butt fired." And he said, "How would you like to go to work for the Philip Morris Company?" I said, "I would love it. When do I start?" He said, "What about tomorrow?"

So I rushed home and told Mother and Dad, who incidentally were very sympathetic about my firing and they wished me the very best, which made me feel very good because I felt as if I had let them down. The next morning I went to work for Bill O'Neill at the Akron sales office of Philip Morris. The office was in an old funeral home, actually it was simply a room, and they had done the embalming in that room.

There was still the gutter in the floor where all the embalming fluid used to run out of the table on which the stiffs were laid. It was rather a macabre place, but regardless, Bill had his desk there and I had a little table or something.

My job consisted of calling on every store in Akron that carried cigarettes and tobacco. I had no car, but I had plenty of bus fare. So I would take the bus to the far ends of town, lugging a heavy sample case full of cigarettes and samples of pipe tobacco, get off the bus and start walking back in toward town, calling on every store, saloon and candy shop. I believe I was making eighteen dollars a week, and in those days that was not too bad. I got plenty of exercise and learned a heck of a lot about human nature.

And incidentally, having been fired made me make a vow to myself which has stood me in good stead to this day. And that vow was simply this: Grow up, be careful what you're doing, don't make mistakes and make yourself as indispensable to your boss as you possibly can. . . .

I asked my mom if coming to the Top had been a luxury for them back then—if going out for a big steak dinner in a restaurant was something they did all the time, or whether it was a treat to be budgeted for.

"This was sort of a gathering place," she said. "We

came here whenever we could. When it was new, it was where all of our friends would come on a Friday or Saturday night. It was the hot new place."

I thought about him, coming out of the Depression, his future, like the futures of all those men who grew up in those years, far from certain. Were he sitting with us tonight—had this dinner been taking place ten or fifteen years before—I probably wouldn't have given a thought to the forces that brought him here. How he had managed to get himself started in the business world would not have been anywhere on my mind. I probably would have been talking about the day's news.

But tonight I saw my mom looking across the table at the seat I knew she wished he was in, and his voice was in my head. The young man trying to catch on with a company that might value him:

. . . I finally became fairly well known in Akron as being the Philip Morris representative, and I don't know how good your memory is, but the trademark of Philip Morris was a bellboy, a very beautifully uniformed midget who called out, "Call for Philip Morris." And so every time I came into stores, the people who I had dealt with used to make that call, which made me feel pretty good, being identified as the Philip Morris representative.

One day Bill O'Neill came to me and said

there was an opening in Lima, Ohio, and would I like that job. Well, I said yes, and will I be making any more money, and he said yes, you'll be making a little more money and you're going to be your own boss. And we're going to give you a car, and you will have a territory that would comprise the northwest part of Ohio, down to Marysville and over to Grand Lake and St. Marys and so forth. That sounded very interesting, because that would be the first time I ever left home.

So I went home that day, my mother was home, and I said, "Mother, I've got a new job and I'm leaving this afternoon." Well, she couldn't believe it, because that was a pretty quick move, but I had no choice.

Bill O'Neill and I went for the long ride to Lima, so that he could get me established there. We took a newspaper, looked for rooms to rent, and found a lovely old house on Market Street in Lima, and I became a roomer. And a roomer I was, because I had a bedroom on the first floor, I think three towels, and the use of a bathroom on the second floor. I believe that was in the summer of 1938. I had my own car there, which was a really snappy maroon Ford convertible coupe, and then later I had a company car, which was a panel truck in which I carried a stock of cigarettes. Bill O'Neill left the next day after getting me all set up in Lima and said, "You're on your own." All of a sudden I think I grew up.

I didn't know a soul in Lima, not one soul, and the places to meet people were in the hotel bars. I was kind of a popular guy because part of my job was to give away samples of cigarettes, and everyone wants something for nothing. That stood me in good stead in the bars, especially the hotel bar where all of young Lima congregated.

Another big meeting place was Indian Lake, a resort south of Lima, where a lot of people went to hear big bands, which played every weekend. Now, these were the big bands of fame. And it was a wonderful thing to see hundreds of young people crowded around the bandstand and listening to the likes of Benny Goodman, Gene Krupa, the Dorseys and the like. Those days were never to be repeated, but of course we didn't know that.

And in the far distance was rumbling a war, because this was summer at the end of the 1930s, when all hell was breaking loose in Europe. . . .

The Top had not been crowded on this night; forty years down the road, the steaks were still good, but it's not the hot new spot in town. Never would be again.

My mom and I walked out and I took her home,

and when she said she was ready for bed I headed back to the place where I'd been with Tibbets in the afternoon. For some reason I was very much in the mood to hear his voice.

I saw him before he saw me. He was walking quite slowly toward the lounge where we had sat before. I had made it a point to be a few minutes early; so had he.

So I followed him in—"Oh!" he said when he saw me. "Didn't know you were behind me!"—and we sat down, and I told him about my dad and that first real job, and about the "Call for Philip Morris!" thing—about how the store people, in the 1930s, would sing out "Call for Philip Morris!" when they saw the young salesman coming.

It was how he became a salesman, I told Tibbets—teaching himself, giving away free samples.

"That's how I started, too," Tibbets said.

"Being a salesman?" I said.

"No," he said. "Being a pilot. But I was giving things away just like your dad."

"How?" I said. "I don't understand."

The sound of this eighty-four-year-old man's words was something that felt exceedingly good to me right now.

"Well . . ." Tibbets said.

He stopped himself.

"Are you in a hurry?" he said.

"Farthest thing from it," I said.

TEN

I dropped Baby Ruths," Tibbets said.

"What do you mean?" I said.

"Baby Ruths," Tibbets said. "The candy bars."

"You dropped them *where?*"

"Out of an airplane," he said. "Your father gave away cigarettes, I dropped Baby Ruths. It was how I first found out that I loved flying—it was the first I knew what I wanted to do with my life."

In the lounge, I asked him to tell me how it had happened.

"When I was twelve years old, my father was a wholesaler of confectioneries, and we were living in Miami, Florida," he said. "My dad distributed for the Curtiss Candy Company. They had a candy bar that was being introduced—Baby Ruth—that they wanted to promote to the public.

"Someone had the idea that a pilot should take a biplane up over the Miami vicinity, and throw Baby Ruth bars out of the plane over areas where there were a lot of people. So a pilot by the name of Doug Davis was hired. He showed up at my father's office the day before the flight. He said that he wanted tiny paper parachutes tied to each Baby Ruth, so that they would float to the ground rather than drop down real hard.

"I volunteered for the job. I sat there and I tied

those paper parachutes to every Baby Ruth. It was tedious work. Then Davis told my dad that he needed someone to come up with him as he flew the plane—someone to throw the candy bars out. Kind of like a bombardier.

"I immediately said that I was the man for the job. My dad didn't want me to do it—he really didn't like the idea of flying. But I talked him into it, with the help of Doug Davis.

"The next morning we went to an airfield in a place that felt like a farmer's pasture. We loaded the open biplane with all the Baby Ruths with the paper parachutes I'd tied on. We climbed into the plane.

"Davis told me to get ready for our takeoff. We were going down the runway over some pretty rough ground—I remember the fence posts going by as we bumped past them. Then all of a sudden, the fence posts were gone, and the ground wasn't bumpy anymore.

"I said to Doug Davis, 'We're standing still.'

"And he said, 'No—we're flying.'

"I have never had a feeling like that in my life— the feeling of being off the ground, of flying through the air, above everything down below. Doug flew the plane to the Hialeah racetrack, where the horse races were going on. The grandstand was full; Doug banked the plane and told me to get ready, and he flew over the grandstand and called to me: 'Throw 'em!'

"I did—I started heaving those Baby Ruths out of the plane as fast as I could, aiming for the people below. Most of the parachutes worked—I could see the people in the grandstand looking up, and watching the candy bars float down, and trying to grab them. We made another pass over the race-track, and I threw more of the candy bars, and then Doug flew us over to Miami Beach. We flew low over the beach and I threw the candy bars that were left to the people in their bathing suits who were on the sand next to the ocean."

As he told me this, I tried to imagine such a scene today—an open airplane flying at an extremely low altitude, buzzing a public gathering where large numbers of people are congregated, and someone in the plane throwing hard objects from the plane into the crowd. Not only would the pilot likely be arrested as soon as he landed—but attorneys would be lining up to file lawsuits on behalf of people who were struck by the falling objects.

But if that thought—the thought of a person tossing things out of an airplane at strangers below—was enough to give pause, then a second thought was even more provocative:

The thought of the boy—so excited and happy about dropping candy bars from a plane to hungry Floridians on the ground—ending up as a man who, half a world away from Florida, drops an atomic bomb on people standing on the ground below with no idea of what is about to transpire.

"Doug Davis flew back to the airfield after all the Baby Ruths were gone," Tibbets told me, his eyes somewhere else. "That was the day I knew. I had to fly airplanes. That was the day that changed my life. I knew I was going to fly."

My father had spoken with such obvious affection and wistful nostalgia about his beginning days in the work force; Tibbets' voice, as he told me about the Baby Ruth flight, had the same lilt as my dad's when he had described being a young man starting out.

I found myself wanting to know if Tibbets felt the same way about the places where he had done his later, more important work. Wendover, for example—the barren part of the Utah salt flats where he had assembled and trained the atom bomb flight team. Did he frequently go back there for visits?

"No," he said, a look of something close to contempt on his face. "I think I've been there three times since we left there."

"Why so few times?" I said.

"You ever been to Wendover?" he asked rhetorically, as if to say that had I ever been there, I'd know why he avoided it.

"Actually, I have," I said.

"Really?" he said, disbelieving.

"I can see why you stay away," I said.

Wendover—West Wendover is what the part in Nevada is called, just a few feet past the Utah line— is as desolate and remote a piece of land as you are ever likely to find. It feels separate from everything; the heat rises from the highway in waves you can see, the nearby Bonneville Salt Flats stretch to a blank horizon. The Nevada part of Wendover seems to exist for its casinos—for people coming from Salt Lake City, it is the closest place where gambling and its peripheral pleasures are legal. Utah residents drive for hours from Salt Lake City and beyond, across the melting highway through countryside all but devoid of scenery, looking for the state line. One of the first casinos they encounter is in fact called the State Line: supply and demand, hidden human needs fulfilled on the parched desert.

A novelist named Peter Rock, who set his book *This Is the Place* in Wendover, once said of the city: "It always seemed like a place where the dark lands begin. It's such a sad place. When I was writing the book, when I decided to set it there, I moved there. But after three days I realized I couldn't do it, so I left." When I was in Wendover myself, I met a schoolteacher who told me, "It's the children here I worry about. Not only that it's so far removed from the rest of the world out here, but so many parents work for the casinos, and are at work all night when the children are at home. . . ."

Wendover seems irrevocably distant from any-

where else, feels like a place no one would come to
if they didn't have to: a place that easily confers privacy, unsolicitedly offers up secrecy. A place you
would instinctively seek out if you didn't want to be
seen.

"We had that place so beautified," Tibbets said.
"The base we put together . . . I was really proud of
what we built.

"I went back there in 1990, and the sight of our
old base made me sick. A bunch of rundown shacks.
Holes in the buildings. When I say it made me sick,
I mean it—I was literally sick at my stomach, looking around. My old headquarters didn't exist."

What was his first thought, upon looking at the
casinos rising near where he had trained his men? I
told him that, from the guest rooms of some of the
casinos, you can see the remnants of the base he had
set up.

"It just felt bad," he said. "When I first saw what
they had done in Wendover, it felt very bad. No
casino has ever gotten a nickel out of me—I think
people who gamble are a bunch of damn fools,
throwing their money this way and that, watching
those stupid wheels turn around.

"I didn't like it. I didn't like being around it. I
just wanted to get out."

What about Tinian? What about that distant island in the Pacific, from which he had made the
most important takeoff of his life—the most impor-

tant takeoff of World War II? Had he gone back there to visit?

"I have not," he said. "I've been there, and I've seen it. In 1945. Not since. I'm a lousy tourist."

He looked at me with a smile and said, "You may have seen Wendover, but I know you've never seen Tinian."

"Actually, I saw it just the other day," I said.

In the 1940s, the United States struggled with almost unimaginable resolve to send men, machinery and weapons halfway across the globe and onto Tinian, so that Tibbets and his crew could stage the raid on Japan. Tinian was, and is, a speck in the Western Pacific Ocean, a piece of sea-surrounded land that was furiously fought for by American troops. It was because those troops were able to take Tinian and the other Northern Mariana Islands from the Japanese in 1944 that the U.S. airstrip could be built on Tinian. Soldiers, sailors and airmen were transported there—as was a certain B-29, as was the atomic bomb.

So far away, so remote and small in the middle of the ocean that it is difficult to find it on a map—yet the United States, battling hurriedly against space and time, moved all those men there.

And now, half a century later, I had gone to my office at the *Chicago Tribune* on the morning my series of stories about Tibbets began to appear, and among the e-mails about those columns was one from a man on Tinian.

His name was Jim McCullough; he wrote that he was the librarian for the elementary school on Tinian. He said that he was a regular reader of the column via the electronic version of the *Tribune*—he sits on Tinian, hits the keyboard, and there, in an instant, is the story I have written in Chicago. The concepts of distance, and time, and scope. . . .

"Tinian is a sleepy little island of about 2,500 people," he wrote in his e-mail. I began to correspond with McCullough, to ask him some questions about the island; he said that "While we who were born in the U.S. view Saipan and Tinian as one of the final stepping stones to victory in World War II, the Japanese see the islands as the location of one of the last gallant defenses of their homeland."

Life on Tinian, he wrote, is peaceful and pretty:

It's like living in any small town Stateside. Except you can't get in your car and drive to the next town. Being in the middle of the Pacific Ocean has some disadvantages and some advantages. A disadvantage is that if you go anywhere—the beach, for example—there will be no one there and nothing going on. What a bore.

On the other hand, one of the *advantages* is that you can go just about anywhere—the beach, for example—and no one else will be

there. No surfers, boom boxes, wall-to-wall
sunbathers to distract you from enjoying some
peace and quiet. From each beach or hillside
you get a magnificent view of endless blue.

McCullough wrote me that a casino (apparently
you can't escape the things anywhere in the world,
from Wendover to Tinian) had recently been built
on the island, in an attempt to draw tourists from
Japan and Korea. There are not many remnants
from World War II, he said—and then he wrote
something too strange to make up: "Most of the real
U.S. military hardware such as trucks, Jeeps, buildings and aircraft wreckage was resold to the
Japanese after the war as scrap metal."

I sent him a question about the airstrip itself—
the runway from which Tibbets and his crew had
taken off on that black August night in 1945, on
their way to win the war.

Instead of answering me with words, Mc-
Cullough went out onto the island with his camera.
The next morning, when I got to work, there it was
on my computer screen—a color snapshot of the island as it appears today. He had taken the picture
and sent it to me over his computer.

"[The airstrip] is in very good shape, considering
the time span involved," he wrote. "The top layer is
broken up somewhat, so I would compare it to a
large highway with pea-sized gravel scattered
about. It is very easy and safe to drive on."

A safe and pebbly roadway—in a world that is tiny and incomprehensibly huge, all at the same time.

"So I have seen Tinian," I said to Tibbets.

"They're driving cars on the airstrip, the guy told you?" he said, shaking his head.

"He taps his computer key on Tinian, and in Chicago I'm looking at the airstrip," I said. "In seconds."

"As I recall, our trip took a little longer," he said.

As we talked, I looked at Tibbets and I thought about photographs of him I had seen from the war—photographs of him as a young pilot. I could still see that young man in his face—the young Tibbets' face was still there, underneath the years. It was like that portrait of my dad that had been painted in Italy—as old as he got, as sick as he got, I could always look in his face and see the young soldier in the portrait.

But I didn't know what my dad saw—I didn't know if, to my father, the young man was still in the mirror. I decided to ask Tibbets what he saw— who was in his mirror every morning when he first woke up to start a new day?

"When I look in the mirror in the morning, I see myself," he said. "Let me put it this way—I figure that if another morning has come and I'm seeing something look back from the mirror, then I'm lucky that I'm looking at it."

"Do you like what you see?" I said.

What I meant was: Does the old man represent the young man pretty well? Is the life he has led reflected properly in the face in the mirror? But he answered in a way I hadn't anticipated.

"I've lost so much bone in my mouth," he said.

I didn't understand.

"I'm embarrassed to have my picture taken," he said. "My mouth goes in."

Apparently there had been some bone erosion above his upper lip. I hadn't noticed it—either before or right now. Even as he was saying the words, I looked at him and did not observe anything really wrong with his mouth.

"It's embarrassing to see me smile," he said. "That's why I don't smile very much in pictures."

You never know what another person worries about; you never know what another person thinks the world is seeing, and thinks the world finds lacking. I asked him, if he had a choice, whether that would be what he would change. Whether, if he could have something back, it would be the bone in his mouth structure that he seemed to feel was such a problem.

"No," he said. "My mouth, I can live with. But the hearing—the hearing is such an embarrassment for me. It's embarrassing as hell. I'm with people who I'm trying to have a nice time with—and I can't hear them. I have to ask them to say things over again. You've seen me do it with you—you'll say something to me, and I'll tell you that you have to say it again. It just makes me feel terrible. And then I'll have to do it again a few minutes later."

My father had the same problem as he grew older; conversations, especially in settings where there were many voices, such as in restaurants, were difficult for him to keep up with. He would become annoyed; especially with my brother or sister or me, if we were talking and he was missing sentences, he would occasionally get angry, as if we had somehow conspired to talk in a way that was designed to leave him out of the discussion. It was as if he—knowing how unclear our words were—believed that we knew it too, and were talking that way on purpose.

"It was all those years of pistons banging away next to my ears," Tibbets said. "From the airplane engines. There wasn't much I could do about it— and you don't realize at the time what effect it is going to have on your life. But that's what took my hearing away. That's what the doctors have told me."

"Would you be seventeen or eighteen again if someone could give you the chance?" I asked.

"No, but I'd like to be forty-five or fifty," he said. "By that time, I think I had a little sense. By the time I was forty-five or fifty, I appreciated the things around me more than I did before. But to be eighteen or twenty again? No way. I wouldn't want to be that age and have to think about raising a child today. Not in this world."

I asked him what physical changes he noticed as he grew older—what a man in his eighties observes about himself that's not visible to the outside world, but the man is conscious of every day of his life.

"I don't have the endurance I used to have," he said. "And I can't recover from being sick or hurting myself as quickly as I used to.

"But most of all . . . I could still *hear* when I was forty-five years old. A man has got to be able to *communicate* properly, and so many times I feel that I just can't, because of my hearing. You have no idea how much it bothers me. It bothers me every single day."

Thinking about that portrait of my dad, I tried to come up with anywhere else in his house where there had been a sign that he had been in World War II, and that it had been profoundly important to him. I couldn't think of anywhere—I knew there must have been places around the home in which he and my mom lived where there were artifacts from his war days, but if there were, I couldn't recall them.

I asked Tibbets about his home. How much war memorabilia did he keep around?

"None," he said.

"None, or very little?" I said.

"Nothing," he said. "There's not any indication in my house that I was ever in the service."

I knew that he was married for a second time, to a woman he had wed after being divorced from the woman who was his wife during World War II. I didn't know whether that had something to do with it—not having reminders of a first marriage in the home where a second marriage lives.

"That's not it," Tibbets said. "I just learned during the war—I had to move around so much, all the time, that taking things with me was a bother. The things that people call 'memorabilia'—it's not memorabilia at the time, it's just things you pack up and carry to the next place.

"I didn't want to carry all that stuff. So I didn't. Every time my orders said that I had to move on to the next place, I would just leave everything behind except for what I really needed to do my job."

But wouldn't some of those things be meaningful to him now—if he could have some artifacts from his war experiences in his home, would those artifacts not be evocative?

"It doesn't mean so much to me," Tibbets said. He pointed to his head. "I've got it all up here, anyway. I don't need to be reminded.

"I've gone into some people's houses—people my age, people who were in the war—and you'd think there was a damned shrine in the house. Walls!

Bookcases! All filled with things from their time in the service.

"I have never believed in that. I don't know what it is—do they want people to think that they're great big shots or something? That must be it. I don't want that. Not for me."

"So you think that's really why people do it?" I asked. "To impress visitors who come to their houses?"

"Oh, it's probably even worse than that," Tibbets said. "It would be bad enough if they set up these shrines to their war careers to convince other people of what a great job they did.

"But a lot of it is probably not to convince other people. It's to convince themselves."

Tibbets had made a note about something. I saw it on top of the table where we were sitting; the handwriting was neat, careful, almost pretty.

It had been that way when he had sent the hand-written greeting to my father. His penmanship was so lovely that it didn't necessarily seem to match the man. He was, after all, eighty-four; he also was a rough-hewn kind of guy, a combat-pilot/no-pretenses/anti-ornate person who, you might assume, expressed himself on paper with a direct and impatient scrawl.

But there it was: handwriting so elegant and delicate that it might belong to the most conscientious and eager-to-please schoolgirl at a top-echelon finishing school.

I asked him about it.

"I try to do things right," he said.

Simple as that. Pure Tibbets.

"My father had the best penmanship I ever saw," he said. "That is something I remember about him very well—how beautiful his handwriting was."

"Do you think a man's handwriting has anything to do with what kind of person he is?" I asked.

"Yes, very much so," Tibbets said. "More than anything else, if a man has good penmanship, it means that he's careful. He cares."

"He cares about what?" I asked.

"About himself," Tibbets said. "He cares what people think about him, and what conclusions those people might draw about him if they were only to see his handwriting."

I folded my arms over some pieces of paper where I'd written a few things down. I didn't want Tibbets to see the sloppy, rushed, all-but-indecipherable scrawl.

ELEVEN

We stayed late that night. I would ask him questions about the war, and he would search his memory and come up with bits and pieces of things that happened more then fifty years before; he would mention names and places and sometimes even specific dates, but there is one thing that he never talked about: being afraid.

So I asked him. What was he afraid of? Both now and then—what scared him?

"I'd have to tell you: nothing," Tibbets said. "What would there be for me to be afraid of?"

The answer to that one seemed beyond obvious: Back then, the German Luftwaffe and the Japanese air force would have seemed to present something to be mightily afraid of. Both—literally—were out to kill him. And now? As an eighty-four-year-old? People of that age have the right to be afraid of a lot of things. The uncertainty of their years, the thought of being eventually alone, the state of their health, something as elementary as walking down a city street at night.

"My mother told me, 'What is to be will be,'" Tibbets said. "I always took that to heart. In the war, and after the war. You can't change what's going to happen, so there's no use being afraid."

"Everyone's scared of something," I said.

"Well . . . I don't like snakes," he said. "But I wouldn't say I'm afraid of them."

"Do they spook you when you see them?" I said.

"No," he said. "I just don't like being around them. I've been in the Everglades, and I'd prefer not to be around those snakes, but they certainly don't put any fear into me."

"I can't believe that you feel just as safe on the streets at night now as you did when you were a young man," I said. I was recalling the look I often saw in my father's eyes, in his later years, when boisterous groups of young people would appear coming around a street corner. It bothered him that he, objectively, was now no match for them; it bothered him that in many ways he was dependent on their goodwill—or at least on their passivity.

"I'm more cautious now," Tibbets said. "But being cautious isn't the same as being afraid. It's just good sense.

"To me, fear paralyzes your mind. If you're afraid, you can't think straight. Literally—your thoughts become all confused if you're afraid. Do you think I could have flown those B-17 missions in Europe if I had allowed myself to be afraid? With all the decisions a man has got to make on missions like those?

"I don't care how old you are—being afraid can do nothing but cause you problems. I want to be able to think—I don't want to be a prisoner of some sort of fear. You've got a better chance to think your way out of a situation than to get out of it based on some kind of fear you're feeling."

He remained silent for a second or two, and then said:

"Bobcats."

"What about bobcats?" I said.

"If I was supposed to walk through a place where there were bobcats, I'd be afraid," he said.

"Why bobcats?" I asked.

"Bobcats are the dirtiest animals there are," he said. "If I had to be around bobcats, that would scare me to death."

"How about foxes?" I said.

"No, no," Tibbets said. "A fox is just a dog."

"Come on," I said. "A fox is definitely not a dog."

"Might as well be," Tibbets said. "A fox is no more dangerous to you than a dog would be."

This was a man who was not especially afraid of Hitler's fighter pilots, of the emperor's dive-bomber squads.

"I would do just about anything to avoid being around a bobcat," he said. "Take my word on this one—a bobcat is something to be afraid of."

I had never asked a pilot what it was like to sit in the back of a commercial plane when someone else was flying the thing. Tibbets clearly had always been a man who needed to be in control of every situation he was a part of. Did he feel differently about airplanes when he wasn't the one in the cockpit? Did something that filled him with such confidence—the act of flying—become something a little different on days when he wasn't the aviator?

Bobcats aside—as a passenger back in coach, did flying ever give him the jitters?

"Not a damn bit," he said.

He never noticed his hands and feet shifting involuntarily, in response to a motion the airplane in which he was a passenger was making—or not making?

"I know airplanes a little bit," he said. "I know that they're built to fly, to stay up in the air.

"And I know that the chances are good that the pilot up in front is a married man with a family. He's not up there to commit suicide.

"I know what he's doing up there, and what he's thinking. I'm as relaxed as can be, back in the passenger section. Flying the plane is not my job—it's his job. And he's not going to do anything that would kill himself."

"So you never notice little sounds when you're a passenger?"

"Yeah—but I know what they are," Tibbets said. "They're never a problem."

"You saw so many planes go down during the war," I said.

"Someone was shooting at them," he said.

• • •

The word he had used—*suicide*—brought my thoughts back to that small box of pills the flight surgeon had given him before the *Enola Gay* took off. One pill for each man—one pill for each member of his crew.

Because the mission had been a success, the decision about whether to take the pills had not come up. But I wanted to know whether Tibbets had given much thought to it at the time—to the question of killing himself had the Japanese military captured him.

"That wasn't the question I asked myself before we took off for Japan," he said. "The question I asked myself was, 'Are we going to come back or not come back?' I thought we were."

"Did the flight surgeon go over all the possibilities with you?" I asked.

"Not really," Tibbets said. "He just came out right before the flight and handed me the pillbox. He said, 'If you get shot down, these will do the job for you.' I took the box from him, but I wasn't really thinking about him, or about the box. I was ready to take off—ready to go.

"I remember him telling me that if we just bit into the pills, that's all it would take. He said, 'You will feel nothing.' Meaning that we would die painlessly."

"Would you have done it?" I asked. "If you had been captured, would you have taken the pill?"

"I don't know," he said. "I made sure it didn't come to that.

"But if we had been shot down, and the bomb hadn't detonated, and the Japanese had been ready to capture us and take us prisoner—I suppose I would have swallowed one of those pills. Think of the alternative—they would have done everything they could to get all the information out of us about the atomic bomb."

"Your crew members didn't even have much information about it," I said.

"The Japanese wouldn't have known that," he said. "In a way, the crew would have been better off dead than captured, because in captivity they'd be tortured until they gave up information about the bomb—and they wouldn't even have the information, but the Japanese probably wouldn't have believed them."

"You did know about the bomb," I said.

"I'm about the only one who did," Tibbets said. "Which makes me think that I would have taken the pill before the Japanese got the chance to start getting answers out of me."

"It would have worked that quickly?" I asked.

"That's what I was told," he said. "The flight surgeon assured me, 'You can swallow this thing and die within three minutes.'"

"Some assurance," I said.

"It was a cold-blooded fact," Tibbets said. "It was something I had to know. Same way I had to know how to fly the plane there and fly it back. If I had failed to do that, then I had to know how quickly the pill would kill me.

"It wasn't a choice, really. It was a cold-blooded duty."

Because he had not been put in the position of taking the pill, he flew the *Enola Gay* back to Tinian—only to find that the Japanese government and military leadership, even with all the carnage and death in Hiroshima, were refusing to surrender.

Which made the next step all but inevitable:

Do it again.

The question was, where? Which Japanese city would be the target for the second atomic bomb?

"Some people were saying Tokyo," Tibbets said. "To me, that made no sense at all. Yes, we had proven what the bomb could do. But let's say we had chosen to hit Tokyo—and we had killed the emperor.

"Who the hell were we going to make the peace with?"

So Tokyo was out. The second atomic mission—for which Nagasaki was selected as the target—was flown three days after the Hiroshima flight.

"Did you want to fly the second mission?" I asked Tibbets.

As I asked the question this was another moment—and there would be plenty of them during

the times when I was in his presence—when the in-
congruity of the situation was almost too much to
process. Elderly man sitting in a central Ohio bar,
talking with a younger man who must raise his
voice in order to be heard. Barroom close to empty,
with the smattering of people who are present completely oblivious to the identity of the older man. If
the other patrons are having any reaction at all, it is
annoyance at the noise—they're trying to watch TV,
and the younger man is speaking so loudly to the
older man. Had the other people been paying attention, they would have been sucked into the surreal
context of all this—they would have figured out
that the elderly man was discussing not health
problems, not sports, not family matters—but how
he had dropped the atomic bomb.

"No, I didn't want to fly to Nagasaki," Tibbets
said. "That was never the plan. I knew that I
should fly the first one, to prove that it could be
done. But I could not let my men think that I was
trying to hog all the glory. So I knew that the second flight—if one was necessary—wasn't going to
be mine.

"General Curtis LeMay was under the impression
that I *was* going to fly the second mission. But
Chuck Sweeney flew the Nagasaki mission, which
had been my plan."

There it was again—the planning part. The macho
aspects of flying a B-29 were almost a given with
Tibbets—or, more exactly, with the young Tibbets.

But, at least for me, it always circled around to the leadership qualities that had been expected of him. You, colonel—you're going to fly a nuclear weapon to Japan in an effort to win the war. And—oh—could you please be the chairman of the board of the unit that is responsible for this, too?

"It never occurred to me that being the leader was going to be a problem," Tibbets said. "When I was a kid, I was always the leader of the gang. I wasn't appointed—it never occurred to me *not* to be the leader.

"In the military, you ran into the situation all the time—you trained people to be leaders, but in your heart you knew that you can't do such a thing. Leaders can't be trained. Managers can—it is fairly easy to train a manager to do a manager's job."

"What's the difference?" I asked.

"Between a leader and a manager?" Tibbets said. "In the business world, it ends up being measured in salary, or title, or who has the best office. Career-oriented things. That's where you see the leaders and the managers split their ranks.

"But in the military—especially in war—the difference between leaders and managers is very simple. The difference can be the difference between life and death. So you'd better be certain that you have the real leaders in the positions where they are needed."

"You're convinced that it's nothing you can pick up by learning it?" I asked.

"I'm afraid not," he said. "You can't go to a businessman's school and walk out with it unless it's already inside you. They can give you an MBA—but they can't give you that."

I asked him—in the event that General LeMay had insisted that he fly the Nagasaki mission—whether he would have felt up to it. After all, he had carried out the culmination of the entire operation only days before—he had flown the long journey to Japan, had dropped the bomb, had flown back . . . might he not, objectively, have been too tired to effectively pilot the Nagasaki mission?

"Why would I be tired?" Tibbets said, with genuine curiosity in his voice. As if it were a trick question.

"Because of what you had just done," I said.

"I'd had a good night's sleep," he said. "Several of them, really."

"But you had to have been very, very tired," I said. "You just had to be."

"This was World War II," he said. "In my mind, it was illegal to get tired."

I had no doubt that Tibbets' ability to keep the details of the atom bomb project to himself had been absolute during those months of putting the 509th Composite Group together in 1944 and 1945. The information—the information that would change the world forever—flowed from his superiors to him, and stopped there.

But what of the 1,800 men who worked for him in Wendover—the men of the 509th, the men he had entrusted to make the mission a success? A cornerstone of his planning was his refusal to let them in on what exactly was going on—when they had signed on, it had been with the understanding that they would not be told exactly what they were trying to accomplish out on the salt flats.

Yet—human nature being what it is—had Tibbets not been afraid that even the little his men did know might get out, and compromise the whole project? Each man had to have figured out at least bits and pieces of the story of the atomic mission— each man might not have been aware of what the final picture would look like, but if enough individual observations were joined together, the story would be there. Had Tibbets simply taken it on faith that the men would obey him—that when he ordered them to tell no one anything about where they were or what they were doing, they would obey those orders without fail?

"Of course not," he said.

How, then, had he maintained secrecy?

"I told each man when he signed on that we would find out anything he might say to anyone outside our unit," Tibbets said. "I assured each man that we would know. I didn't say *how* we would know—but I told each man that this was no empty talk on my part.

"I set up a security organization for this very purpose. It was run by a man named Bud Uanna, and he had about thirty special agents working with him. Their job was to infiltrate what we were doing—to know everything.

"If one of our men received or sent mail, we read it. If a phone call came in, we listened to it. If a couple of guys were sitting around talking on the base, they were being heard. It had to be that way."

"But what about when the men left the base?" I said. "On the base, at least they were talking to each other. But off the base . . ."

"That was the key to everything we did," Tibbets said. "Shortly after the 509th was assembled in Wendover, I announced that I was allowing Christmas leaves for the men. They got to go home.

"I had a reason for doing this—and it had nothing to do with trying to be nice to them. Wendover was so isolated that there were really only two ways to get out—through the train station or the bus station in Salt Lake City, or through the bus station in Elko, Nevada.

"So the men left Wendover, and they went to Salt Lake City or to Elko. And if they had a drink in the bar of the train station, you can bet that the fellow on the next bar stool was one of our operatives. If they leaned back during the long bus ride out of Elko and the man in the next seat asked them what unit they were assigned to, you can bet that this man was working for us.

"And we found out who talked and who didn't. The men got home for their Christmas leaves—and the ones who had talked got telegrams, ordering them to report back to the base immediately. There was no indication in the telegram of why they had to come back.

"They got to Wendover, and I called them in. I would say, 'Did I not tell you to keep your mouth shut?' And if they would tell me that they *had* kept their mouth shut, I would tell them exactly what they had said, and when. How I knew was none of their business. It was my business.

"I wanted them to sweat. That was the whole purpose of this. I didn't want to go through it twice—I wanted to put so much fear in them that they would never talk about our unit again."

"So you never really believed, at the beginning, that they would keep silent the way you ordered them to?" I said.

"I knew very well that some of them were going to talk," Tibbets said. "You can't have that many men and have all of them obey. But if you put real fear in them—if you make them understand the lengths to which you will go to maintain security—then they won't do it again. Those who I did sense might do it again were shipped out. Some of them to Alaska, where there was no one to say anything to. But the rest were confined to the barracks for a while, and allowed to come out only to eat their meals in the mess hall, and after that it was up to them to keep quiet. Which they did."

"Did you let up on them after that first Christmas leave?" I asked.

"No," he said. "We never let up. We couldn't afford to. And we let them know it, in little ways.

"A man might call home, and his wife might tell him that she was pregnant—that she had gotten pregnant during his Christmas leave.

"And the next day one of us might see the man and say, 'Oh, your wife is going to have a baby. That's wonderful.'

"He'd know. We'd been listening to the phone call. We'd congratulate him on his wife's pregnancy, and it had nothing to do with offering best wishes. It had everything to do with letting him know that nothing got past us."

It sounded lonely. For all the swashbuckling aspects of the stories that Tibbets had been telling me—both the combat-pilot parts and the top-secret-commander parts—it sounded, to me, like just about the loneliest duty a man could have.

"Yeah," he said. "I felt pretty alone. A lot of the times I felt this real need to talk to someone about what I was going through—and there was no one I could talk to.

"Because of the orders I had been given, I really was alone with the knowledge of what we were doing and why. Most of the people who knew what I knew weren't with us in Wendover—they were in Washington, or Los Alamos. When I would fly there for meetings, I would be with people who knew the story. But then I would go back to Wendover—and even the people I trusted the most, even the people who worked with me the most closely, didn't know everything and couldn't know everything."

"Did you ever come close to cracking?" I asked.

"Look, we had a special job to perform," Tibbets said. "It had been told to me quite directly: If we were successful, we were going to hasten the end of the war. That was worth the loneliness.

"And please understand this: Any commander is lonely. When a man is in command, he sits in a position where he cannot have friend or foe. Regular human relationships do not figure into it. So you can't worry about what people think of you, and you can't lie awake and have sleepless nights. The job of being in command is lonely by definition.

"This one was just a little lonelier than most."

"And you were twenty-nine," I said.

"So were a lot of other guys," he said. "Twenty-nine didn't seem so young that year."

Which summed up something I had been thinking about all evening—really, since the

day I had met Tibbets, but especially tonight, after
dropping my mom off at the home she and my dad
had shared, and coming back here to meet him.

They all seemed so much older at such a young
age back then—the feeling I was having tonight
was a permutation of what I had always felt when I
had looked at the oil portrait of my dad in uniform,
but it went well beyond that. The American men of
their generation—or so it seemed—strove purpose-
fully to come off as older than they really were.
Maybe it was because of the war, or maybe it pre-
dated the war—but the emphasis on youthfulness
that took over the American culture in the years
after World War II seemed almost the mirror opposite of what had come before.

It was as if your dad, when he was a young man,
wanted nothing more than to be mistaken for his
own father. In mannerisms, and seriousness of purpose, and desire to join the society of adults—in just
about every way, or so it appeared when looking
back on them from a distance of fifty years, those
young men were intent on being not so young at all.

Or was I wrong?

"Some elements of that are true," Tibbets said.
"You can't generalize—it wasn't true of every man.
But I think it was true of a lot of us.

"Maybe we had more of a reason to be serious.
We were coming out of the Depression when the
war began—we were serious even before we went
into the service, because we grew up having no idea

whether we would be able to go out and earn a decent living and support a family.

"That'll make you old inside—growing up worrying about that. Today . . . look, I don't want to be critical of young people who are growing up today. They have been handed a different set of circumstances than we were.

"But what I see, and I don't like, is this constant sense of *entitlement* that people who are younger than your dad's and my generation seem to have. Where did this belief that a person deserves *entitlements* come from? The queen of England may be entitled to something, but I can't think of many other people who are.

"Here's the difference—when I was running my company after I retired from the service, young people would come in to apply for jobs, and what do you think they always asked, right away? 'What are your benefits and workplace conditions?' That's what they would say. And they thought that's what they were supposed to say.

"I don't think we did that—I don't think that when your dad and I were looking for our first jobs, those were the words we said right away. What we said to a man we wanted to hire us was, 'I can do this for you.' 'I can help you out by doing this or that.' When you are raised during a little harder times . . .

"Well, you're a different person than if you were raised when things were easy. So, yes, I suppose we were different. With good reason."

TWELVE

When you are a child, you think your father can do anything. Anything in the world.

And, in every childhood, there comes a time when you first realize that you have been wrong. Your dad can't do everything. It was an illusion—an illusion willfully created by you.

Sometimes that realization arrives with great drama, at a life-changing juncture; more often it arrives quietly, in a moment that seems to mean nothing.

When I was four years old or so—maybe a year or two older—I asked my father to build me a rocket ship. He said he'd be glad to; he would build it in our garage. As soon as the weekend came, he would build it for me.

Waiting for Saturday, I was filled with excitement. I had the rocket ship in my mind, exactly as it was going to be: six or seven feet tall, made of wood (my dad had told me he would use wood), with a hatch through which I could climb in, and a seat in front of a steering wheel, and a control panel made of metal and glass. I knew the rocket ship wasn't going to go anywhere—I knew that it was just going to be one to get inside of and play with and pretend. But I couldn't wait for him to go out to the garage with me and for him to put it together.

Saturday came. He didn't forget. The two of us went out to the garage, and he pulled out his tool box and some pieces of lumber that were lying around.

He cut the lumber with a saw; he shaped it with a plane. He nailed a few pieces of the wood together, and there it was:

A toy rocket ship. About ten inches long. A rocket ship you could hold in one hand—a rocket made to a child's scale.

I don't know if my face showed anything that day. I'm certain I didn't say anything. But there was the rocket ship he had made me: not much bigger than a flashlight. It occurred to me that of course he hadn't known I was thinking of a big, elaborate rocket ship you could climb inside of; of course he hadn't been able to read my mind. And even if he had, he would not have been able to go out into the garage and make such a thing. It was beyond him—it was beyond what a dad could do.

That was the first time I knew: He could not do everything. I should not expect him to. My view of his abilities—like every child's view of his father's abilities, until a certain day arrives—had been over-large.

Not his fault. Not my fault. Just the way the world works. And that first time gets you ready for what almost without question will come; that first time you realize your father can't do everything for you gets you ready for the day, many years down the line, when he can do just about nothing at all for himself. When the man you first assumed had no limitations turns out to have nothing but limitations, as he comes closer and closer to the day he will die.

They were raised during times that were a little harder, Tibbets had said; as far as work was oncerned, the men of his and my dad's generation did not go in to a potential employer demanding things.

My father's voice—talking about the job offer that had gotten him out of Lima. A couple named Violet and Sam Shinbach, who lived in a suburb of Columbus called Bexley, were starting a company that specialized in metal plating. The company would do standard silverplating of household dinnerware, but the thing that was going to make it different, or so the Shinbachs believed, was their idea for bronze-plating baby shoes. They thought that parents might want to preserve their children's shoes as family heirlooms; this new firm of theirs, which they planned to call the Bron-Shoe Company, might offer prospects for the future for an employee who worked hard at the beginning. Or so my father seemed to believe:

One good thing I always remember, I didn't have any friends when I came to Lima, but when

I left town a year and a half later these kids gave me a party at the Kirwan Hotel, in the bar, as a going-away gesture, and it was absolutely lovely. It was a good feeling to leave Lima knowing that I had some excellent friends remaining.

Violet and Sam Shinbach were in need of someone who had sales-promotion experience and ability, and having been with Philip Morris I seemed to fit the bill and I was available— cheap. So I left Lima to come to Columbus to join the then very tiny Bron-Shoe Company. There were exactly four employees.

Sam and Violet were good enough to let me stay at their house, where I had a bed underneath the stairway and all privileges of their home on Fair Avenue. This was the summer of 1940, and at the beginning of that summer I bought a new car on one of my trips back to see the folks in Akron, and it was a splendid Ford convertible coupe painted cigarette cream, which actually was a bright yellow. And my friends in Lima had immediately tagged and labeled the car as the flying omelette, and I indeed did fly around in that car the summer of 1940.

I was working pretty hard over the summer with Sam Shinbach, and at the end of the summer we went on a long business trip to the East Coast with Violet, and I started learning the business in earnest.

I shall not attempt to go into a history of the

early part of World War II. Suffice it to say that the draft came along, and every able-bodied young man had to register for the draft, which of course I did. As the fall wore on they started to pick the numbers out of the big fish bowl in Washington, and lucky me, I was number one draft in the Bexley area. . . .

I hadn't been too crazy about the confinement of the Bron-Shoe job as compared with the freedom I had had with Philip Morris in the Lima area. But little did I know what was going to happen. I was called up, and on January 28, 1941, I entered the Army and was sent to Camp Shelby in Hattiesburg, Mississippi, that same day or a few days later. . . .

I have seen some impressive things in my life. I have never seen anything to match the way my mother cared for my father in the months of his dying.

When he became totally bedridden, virtually everyone to whom she went for advice—his doctor, our relatives, her friends, in the end the hospice people—told her the same thing: You must make some time for yourself. If you try to do everything, if you try to be with him every minute, you will exhaust yourself, deplete your strength and health, perhaps even shorten your own life. For his sake as well as your own, you must regularly step away—you must breathe.

She said yes. She said of course she knew that was true.

And then she didn't do it.

With the exception of when she took a shower, or went to the grocery to buy food, or had to leave the house for an essential errand, she did not leave him. He became more emotionally dependent on her than he ever had been; he became frightened and disoriented when she would leave the room. We had hired a man to come to the house every day to do the things she was not physically strong enough to do—lift him from the bed, assist him with the bathroom functions that must be tended to—there was time for her to give herself some peace. She didn't want it. She wanted to be with him.

As his confusion grew, he began to ask her the same questions, over and over. This was a man who never forgot a detail—and all of a sudden he was interrogating her about things that made no evident sense, and when she would offer some explanation to calm him, he would nod—and then, within minutes, ask the same questions once more.

And she would hold his hand and answer. Softly, lovingly, without rancor—she would go through everything again.

He would ask: What about the third floor? Was the third floor cleaned up? It was important—the third floor had to be straightened. Had she done it yet?

And she would explain with gentle patience: Their house did not have a third floor.

The mailman—had she given the mailman the notice yet? If the mailman came and she didn't give him the notice, he didn't know what they would do. Was she certain the mailman hadn't arrived yet?

And she would ask him what he wanted her to tell the mailman—and he would look off, not being able to think of it, and finally say that he guessed he was mixed up—he guessed it didn't matter. Then: Had the mailman come yet? Had she remembered to tell the mailman what he had asked her to tell him?

The white pipe that he wanted her to adjust; the geometric forms that he wanted her to explain. In his dying he became stuck on these things, things that defied logic, and she would sit and talk with him about them as if it were forty years earlier, and they were talking about their children, or their vacation plans, or their hopes. From the sound of her voice, you would think that these awful conversations were the most wonderful moments she could ever spend. She was talking with her husband.

She assured us that this was fine; she assured us that this was what she wanted. Often he would wake her up at 3 A.M. or 4 A.M. and start with his questions. The third floor; the mailman; the white pipe. She was getting no sleep, but she wouldn't leave the room. Don't worry, she told my brother and my sister and me; I sleep during the daytime, when he sleeps.

One night I called and there was something changed in the way she sounded. She was near tears. He had been asking her questions for twenty straight hours, she said; she would talk to him and soothe him and answer the questions, she would assure him that the fears upon which he was basing the questions were not real, and he would seem to understand—he would thank her. But the period between the bursts of questions had shrunk to virtually nothing; within seconds the same questions would start again. She was bone-weary, close to desperate.

She had gone out to the living room to lie down, just for a second, and had drifted off to sleep when I had called. She was telling me about all this, and the hollowness of her voice frightened me. In the background, I could hear him calling to her from the bedroom. Where was she? He needed to talk to her—he needed to ask her about some things. This was the ultimate terrible extension of Organize, Delegate, Supervise, Check: He was still doing it, except what he was supervising, what he was checking on, had only the most tenuous connection to reality.

"I'll be OK," she said.

I said I would get the next flight to Columbus. "Really, I'll be OK," she said. "This has just been a bad day." I said I'd be there anyway.

• • •

On the tape he made telling his life story, you have to jump past his induction into the Army to find his first reference to her.

It comes after he has been at Camp Shelby for a while; it comes as he is describing a trip to Columbus he had taken when the soldiers had been granted a leave.

In Columbus I had met a certain Phyllis Harmon, and I thought she was kind of nice. I had taken her to the movies on one of my previous trips to Columbus when I was first visiting Violet and Sam.

She seemed like an OK gal, but I didn't pay a hell of a lot of attention to her because I was still squiring around a girl named Nana Bowler, who lived up in Lima.

Well, I didn't think a heck of a lot about Phyllis Harmon until after I had been in the Army for about six months, and I believe she and I started corresponding with each other.

One fine day when I was on leave in Columbus, she volunteered to drive me to Union Station where I would catch a train to go up to Akron to see my folks. I remember the old blue/gray Pontiac she was driving, and I also remember she looked pretty damn good to me, and I said to myself, I think I'm going to marry that gal.

Little did I know that I really was going to. I believe that that little ride to the train station from Violet's house with Phyllis was the luckiest thing that ever happened to me. That fact has proven itself time and time and time again over the years.

I remember that once I was visiting my parents— this must have been when he was in his midseventies, getting noticeably older but not yet really ill—and I was staying in my brother's old room on the basement level of the house.

One of the lightbulbs in the bathroom down there had burned out—it was a special kind of bulb that had to be replaced in a specific way. I mentioned it to my parents at breakfast; my father said that he would take care of it.

We went down to the basement and he stood on top of a chair and asked me to hand him a new bulb and a tool of some sort.

"Don't let him stand up there and do that," my mother said to me, which was my thought exactly. I had no idea how to replace this particular bulb, but it was obvious that my dad—who had been having some trouble with his back and neck, as I recall—should not have been the one up on the chair performing this task.

"Let me get up there and do it," I had said.

"You'd screw it up," he said, which was true.

"Just tell me how to do it and I'll do it," I said.

"Give me the bulb," he said.

My mother whispered to me: "I mean it, you do it—he shouldn't be up there."

So I said, "Come on, get down—I want to do that."

And he—I can hear his words right now—said:

"I'm running this lash-up."

What a phrase. It sounds more Navy than Army—*running this lash-up*. In the middle of his seventies, so many years removed from military service, yet when he wanted to make a point, that's the language he reverted to. When, for example, he wanted to let us know that there was a person he didn't like—this could be someone our family had known for years, or a waiter in a restaurant whose attitude seemed lackadaisical—he would say to us: "I don't like the cut of that guy's jib." Again, Navy—which he was never in. But those were the references—military references.

He was kidding, at least a little bit, when he said them; he knew that changing a lightbulb hardly constituted a lash-up that had to be run, and he knew that the cut-of-his-jib line always made us smile. But when he used those phrases it was almost as if the words were not meant for us, but for himself. As if he were having a private conversation with himself that no one else was supposed to hear—or, more accurately, the emotional meaning of which no one else was supposed to be able to translate.

• • •

On the troop train to go down to Camp Shelby, Mississippi, all I could hear was a lot of griping about the Army, and not much foreboding, but a lot of dissatisfaction because it was kind of an uncomfortable ride down to Hattiesburg. Upper and lower berths, two people to a berth. . . .

After we got down to Camp Shelby, it was an entirely new world. The camp had recently been gouged out of cornfields and cotton fields, and consisted of miles and miles of perimeter tents with wood-and-coal-burning stoves in them. And that was our introduction to Army life. The first thing we noted was a cloud of black smoke over the whole area as far as you could see, a result of the soft coal that was being burnt in those stoves. It was the middle of winter, and while the camp was in Mississippi it was still a very cold place, and the stoves were badly needed.

We lined up and were assigned certain companies. . . .

They were getting used to the cut of each other's jibs—young men who, weeks before, had been working in cities and small towns and farm communities all over the United States were now inex-

tricably connected with one another. From the
sound of my father's voice, it seemed that this
lash-up was something that held unexpected revela-
tions for him.

In the meantime, a strange phenomenon occurred. As you know, the favorite thing for a
soldier to do is gripe, and believe me, this division made up of fifteen thousand recent civilians and a handful of regular Army officers and
enlisted men did very little else but gripe. The
weather was terrible, the jobs onerous, the
drills and hikes very bone-wearying, and in all
it was a hell of a way to live.

But the phenomenon I mentioned to you was
just this—strangely enough, I started to like it.
I don't know why, but it just seemed to me that
I was free.

Although I had to obey orders and do everything a soldier must do, it was kind of a new-
found freedom. Everyone was alike, nobody was
given any privileges other than what they deserved or earned, and I was not fettered by a job
that I did not like. So going into the Army, believe it or not, was kind of a relief for me. . . .

Listening to his voice—in the months after he
was gone—made me think about the fine grada-
tions in a man's life, the never-anticipated changes a
man may encounter, changes that transform him

from the person he was before into the person he will be forever after. Showing up for Army training in Mississippi and finding it liberating, finding it freeing . . . it's the kind of moment in a man's existence that they don't make movies about, I thought, but one that bears more quiet power than any dozen action films.

And then I thought about a man they did make a movie about. There were some questions I wanted to ask—about the movie, and about the man who was portrayed in it—the next time I saw him.

THIRTEEN

The movie—black-and-white—starred Robert Taylor in the role of Colonel Paul Tibbets. It was called *Above and Beyond*, it was produced by MGM and released in 1952, and you could see traces of *The Best Years of Our Lives* all over it—at least you could see how the MGM marketing department was trying to link it with *The Best Years of Our Lives*.

The Best Years of Our Lives had won the Academy Award for Best Picture of 1946. A beautiful, movingly lyrical film—it holds up even now—it told the story of three servicemen returning to the same small town after World War II had been won. The problems and eventual triumphs of the three characters—a bank executive played by Fredric March (who won the Oscar for best actor), a drugstore employee played by Dana Andrews, a kid just out of school played by Harold Russell (a young veteran who won the Oscar for best supporting actor and who, like the character, had lost his hands in the war)—captivated audiences all over the United States. How these men adjusted to the America they had left behind—and to their own families—touched emotions deep inside a nation that understood the plot only too well.

So when the story of the *Enola Gay* mission was

brought to the screen, it was following in the steps of a proven feel-good movie about the U.S. after the American victory.

But how to make Americans feel good about the devastation and death that Tibbets and his crew had left behind in Japan?

And—more to the point—how to make Americans feel good about Tibbets' family life?

The preview for the movie is startling to view today. It begins on a note of romance, with the Tibbets character saying to his wife, Lucy (played by Eleanor Parker): "If I didn't have you, I wouldn't have anything."

"Oh, Paul," she replies passionately.

Almost immediately, though, the tone of the preview shifts. The deep, portentous voice of an unseen announcer informs the audience: "In his heart was locked the world's best-guarded secret. On his shoulders rested a responsibility greater than any man had ever carried. From here on he had no wife, no loved ones, no friends. Just duty—above and beyond." Next the audience sees Paul and Lucy Tibbets at the air base in Wendover. He is angrily speaking to her.

"Go home!" the Tibbets character says. "Stay home! And keep your nose out of this base!"

The Lucy character, not even trying to hide her contempt for her husband, says: "Is it really necessary to play it this big, Paul?"

"They told me not to bring you out here in the first

place," Tibbets says. "Maybe they were right. . . . For the last time, stay out of my business!"

"It's my business, too!" Lucy says. "Now I'm beginning to understand a few things I couldn't face before."

"That's enough!" Tibbets says.

"Everything they say is true!" Lucy says. "You're not the man I married, not anymore. You're ambitious, you're cold, you're unfeeling. . . ."

Some "best years."

The studio—seeming to realize the problem it had on its hands—endeavored to market the movie to a female audience, in the hopes that enough women would want to see a motion picture about a troubled wartime romance that the film might turn a profit. The line used to promote the movie was: "The love story behind the billion dollar secret." MGM tagged endorsements by prominent women reviewers onto the end of the trailer:

" 'A love story with tenderness and heartbreak. Ladies, take a couple of hankies with you, you'll need them.'—Hedda Hopper, syndicated columnist."

" 'Picture of the month . . . a love story no woman will ever forget.'—Louella Parsons, *Cosmopolitan*."

" 'The love interest is very real. Every woman should see it.'—Ruth Harbert, motion picture editor for *Good Housekeeping*."

I knew that Paul and Lucy Tibbets had been di-

vorced after the war; still, it was surprising to see
the brittleness between them depicted on a movie
screen. *Above and Beyond* didn't do much at the box
office in 1952; you virtually never see it on television these days, and video stores don't regularly
stock it. Yet as I watched the movie—looking at
Robert Taylor on the screen playing the young
Tibbets, thinking of the Tibbets at eighty-four
whom I had been getting to know—I thought
about something else, too: of my parents, and their
closeness and love that had begun during the war,
and that had lasted all those years.

For the last time, stay out of my business! . . .

**You're not the man I married, not any-
more. . . .**

I could hear the echoes of the cinematic Paul and
Lucy Tibbets, and I knew I had to ask him about it.
Tibbets may have won the war; I couldn't help
thinking that my dad was able to win something
else, something that had eluded Tibbets.

I'm afraid that I treated Lucy very badly," he said.
I could tell that he didn't want to spend much
time on this; he was as direct as always, but it was
plainly far from his favorite subject.

"Look," he said. "I've told you about the secrecy
that I was asked to maintain. I took that as seriously
as a man can take anything. Please think back to
1944 and 1945. There were very few people in the

world who were aware that we were well along in developing a bomb that could end the war. If I couldn't tell any of the men who were serving under me, I certainly couldn't tell my wife."

"I never knew how things like that worked during the war," I said. "Whether there was kind of an understanding that of course a man would tell the truth to the person he loved the most—of course he could trust her to keep the secret."

"You're right—you don't know how things worked," Tibbets said. "No, you didn't tell your wife things. What do you think I was explaining to you when I told you about setting up the operatives at the train stations and the bus stations? About listening in to the men's phone calls and reading their letters? If you were told not to say anything to anyone, that included your wife. You never knew who a guy's wife was going to talk to after she had talked to her husband."

"So how did you handle it?" I said.

"I wouldn't talk to her," Tibbets said.

"You mean about the mission?" I said.

"About anything, I'm afraid," he said. "Especially when she was in Wendover—I found myself shutting down completely. I couldn't talk to her about the things that were most important to me, so I found myself not saying very much of anything to her about other things, either. It wasn't fair to her— it also probably wasn't fair to me, being put in that position, but I know it wasn't fair to Lucy."

I was aware that Paul and Lucy Tibbets had had two sons who were very young during the war. I also knew that, in the years after the war and after the divorce, there had been a considerable emotional breach between the sons and their father, and that they did not see much of each other. Although there had been something of a reconciliation, the chasm in many aspects still remained, or so I had been told.

"Did the problems between you and your sons happen because of what they lived through when things were bad with you and their mother?" I asked.

"I think so, to a large extent," Tibbets said. "I was not a good husband, and I was not a good father. I was so wrapped up in doing a good job in what I was entrusted to do in the war that I did not do a good job with the other things.

"I've told my boys: Your mother got a bum deal."

"You say that you don't think you were a good father, either?" I asked.

"No, I wasn't," he said. "Not the best."

"Why?" I said.

"I don't know," Tibbets said. "Don't ask me."

"But I am asking," I said.

"I was just . . . I was just distant from the boys," he said. "I didn't know how to show them any affection. I'm from the generation that, you know, if a man kisses a man—his son—that was considered a sissy thing."

"Did you know back then that you weren't doing so well with your sons?" I said.

"I didn't see them almost at all for years," he said. "I was flying those missions in Europe, and then there was Wendover—it's not like I had the chance to do well or not well with them. I wasn't there. I was in the war."

"When the war ended was it too late?" I asked.

"It might not have been, had I known how to be any other way," he said. "But I didn't. At the time, I thought that was how a father was supposed to be. I think I was probably wrong. But I didn't know. I didn't know how to do it."

I could sense his discomfort, just talking about it. So I shifted the subject. Instead of asking him about his relationship with his wife during the war—the relationship that had been portrayed in the movie—I asked him about the feeling of being depicted in a movie in the first place. What was that like, for a man who grew up in a movie-worshiping America—what had it been like, in 1952, to know that at least for a while, someone pretending to be you was being seen on screens in every downtown and neighborhood in the country?

"I found out right away that they took liberties," Tibbets said. "They made things up. Things about the flight—at first I felt like correcting them, but then they explained to me that this is the way the movies work. To make it more entertaining, and to make it move along. So I just accepted that, and watched it as a movie."

"Did you ever think you were similar to a certain movie star?" I said.

"Well, I liked Robert Taylor," Tibbets said. "He was a nice fellow."

"I'm talking about now," I said. "Is there anyone out there who you think has your personality?"

"Like who?" he said.

"I don't know," I said. "Maybe Clint Eastwood . . ."

"Well, I'm a stubborn man," he said. "I'm stubborn in my own way. I don't know if that's what you're asking, but I would say my stubbornness is the main thing about me.

"And I do like actors who don't use a lot of words. There's no use in wasting a lot of damn words when you can do something instead."

I brought up the *Best Years of Our Lives* comparison to *Above and Beyond*. I told him I'd noticed that *Above and Beyond* had even tried to emulate the inspiring symphonic sound that had served as the background music in *The Best Years of Our Lives*. It hadn't quite worked—Hugo Friedhofer had won an Academy Award for his heart-stirring score in *Best Years*, but the strings in *Above and Beyond* had merely felt weird and out of place. At least to me.

What had Tibbets thought of *The Best Years of Our Lives*?

"I never saw it," he said.

"You never saw it?" I said. "It was the best movie ever made about coming home from the war. How could you not see it?"

"I guess I wasn't interested," he said.

"What war movies have you seen?" I asked.

"Name some," Tibbets said.

"*Thirty Seconds Over Tokyo*," I said.

"Never saw it," he said.

"*Saving Private Ryan*," I said.

"I did not go," Tibbets said.

"*The Thin Red Line*," I said.

"No," he said.

"You just don't like war movies?" I said.

"They're a bunch of bullshit," he said. "To make a movie about war, you have to glamorize it. You have to take the leading man and make him a hero."

"You'd think that would be pretty easy in a war movie," I said.

"That's not necessarily the case," Tibbets said. "In war, there are a bunch of bastards on *our* side the same as there are on the other side. Guys who are looking out for their careers—just like in industry. Guys who cut your throat if you get one-up on them."

"Not literally cut your throat," I said.

"No," he said. "In the same way people do it in business, though, people do it in the military."

"Did you at least like John Wayne movies about the military?" I said.

"Not really," he said. "At least Bob Taylor had served—by the time he played me in the movie, he had been in the Navy. John Wayne was a cowboy actor. Shoot 'em up.

"Maybe that's why he did so well when he was playing soldiers. A cowboy is a hero. People like cowboys. In a real war, you don't see many cowboys. A cowboy is a romantic kind of fellow.

"You don't find a lot of romance in a real war."

What had been on my mind—what I had been waiting for the right moment to talk to Tibbets about—wasn't war movies, and wasn't marital difficulties.

It was this:

Every time Tibbets spoke of his lingering thoughts about the aftereffects of the *Enola Gay* mission, it was with some variation of the I've-never-lost-a-night's-sleep line. He had been saying that for years; he had been saying that his conscience was clear, that he had done what his country had asked, that he had helped save many lives by bringing the war to an end.

And I believed him. For all the reasons we had talked about, and more, I knew that he was proud of what he had done and that he was honored he had been the man his country had asked to do it. It wasn't just American lives he had saved—not just the lives of the U.S. soldiers who would have been killed in a land invasion of Japan. He most likely had saved many Japanese lives, too—the lives of

Japanese soldiers and civilians who would have died had the fighting moved on to Japanese soil. An argument can be made that many more Japanese lives would have been lost in conventional warfare once the land invasion began than were lost at Hiroshima and Nagasaki. The dying just would have stretched out over a much longer period of time.

And yet . . .

Some of the letters I received after my newspaper columns about Tibbets ran were from Japan; the columns appeared over there, so readers picked up their papers one day to see the stories about the man who had dropped the atomic bomb on their country.

The reaction from Japanese readers was not angry, or even resentful. Many said that they agreed Tibbets had been acting as a good combat pilot should, and that they understood, in the context of World War II, why his country asked him to do it. Some said that had Japan possessed the atomic bomb, the Japanese military leaders certainly would have tried to drop it on the United States; some said—as Tibbets had—that in the end, Japanese lives may have been saved by the bomb bringing a swift end to the war.

But the letters from Japan were not really about that. The letters were the Japanese readers' accounts of what happened. Some were firsthand, some had been passed down from older family members. They weren't about politics and they weren't even about warfare. They were human stories about what occurs

when an atomic weapon is dropped onto an unsus-
pecting city.

Some of them kept me awake far into many
nights. One in particular—it was a letter from a
Japanese woman named Hideko T. Snider who
had moved to the United States in the years after the
war—stayed with me for days after I first read it.

I wanted Tibbets to know about it, too. This was
not a woman who hated him, or who didn't understand why he did what he was asked to do. But I
wanted him to know about her letter. So I brought
it with me on my next visit to him:

> . . . On the morning of August 6th, 1945, I
> was a child in Hiroshima, just returned on the
> previous day from a far-away village where I
> was evacuated. We had no idea *Enola Gay* was
> on its way with its grave mission.
>
> When the bomb was let go in the mid air
> over the sky of Hiroshima, it unleashed the
> power so horrific that it defied a language of
> description. Even those of us who lived
> through it could not fathom our own experi-
> ences. Some people evaporated at the center.
> Hundreds and thousands were charred and
> naked with physical distinctions no longer rec-
> ognizable. Their arms stretched forward, mov-
> ing slowly, they fell to the ground and floated
> on the rivers. My brother, cousin and other
> cousins were among them. We were unable to

rescue those buried alive under the collapsed buildings and burned to death. My mother was one of them.

We did not know this was only the beginning. We did not know that the lethal power of radiation had penetrated to the marrow of our bones, destroying our organs and changing our DNA. People continued to die suddenly and strangely, bleeding from the mouth and often from every orifice. I nearly died myself, in a semi-conscious state running extremely high fever for days.

The strange phenomenon continued with increased number of cancer deaths, first leukemia, breast and lung cancers not only among the survivors but among those who entered the city after the explosion, such as those searching for the family members. They, too, breathed the poison and were affected by it. . . .

Strangely, the plants and flowers bore misshapen and misfigured offsprings. Three years after the A-bomb explosion, the banks of the river in Hiroshima were covered by 4-, 5- and 6-leaved clover. I know. I picked them up and kept them in my Bible. In Nagasaki, they detected the presence of radioactive poison in their water reservoir and in the soil more than 30 years later.

It is an irony that my mother, who loved Wordsworth and even *Gone With the Wind*,

never took a gun or spoke ill of the Americans
or the British. My male cousin, who was only
12 and was burned alive by radiation, loved to
watch the B-29 and its mechanical wonders.
He used to climb to the rooftop to watch them
at his own peril. There were many formations
passing over our sky. . . .

It was the image of the boy—the image of the
boy waving to the B-29s as they passed overhead—
that haunted me. I had called Hideko Snider and
spoken with her about it; she told me that apparently in the days and weeks before August 6, there
had been a number of B-29 reconnaissance missions
over Hiroshima, in which no bombs were dropped
or shots fired. Many residents—like her twelve-
year-old cousin—began not to fear the sounds of the
B-29s; they thought they had learned that the
planes were merely traveling by, on their way to
somewhere else. Her cousin loved airplanes. From
the roof he would wave hello toward the pilots.

And then the *Enola Gay* came.

I wanted to talk to Tibbets about the boy on the
roof.

So the boy was watching the other B-29s when they
flew by," he said, his voice sounding different.

There were times when I was speaking with Tibbets
that he seemed like the young aviator of the 1940s—

full of self-assuredness, bluster, literal combativeness. On this day, though, he was all of eighty-four.

I had recounted the story to him; he got quiet and there was a softness in his eyes. He said that, yes, there had been many flyovers of Hiroshima; yes, as far as he had been told, the citizens became so accustomed to the B-29s overhead that they assumed they were in no danger. That was the point—to lull the people on the ground so that on the day the *Enola Gay* arrived it would seem routine.

"Does it bother you at all, that story?" I said.

"Bother me to hear it?" he said. "Yes, it does. Of course it does.

"I can picture him doing it. He was encouraging the B-29s to fly on. I can see him up on the rooftop waving. . . ."

"I know you've lived with this for a long time . . ." I began.

Tibbets interrupted.

"You know, I was told that there were American prisoners being held captive near Hiroshima," he said. "The generals told me that the prisoners were there, but they said 'We don't know where.' They said that when we dropped the bomb, there was a good chance that we would be dropping it on American prisoners.

"And then they said to me, 'Will that bother you?'"

"What did you say?" I asked.

"I said no," Tibbets said. "I said it wouldn't bother me."

"Was that true?" I said.

"I had to make it be true," Tibbets said. "Because if it wasn't true, if I let it bother me, I might flinch. I might deviate from the job I was supposed to do. They asked me if I would be able to drop the bomb, even knowing what might happen.

"And I said, 'Yes. Of course.'"

"Were you at all sorry at the time that you were being put into that position?" I asked.

"That wasn't my business, to be sorry," Tibbets said. "My business was to hit them."

I told him that Studs Terkel had once written a fine book called *"The Good War."* It was about World War II—but what many people, even those who had enjoyed the book, had not noticed about it was that the phrase "The Good War" was in quotes. It was Terkel's way of making a point.

"His point was that no war is good, wasn't it?" Tibbets said.

"Yes," I said.

"He's right," Tibbets said. "There is no such thing as a war that is good."

I asked him if he thought that people who anguished over the suffering that was caused by the bomb he and his crew dropped—people like the woman who had written me the letter about the boy on the rooftop, people who sincerely feel that no victory was worth the human damage that Tibbets and his crew caused—were wrong to feel that way.

"No," he said in something close to a whisper. "They're not wrong. Why should they be?"

"Because of all the things you've told me," I said. "Because of the necessity of ending the war."

"Their relationship to that day is different than mine," Tibbets said. "I had a different relationship to that day than they do.

"But that doesn't make them wrong. I don't know who's wrong or what's wrong.

"I don't know that I'm right."

He looked at me.

"Do you understand what I'm trying to say?" he said.

I said I thought that I did.

And I said I had one other letter to ask him about.

It had come from a high school student—a seventeen-year-old boy by the name of Patrick J. Walsh. He, too, had read the newspaper columns I had written about my first visit with Tibbets; his letter was full of praise for Tibbets' bravery, and full of appreciation for the ending of the war that followed the mission. He wrote that if it were not for Tibbets and men like him, "our country would not be free from tyranny."

And then he ended the letter this way:

I have just one question, Mr. Greene. I am

an Irish-Catholic. I believe in God. I believe in the existence of heaven.

I would like to know if Paul Tibbets ever thinks about going to heaven? I have asked myself this question, but have not come up with an answer.

So I did ask Tibbets, on behalf of the young man: Did he ever think about it? Did he think he would be going to heaven?

He sat silent for a few seconds. Then he said:

"I never planned my life the way it happened. I never planned it so that I can go to heaven."

"What should I tell him?" I asked Tibbets.

"Tell him that heaven is here on Earth," Tibbets said. "Tell him that, yes, I think I will go to heaven.

"But tell him that your happiness is here. It's here, not in heaven. It's up to you to find it."

I asked him when the last time was that he cried.

"Don't ask me that," he said.

"You don't want to talk about it?" I said.

"I don't know when it was," he said. "I don't remember."

"I can drop the subject," I said.

"Just because I never was emotional and I never burst out into tears doesn't mean I don't feel certain things inside of me," he said.

FOURTEEN

Sometimes, when I was very young, my father would pick me up in his car after I had been playing at my best friend Jack Roth's house.

We played Army—we played war. We had seen the movie *To Hell and Back*, which starred World War II combat hero Audie Murphy portraying himself. In the movie, Murphy had seemed to run all over every overseas battlefield there ever was, mowing down the enemy, leaping for cover, tossing grenades and diving away from the explosions. He was who Jack and I pretended to be—he was the perfect representation of the courageous American soldier.

Jack's house had a little sloping hill just off to one side of the front yard. It was about as gentle as an elevation could possibly be—the rise from the sidewalk to the top of the hill was probably no more than a foot. But we were very small, too, so we would stand on the sidewalk and then charge up that hill, sometimes holding cap guns, sometimes holding sticks or overgrown twigs from Jack's parents' trees.

My dad would show up to bring me home for dinner, and he would stand beside his car and watch what Jack and I were doing. He never said much about it; he just stood and watched, as if it reminded him of something.

From his description of the first days of training at Camp Shelby, when he and the other draftees and enlistees had arrived at the base, in an America that did not seem all that expertly geared up to fight a war on foreign shores:

. . . To show you what kind of equipment we had, we used broomsticks for rifles and also to simulate 37-millimeter anti-tank guns. We used World War I underwear, wrap leggings and helmets. . . .

On we went with our training day after day until we finally went on what was called the Louisiana maneuvers. Many, many divisions packed up lock, stock and barrel and descended into the murky swamps and badlands of Louisiana where maneuvers which proved to be the largest in the history of the United States started to unfold. This was a very exciting time because we were all issued new equipment including real rifles and the new helmets. Of course that was a morale booster because before it was as if we were just playing soldier, but this time it looked like it was for real. . . .

The maneuvers were as close to actual battle as we could possibly be until later on we actually got into combat. . . . These were exercises in which live ammunition was used. . . . So here we are, we're running up and down the roads and byways of Louisiana not realizing that very, very shortly something bad would happen and would affect the lives of not only us, but everybody in the whole world. . . .

Less than ten years after the war ended, he would take my sister and me—my brother was just a baby, he was too young—to an amusement park called Norwoods.

This was in the days before the giant theme parks; Norwoods was as local as local could be. It was just a few minutes' drive from our house, with its front entrance on Main Street and its eastern boundary butting up against a tree line that led down to Alum Creek.

There was a not-very-tall ferris wheel, a merry-go-round, a "thrill ride" that mainly consisted of a two-minute trip through a lightless, overly warm room that featured one skeleton that lit up on mechanical cue, one recorded transcription of a woman screaming, one wooden hand, attached to a pulley, that came out of the wall at its assigned time, and, if memory serves, one hanging rubber mat with fringe on the bottom that swept across you as the car moved past.

There was more at Norwoods—bumper cars,

Skee-Ball machines, the shortest miniature railroad in the history of amusement parks—but I think what I remember most was the smell of gunpowder.

It was from the shooting gallery—a place where men and older boys aimed rifles at moving targets that proceeded horizontally across their line of sight. There were white rabbit-shaped objects, and bull's-eye devices, and—I don't know why—figures that looked like horses. Why anyone would want to shoot a horse . . .

And it is difficult to believe, recalling Norwoods now, that the gunpowder was genuine; it is difficult to believe that real bullets were being fired in a place with so many children wandering around. But the smell was real; the scent of the gunpowder was so overpowering, so thick, that when you would get home from Norwoods your clothes would still smell like the shooting gallery.

There were exercises in which live ammunition was used, he had said. I think of him—still a relatively young man, he was in his thirties when, back from the war, he would take us to Norwoods—and I try to imagine what he was thinking as he heard the rifles going off, burst after burst, to the sound of laughter and shouts from the people trying to kill the metal rabbits. His clothes would smell, too; when we would get home for dinner—such a short drive from the place with the shooting gallery—his clothes, like his children's, would carry the memory of the gunpowder. And we would sit down and eat.

· · ·

He had been on a weekend pass from Camp Shelby with some of his new Army buddies when the news came. They had been in New Orleans.

For a kid from Akron whose idea of someplace worldlier had been his fledgling life in Columbus, this had to have been something: on the town on Bourbon Street. A young soldier in training for a war that still seemed to be the immediate problem of other, far-distant countries—this wasn't bad: friends he'd just met, government paycheck in his pocket, the uniform of the United States on his back . . . this had to seem, if not fun, at least energizing, venturesome.

They got back to their hotel in New Orleans after an evening at the bars and nightclubs:

 . . . So we got into the elevator and there was an awful lot of buzzing going on by people and someone said, Did you hear about Pearl Harbor? And I said, Who's Pearl Harbor? Because I actually had never heard of the place. . . .

There were squads of MPs rolling around New Orleans urging every soldier to get back to his post. Before packing up, somehow I got kind of sentimental and dashed off a wire to Phyllis saying that Pearl Harbor was bombed but I love you and so forth and so on. Now, that certainly doesn't sound much like me, but I did it and Mother will attest to it, as a matter of fact she might still have that wire somewhere. And after that day, nothing would ever be the same. . . .

In the house where I grew up, there were many occasions when someone in the family—my dad, my mom, my sister, my brother or I—would have to go down to the basement to look for something.

In the basement was a doored-off area we referred to as the darkroom—evidently the family who had lived in the house before we did used it for that purpose, to develop photographs. For our family, it was mostly a storeroom; the things we didn't really need to have easily on hand, things that didn't belong in an upstairs closet, were down in the darkroom.

His trunk was in there. It was a literal trunk—a military trunk, filled with things he had brought home from the war. We seldom opened it.

I think about the trunks that children take with them to summer camp, trunks that families buy to store possessions, and there's a smiling, good-time feeling to those items. They're luggage, meant to convey a sense of vacation, of relaxation.

My father's Army trunk always felt like something quite different. We were too young to know what it really meant; like the duffel bags that were down there, the trunk had been a part of his life when he was overseas—of that, we were aware. But it was almost as if he was consciously putting that World War II life of his away in the darkroom. Upstairs a family lived on a pleasant Midwestern street in a nation just as peaceful as the tree-lined block on which the house sat. Down in the darkroom were the trunk and the duffel bags. They had been to a few places, none of which we children would ever see— none of which the man whose possessions they held would ever want his children to have to see.

I recall that once my sister and I had opened the trunk, and had found some love letters—letters sent back and forth between my father and my mother while he was overseas. We thought they were mushy; we thought they were kind of embarrassing. We read a few of them—I think we must have giggled, we were at that age—and then we became a little bored and closed the trunk.

It was while he was in training to go overseas that he asked my mother to marry him. It was, of course, not done casually; he arranged to get a leave, and came from his military base in the South back up to Columbus to work on making it happen.

From his tape:
. . . Phyllis and I started badgering her parents to let us get engaged, and we were really turned down. I was supposed to go to [her step-

father's] office to "ask for Phyllis' hand"—believe
it or not, that was still being done in those days.

I had to get my nerve up somehow, so like a
damn fool I stopped in the Neil House bar and
had about three quick shots, and I go up to his
office shaky in my shoes.

He was very nice to me, I must have smelled
like a brewery, but I think he was very understanding. . . . He said that he and [Phyllis'
mother] had decided that because I was a second lieutenant by this time, and they had heard
that the length of a second lieutenant's life in
actual combat was twenty seconds—where
they got this I don't know—but obviously they
didn't want their loving daughter to be a
widow twenty seconds into the game.

And so almost tearfully I left the office and
reported back to Phyllis, who also was in tears,
and we just felt that we had to keep on trying.
Well, the bottom line was that just before July
14 they had given us permission to become engaged. . . .

In the last years of his life, he and my mother
would often talk about coming to Chicago to
visit, but they never did. They had come relatively
often when I was first working there—a trip from
Ohio to Chicago was not only no big deal, it was
kind of joyful for them.

But one of the things that happened as he grew older was that the once-simple act of taking a short trip became cumbersome. He moved slowly; airplanes—which were much more cramped than the commercial aircraft of the 1950s and 1960s; the new planes felt as if they were designed to cram livestock in rather than to transport human beings in a gracious and civilized way—were considerable trouble for him to deal with.

It's not that he never traveled in the end; each year he and my mom would go down to Longboat Key, Florida, to spend a few winter months, and they would plan the transportation aspects of their trip well in advance. The actual day of getting from Columbus to Florida was usually an exhausting one for them; once they were there, they knew it had been worth the doing, because they had all winter to relax and not think about going anywhere else.

The short hops, though, became something out of their past. An easy trip never was, not anymore. It wasn't an especially dramatic change—it just sort of happened. One year, or so it seemed, they were a couple who were always traveling around, the next year they were a couple who, because of circumstances not of their own making, tended to stay in the city where they lived.

Back when they were first married—during the war, after they finally had persuaded my mother's parents how important this was to them—they set up housekeeping in Oregon, where my father and the men of the 91st Infantry Division were at that time being headquartered. Transportation for him then was not something to which he had to give much thought; he would not be choosing where he went or when he went there, and he and my mother knew that when the time to move quickly arrived, the arrangements would not be his to make.

. . . We were alerted, first a yellow alert and then a red alert, which meant we were at long last going overseas. Your mother and I would have the radio on every night and hear all the terrible things that were going on over in Italy. Little did we know that that would be our theater of operation. . . . I know it was a dark day for Phyllis and certainly a dark day for me and literally a dark day when I left.

We had a long train ride across the entire United States, and we finally arrived at Camp Patrick Henry, in Newport News, Virginia. It was from that spot we were to receive our final preparations to go overseas. We didn't know where we were going. Everything was top secret, so Phyllis had no idea where I was located and any hints that I would try to give at the infrequent times I could talk to her long distance were quite dangerous, because it was a mortal sin to give any information out about troop movements.

We were to be loaded onto Liberty Ships and go by convoys over the Atlantic to Oran, Algeria, which was our first stop. Now, convoys could only go as fast as the slowest ships. And we, on the Liberty Ships, were the slowest ships. They went about 10 knots, which made us sitting ducks for submarines and air attacks. We were surrounded by corvettes and destroyers, which maintained a constant lookout. And actually nothing happened until we went through the Straits of Gibraltar and then the depth charges were set off which indicated that there were submarines in the area.

A Liberty Ship was nothing but a hastily built tub, and the enlisted men slept on what were called standees. They were cots five feet high. A soldier was assigned one of these cots and his nose would press against the bottom of the cot on top of him, and so on for five layers. It was stifling, it was absolutely terrible, but it was the only way to move the troops. Eat in shifts, go to the toilet in shifts, shower in shifts, and all the time maintaining blackout. This went on for twenty days, and the only time we were allowed on deck was if it was all clear either at night or in the daytime. And believe me that was something to look forward to because it got awful smelly and awful fetid down in the bowels of that ship. . . .

• • •

If the little area in the basement of our house was referred to as the darkroom, then the room where we as children watched our family's first black-and-white television set was always called a name that had nothing to do with TV: It was the library.

It did indeed have bookshelves built into its walls; as small as the room—just down the hallway from the kitchen—was, you could imagine families who lived here before, in the pre-television era, sitting quietly on a winter's evening reading books before bedtime. At least before TV sets became the entertainment focal points of most American homes, a room like this one—a room devoted to books—likely did not feel elitist or stilted. A room like this was where the outside world entered your house; a room like this—before TV—was the place where a family could read and discover a wider world.

My sister and brother and I would sit there and stare at *Rootie Kazootie* and *Ding Dong School* and *Super Circus*—would stare at the outside world being delivered onto a glass screen—and on the wooden bookshelves were the volumes our mother and father had collected over the years.

In the early 1950s, I recall now, so many places of honor in the family library went to books about the war. It was as if my father and mother felt an obligation to keep the narrative of the war in our home; these were not memorabilia specific to my dad, these were not his personal souvenirs. They were instead history—history that at the time the books first came out was still brand-new.

There were memoirs by Eisenhower and by Churchill; there were collections of war correspondence by Quentin Reynolds and other newspapermen who had been at the front. One book in particular I remember; by Ernie Pyle, the greatest chronicler of the fighting men, it bore a title that could not be improved upon. It was called *Here Is Your War*.

Seven or eight years before, all of this had been present tense. Now it was between hard covers: the literature of combat, on our safe little street. *Here Is Your War*. Your war. You, the man of this house.

His voice, on the tape, described the final stage of their troop-ship journey across the Atlantic Ocean:

. . . We finally got there in one piece and of-floaded in Oran, and saw all the wreckage of the French battleships that were in the harbor. We got into trucks that took us out to the countryside. . . . We immediately started training there for the amphibious landings that were to come later.

It was here that we received our first casualties. The area around Oran and Port aux Poules was part of the battleground in the African invasion. And there were many minefields that were still very, very deadly and sure enough I lost three friends because of stepping on mines. And this really sobered us up, we were actually in a theater of war. . . .

He was serious about few people; from the time I was a boy, I could count on him saying something sardonic or amusingly cutting about just about anyone whose name I might bring up. It didn't matter whether the person was Elvis Presley or our milkman—my dad would make a joke out of the discussion, would go for laughs in his evaluation or description of whomever we were talking about.

Not only did he not impress easily—it was hard to impress him at all.

So I was more than a little surprised by his reaction when I mentioned Gary Griffin's dad.

Gary Griffin is the keyboard player for Jan and Dean, the '60s surf-rock duo. For most of the 1990s, I toured the country on summer weekends with Jan and Dean and their band, singing backup vocals during their concerts and eventually being promoted to lead vocals on "Dance, Dance, Dance" and "I Get Around." How this came to pass is a long and juvenile story, one that probably would be better to go into at some other time.

My father thought that the idea of his grown son

singing surf music on stages around the United States was stupid beyond belief; it's hard to argue that he was wrong. But once, after we had played a show in Eaton, Ohio, and I had gone to Columbus the next day to visit with my parents, I mentioned to my dad that I had met Gary Griffin's father at the show, and that Gary's dad had been a Doolittle Raider. At the time, I am ashamed to confess, I did not know exactly what the Doolittle Raiders had done during World War II. I knew they had been a famed unit in the war, but that was about it.

So I had met Gary's dad—a self-effacing, friendly man, a proud father who had come to watch his son make music—backstage at the show, and the next day I told my dad about it.

"Your friend's father was really a Doolittle Raider?" my dad had said.

I had said yes.

My dad—the man who was never serious about anyone—said:

"If he was a Doolittle Raider, then that man is a hero."

I would one day find out for myself—but only after my father was gone.

FIFTEEN

I was having lunch with Tibbets on a Friday afternoon. I had called him at the last minute to say I
would be in Columbus only briefly; we went to a
restaurant called B. J. Young's, and I said I had a
question for him.

"What's your opinion of the Doolittle Raiders?"
I asked.

"They're the real thing," he said. "Why?"

I told him what my father had said about them.

"Your dad was right," Tibbets said. "If ever there
were heroes, the Doolittle Raiders were it. But why
are you bringing it up now?"

"Because I'm on my way to see them," I said.

G ary Griffin had gotten in touch with me,
sounding a little harried.

The surviving members of the Doolittle Raiders—
there had been eighty aviators, but now the number
who were able to travel was down to seventeen—were
being honored at the United States Air Force
Museum at Wright-Patterson Air Force Base in Dayton, down the freeway from Columbus. A monument
to the men was scheduled to be dedicated.

Gary's dad was in charge of this Doolittle re-

union. He had been assured that a master of ceremonies befitting the occasion would be on hand.

But now, within a week of the event, there was no
MC. Somehow, whoever was supposed to make certain that a Pentagon official or a leader of Congress
would be on hand had not gotten the job done. The
last living Raiders were making plans to come to
Dayton for the dedication of their memorial—and
there was no one to narrate the ceremony.

"My dad wants to know if you'll do it," Gary
said.

I was stunned. Whatever the comical line was
from a recent movie—"We're not worthy"—at that
moment became personal. The Raiders must have
wanted Colin Powell, or John Glenn, or Norman
Schwarzkopf—they must have wanted someone on
their own level. Not some guy who writes stories for
newspapers.

I told Gary as much. "I'd feel embarrassed being
up there in front of them," I said. "I don't have the
right to appear at their ceremony."

"My dad's really in a pinch," Gary said. "Can he
call you?"

I said of course. The next morning Tom Griffin
called, and said, "Is there any way you can fly in
from Chicago?"

I asked him whether the Air Force Museum was
still trying to get one of the speakers whom the
Raiders really wanted.

"I keep getting a little runaround," he said. "I

finally found out that they had asked one of the local TV anchormen in Dayton to do it. But it turns out that he's on vacation."

I found myself shaking my head as I listened through the phone.

"I know it's asking a lot for you to come on such short notice. . . ." he said.

By this time I had read up on the Raiders. By this time I knew exactly why my dad and Tibbets would never kid around about these men. *I know it's asking a lot . . .*

"It's not asking a lot, Mr. Griffin," I said.

Meaning: You men, of all people, should never have to be put in the position of asking anyone to do anything.

It is almost impossible—even knowing the facts of what they were ordered to undertake—to comprehend the courage of the eighty men who, under the command of Jimmy Doolittle, took off from the deck of the USS *Hornet* on April 18, 1942.

In the months after the Japanese attack on Pearl Harbor, in which more than two thousand Americans were killed, morale in the United States about the war in the Pacific seemed to sink ever lower. There had been no effective response to Pearl Harbor; the leaders of the Japanese military appeared to believe that they were all but invincible.

American officials determined that a surprise

bombing raid of the Japanese mainland was the way to turn things around. But how to do that—from where to launch the attack?

The only option was from the deck of an American warship. Bomber planes had never done this before. United States commanders concluded that such a feat was technically possible, if B-25s were modified specifically for this task, and if crews were trained to carry it out with no margin for error.

Sixteen five-man crews were selected. They had only three weeks to train for the mission—and the training did not include taking off from ships. None of the pilots, before the day of the raid, had ever attempted such a takeoff, and none had ever seen any other pilot do it. When they flew their B-25s off the deck of the *Hornet*, it would be their first such flights.

The plan was for the planes to drop their bombs on specific targets in Japan—and then to fly to China, and to land at a Chinese airfield friendly to the U.S. There could be no turning back; there was no way that a big, heavy bomber would be able to land on a carrier. The USS *Hornet* and its task force—four cruisers, eight destroyers, two oilers— would reverse course after the Doolittle Raiders took off, and head back to Pearl Harbor.

So on the day of the raid, the sixteen B-25s were lined up on the deck of the *Hornet*, their crews knowing that they had just enough fuel to get to China, and that returning to the *Hornet* was not an option.

And then the news came:

The launch of the bombers was supposed to have come from a point in the Pacific Ocean 400 miles from the Japanese mainland. But U.S. military officials intercepted a Japanese message that indicated the enemy had spotted the U.S. task force.

The Tokyo raid would either have to be called off—or begin earlier than scheduled. Which, ominously, meant much farther away from Japan than scheduled.

From the originally planned-for 400 miles away, the Doolittle crews knew they had barely enough fuel to make it to China. But from farther than that?

If they were ordered to fly, they might not make it out of Japanese airspace after dropping their bombs.

The *Hornet* was 640 miles away from Japan when the official order arrived from Admiral William F. "Bull" Halsey, who was on the USS *Enterprise*:

LAUNCH PLANES. TO COL. DOOLITTLE AND GALLANT COMMAND GOOD LUCK AND GOD BLESS YOU.

And they did it—knowing that they very well might have no chance of landing safely, they took off for Japan. Doolittle piloted the first plane in line, which had the greatest chance of crashing off the deck of the *Hornet*—it had the shortest amount of runway in front of it. He made it off the ship, followed by the next fifteen B-25s.

The men bombed Tokyo and other targets on the Japanese mainland, burning or destroying the

Tokyo Armory, a tank depot, steel and gas works, factories and a harbor installation. In terms of real destruction, the Tokyo raid did not do much to significantly disable the Japanese war effort. But psychologically, what the Raiders accomplished was staggering. Finally, months after Pearl Harbor, the American people could be told that U.S. planes had hit Japan. The United States was striking back.

But the sixteen Doolittle planes were over Japan—and their fuel was running out. There was a storm over China, and thick fog. The planes managed to get past the Japanese mainland—but eleven of the five-man crews had to bail out. Four more crews crash-landed. The sixteenth Doolittle B-25 was able to land within the border of Russia—at which time the crew was taken prisoner, and held for more than a year.

So one B-25 was in Russia, its crew imprisoned. The other fifteen bombers had crashed or been ditched. Two men died as they bailed out; eight more were captured by the Japanese. Three Raiders were executed by their Japanese captors; five others were sentenced to life in prison. One of the five died of starvation in a Japanese prison camp; the other four endured forty months of mistreatment as POWs.

The other Raiders who bailed out made it safely to Chinese soil, and were treated well. The U.S. government, upon recovering these men, sent most of them back into combat; having survived the

Tokyo raid, ten more of Doolittle's men were killed in action later in the war.

The Doolittle raid was regarded as the turning point in the war in the Pacific. And what those men did—taking off from the *Hornet* knowing what lay ahead—inspired Americans in a way that was desperately needed in the uncertain months after Pearl Harbor. Americans, in 1942, might not have always felt they had much to believe in—but they had the Doolittle Raiders. The Raiders represented the very best of how America wanted to see itself.

Each of the eighty raiders—some posthumously—was awarded the Distinguished Flying Cross, and Jimmy Doolittle himself was promoted to brigadier general, and was presented with the Medal of Honor by President Roosevelt. The Raiders, American citizens were being signaled, were the proof that no matter what the odds, the war could be won.

That was a long time ago, though. Doolittle had died in 1993; each year the number of surviving Raiders grew smaller. As they arrived in Dayton for the dedication of their memorial, they were well aware that few Americans knew who they were, or what they had done in 1942.

The night before the dedication ceremony, the seventeen Raiders arrived in Dayton from all over the country. There was a reception for them at an officers' facility at Wright-Patterson.

Gary Griffin and his girlfriend, Carol Huston, had planned a surprise for the Raiders. The kinds of songs Gary usually sang in public were along the lines of "Help Me, Rhonda" and "Shut Down"—I had seen him, with Jan and Dean, sing those songs to cheering, screaming crowds across the United States.

This night was going to be different. Carol is a singer and an actress, too—she starred as Andy Griffith's beautiful young female cohort during the last seasons of the *Matlock* television series—and in the weeks leading up to the Doolittle reunion she and Gary had been working on something.

So as the Raiders arrived for their welcoming reception, Gary and Carol were waiting for them. Gary, on stage, most often wears a Hawaiian shirt and a pair of jeans; tonight he was in a business suit, and Carol was in an evening dress. Gary was going to be playing the piano, accompanying Carol's vocals.

The Doolittle Raiders were in their seventies and eighties. Most of them, it was safe to assume, didn't go out much to concerts anymore. So this concert had been put together for them.

Gary hit the keys, and Carol sang "I've Heard That Song Before." She sang "White Cliffs of Dover." She sang "The Last Time I Saw Paris."

She and Gary had lovingly assembled a program of songs from the 1940s, from the years of the war—the years when these were new songs in the ears of the Raiders and their wives. The idea was to give them a show like one they might have enjoyed when they were young airmen and young airmen's wives. When they, and their world, were full of youth.

Carol sang "Where or When," and "One for My Baby," and "I'll Be Seeing You." She looked out into the eyes of the men and women in her small audience, and she saw emotions so intense that she had to look away.

She and Gary told the Raiders and their wives that there was one song they needed some help on. They asked the Raiders if they would sing along.

Every person in the room knew that it was far from certain how many more of these get-togethers there would be. The Raiders had been holding reunions since 1943, but as their numbers dwindled, the question of how long these could continue was a real, if mostly unspoken, one.

Gary hit the chord he was looking for and Carol sang the opening words of "We'll Meet Again."

> WE'LL MEET AGAIN,
> DON'T KNOW WHERE, DON'T KNOW WHEN. . . .

And in the audience, the Raiders and their wives joined in, singing together.

> BUT I KNOW WE'LL MEET AGAIN
> SOME SUNNY DAY. . . .

• • •

I had taken my mother to dinner in Columbus before going over to Dayton in a driving rainstorm to get ready for the Doolittle Raiders ceremony.

It was to be a morning event; the dedication of the monument had been scheduled to be held outside, next to the monument itself. But the weather was still severe, and no one wanted to subject the Raiders to sitting out in it. The decision had been made overnight to hold the ceremony inside the museum's auditorium. It would be dry and warm— but the memorial would be nowhere in sight.

Something else would be missing, too. The Air Force Museum had arranged for a restored B-25— just like the one these men had flown off the deck of the USS *Hornet*—to fly over the memorial as the dedication was beginning. It was certain to have been an unforgettable moment—Doolittle's men sitting next to the memorial in their honor, while above them roared that B-25.

The flyover was rescheduled so that the Raiders could see the bomber as they were walking into the museum's main building. They had been at breakfast together; a van brought them to the museum, and just as they were getting out, the B-25, flying loud and low on the gray, damp morning, thundered above the roof of the museum. Most of the Raiders looked up toward it; some, having trouble getting around, chose to come inside the building and find a seat.

They walked into the auditorium—some of them helping their wives, who were in wheelchairs or who needed assistance getting down the aisle. The auditorium was not full for this ceremony, but a respectable number of people had shown up. The Dayton news media had been announcing that the ceremony would be open to the public, and some fathers had brought their sons to see the Raiders, and to hear about who they were.

When everyone was seated I introduced myself and read from a script I had been handed by a Wright-Patterson official:

"We ask everyone to stand at this time for the posting of the colors by the Wright-Patterson Air Force Base honor guard."

The color guard, marching crisply and handling the flag with great tenderness, came to the stage to present the colors.

I introduced Reverend Jacob DeShazer to give the invocation. Reverend DeShazer was one of the Raiders captured by the Japanese and sentenced to life in prison; upon his liberation at the end of the war, after Tibbets and the crew of the *Enola Gay* had dropped the atomic bomb on Hiroshima, he had dedicated himself to becoming a member of the clergy.

He blessed the gathering, and then Wilkinson Wright, the grandnephew of Orville and Wilbur Wright, welcomed the Raiders to Dayton. Retired Major General Davey Jones, one of the Raiders, spoke on behalf of the men and their families; Major General Charles Metcalf spoke on behalf of the Air Force Museum.

I did my best to tell them what I, and so many people, thought of them. I mentioned what my father had said about them, how they were just about the only people I had ever heard him talk about with a tone close to reverent respect, and I could see some of them looking at one another and nodding. I told them I had had lunch with Tibbets the day before, and that he had asked me to extend to them his congratulations and his best wishes; there were smiles and murmured conversations among them when his name was mentioned.

"The official announcement of this event says that we are here to honor you today," I said. "But that's not quite right. We are the ones who are honored today. We are honored to be in your presence. The monument is yours; the honor is ours."

I spoke a while more, without notes, just telling the men how I and so many others felt about what they had done, and then I read from the script:

"Everyone please stand while Reverend DeShazer joins us for the benediction, and the playing of taps."

The sound of a million military goodnights—the sound of a million military goodbyes—filled the room as taps was played, and then, still reading from the script, I said:

"Will everyone please remain standing for the retiring of the colors."

This was where the honor guard was supposed to return to the stage to retrieve the flag.

The Raiders and their wives—those who were able to stand—stood at attention and faced the flag.

And the honor guard didn't come.

Silence filled the room.

I looked at General Metcalf. He raised his eyebrows a little bit. I repeated it into the microphone. "The retiring of the colors."

No honor guard.

The flag was on the stage, the Doolittle Raiders were on their feet—and the honor guard had taken off. They were missing their cue; they were nowhere to be seen.

It would have been an awkward moment under any circumstances; here, it was terrible. These men, of all men, would have seemed to deserve a perfect military ceremony. To have every detail right—the way they tried to do it when they took off from the Navy ship in the Pacific that was going to turn around and leave them as soon as they were in the air.

At the back of the room, staff members of the museum looked frantically for the honor guard. They left the auditorium, they went to check the men's restroom. Nothing.

And the Raiders and their wives, men and women of seventy-eight and eighty and eighty-four . . .

They remained standing at attention, gazing at the flag of their country.

They probably didn't mind this as much as I did. After all, on the day they were supposed to attack Japan they were told that they'd have to fly from 640 miles instead of 400. And that they probably didn't have enough fuel to make it to China. Next to that, this little blip of a screwup at their dedication ceremony may not have meant much. If any group of men was used to things going wrong, it was these men.

I looked down off the stage toward them. One of them smiled and winked, as if to try to set me at ease.

"I hope that all of you know that you are our heroes," I said, and, with the flag still waiting on the stage for someone to come for it, I concluded the ceremony. I asked the rest of the audience to remain as the Raiders—slowly—made their way back up the aisles.

There was a lunch scheduled for the Raiders and their wives at a hotel on the base. It was a private event; I went to the same hotel to have a sandwich in the restaurant, and as I passed the door where the Raiders' lunch was being held Tom Griffin saw me and asked me to join them.

I said that I didn't want to intrude; he insisted that I come in. One after another, the Raiders came up to me to thank me for the words I had said about them. One after another, they told me how much they had appreciated it.

And I thought of that letter that Tibbets had sent me, early on:

You made me think, after a word-by-word review, that maybe I am not too bad a guy. Thanks.

As if these men should ever have to thank any of us—as if they should ever have to express a single word of gratitude to us who have followed them. I sat with these men—quiet, courteous men, men with not a bone of self-promotion or self-aggrandizement in their makeup. I watched as the men whose wives needed help getting to the table carefully moved the wheelchairs for the women they loved, patiently assisted their wives eat the sandwiches that the hotel had provided. They did what was expected of them in 1942, and they were doing what was expected of them now, because that is who they were and who they are.

There was a printed program for the dedication ceremony; inside the program were photographs of the Raiders taken in 1942, posing with their planes on the deck of the *Hornet*. I looked at the faces in the overly bright hotel function room, and I matched them with the faces in the program—kids' faces in the program, faces so young and proud and sometimes, or so it seemed, scared, faces peering over the tops of leather bomber jackets.

They weren't young now; the faces in this room were not the faces of kids, and while the faces still seemed proud, especially today, I did not see a single face in this room that appeared scared to me. I thought about that day when, at the request of their country, they had taken off for Tokyo knowing that there would be no turning back. These men in this room—they took off from that deck in the Pacific because the United States said that they must do it for the future well-being of their nation.

I was supposed to get back to Chicago. I said my goodbyes to the Raiders, and left Wright-Patterson so that I could make my flight. On the way off the base I saw a billboard advertising a local car dealership, encouraging Dayton-area motorists looking for a good deal to stop in at Airport Toyota.

SIXTEEN

I had seen a news item about an old sports star's uniform—I think it was the baseball jersey of a Hall of Fame player—going up for auction, with the expectation that it would bring in several hundred thousand dollars.

This didn't seem all that startling. The market for pieces of history, especially sports history, has been escalating rapidly in recent years. Whether it's Mark McGwire's record-setting home run ball from our current world, or Lou Gehrig's Yankee uniform from long ago, people are willing to pay big money to own a piece of the past.

So the next time I saw Tibbets, I asked him the question.

"Where's your uniform?"

"I have no idea," he said.

"You don't know where the uniform you wore in the service is?"

"I took everything to a thrift shop when I left the service and had it sold," he said. "I had no use for my uniforms once I was out—so whatever the thrift shop did with it, those are where the uniforms are."

"You know, I bet if you looked in your closet and found some of your old things, you'd be shocked at what the market might be for them," I said.

"There's nothing in the closet," he said. "I don't have anything left."

I told him about the prices that the clothing and equipment of sports celebrities are bringing in, and about how Americans are now collecting items like that the way art enthusiasts have always collected paintings and sculptures.

He shook his head, with a look that was a combination of amusement and disgust.

"Which uniform did you wear on your way to Japan?" I said.

"On the *Enola Gay?*" Tibbets said. "I just wore an old khaki flight suit. It was going to be a long flight, and I wanted to be as comfortable as I could."

"And what did you do with it when you got back from Hiroshima?" I said.

"Hell, I don't know," Tibbets said. "I suppose that when I got back to Tinian I turned it back in to supply. I didn't need it any more—the flight was over, and I was going to be leaving Tinian."

"So you never got anything for the uniform you wore," I said.

"I probably got a receipt from the supply sergeant," he said.

Sometimes, talking with Tibbets, I felt as if he regarded what he had been through as history with a lower-case *h*. For most of the rest of the world, the events he had been a part of were stories to be found in libraries between hard covers, or in documentary films with trumpets and bugles as a soundtrack. Tibbets, though . . .

Well, his was the receipt-from-the-supply-sergeant view of history. I thought I would ask him about some famous figures from the war years—men the rest of us thought we knew because of the mass-media portrayal of them.

"How about Audie Murphy?" I said, remembering that little hill on the side of my childhood friend's front yard.

"A showoff," Tibbets said.

"Pardon me?" I said, not really wanting to hear such a thing about my boyhood idol.

"Murphy was a showoff," Tibbets said. "He got a lot of medals—and he deserved them. He earned them in combat.

"But the guy wore them everywhere. He craved attention—he wanted to be noticed and praised all the time. That's why he became a movie actor when he got back—he couldn't stand it when he wasn't the center of everything."

"Did you know Ernie Pyle?" I said.

"I was with him in North Africa," Tibbets said. "I watched him write his stories. He was a very quiet man, and very serious about his work.

"As you know, he was trying to write for the hometowns. Most of the war correspondents were writing the big picture, but Ernie knew that the Army was composed of a lot of hometown guys who went off to war. The guys who were really fighting the war—the guys no one ever heard of."

"Did the soldiers treat him differently than they treated the other war correspondents?" I asked.

"He was treated like a GI, which was the highest praise the soldiers could give him," Tibbets said. "Where the soldiers went, Ernie Pyle went. He went out and got dirty with them. He bled with them. And they loved him for it."

"What about Edward R. Murrow?" I asked.

"Never knew the man," Tibbets said. "I had heard him on the radio, obviously—everyone heard him on the radio. He told it so people could understand. That was very important—during the war, it wasn't so easy for the people back home to understand what we were doing over there. Murrow was so good because when he talked, what was going on became clear to his listeners.

"He told it *slowly*. He was careful with his enunciation. The war was hectic and it was fast, and Murrow knew that to make the people back home understand what it was all about, he had to be the opposite—he had to be slow and clear."

"Patton?"

"I knew him at Fort Benning, Georgia," Tibbets said. "He was what he was, and I had to admire him for that. Patton's model was Rommel—the dirty son of a bitch. Patton was a rough, tough SOB just like Rommel, and if you took him for that, he was very good at what he did. He led his troops, I'll tell you that."

"Was he anything like George C. Scott in the movie?" I asked.

"Well, he sure didn't talk like George C. Scott," Tibbets said.

I sat there recalling Scott's gravelly, almost belligerent voice.

"They sounded different?" I said.

Tibbets laughed. "Patton had an effeminate-type voice," he said. "Very squeaky."

"George Patton," I said, thinking that Tibbets was kidding me. "A squeaky voice."

"That's what he had," Tibbets said.

"Did it get in the way of his being a commander?" I said.

"Not at all," Tibbets said. "He didn't give a damn what people thought of him. What you got from Patton was *him*, it was no damn act."

"George Marshall?" I said.

"He was just the other way from Patton," Tibbets said. "He was a diplomatic man, a very intelligent man, well spoken.

"I flew him around for three weeks in '39 and '40. He was very much of a gentleman. I remember that I landed him at an air base in Anniston, Alabama. I was flying a two-seater airplane—just Marshall and myself.

"So we landed at the field in Anniston, and the people were waiting to take him to where he was going. He's wearing four stars, he's big, he's the one they were waiting for as our plane landed.

"But before they could lead him away, he said, 'Wait a minute. I don't want to leave until I'm sure that you're going to take care of Tibbets here. He needs to get some food and some sleep, and someone's got to make sure that his plane is refueled.'

"Now, I could have taken care of all of that myself, but it would have meant talking to people and asking them for favors, and it might have taken me a while. Marshall didn't want me to have to do it myself. I never forgot that gesture."

"Mark Clark?" I said.

"A great, great general," Tibbets said. "A Southern gentleman. Very soft-spoken, never got riled. Never got upset—or if he did, he didn't show it. He had innate politeness.

"He was more than a good general. He was a good man. Of all the military leaders in World War II, Mark Clark is the one who never got the proper credit publicly. He didn't seek it—and somehow he didn't get it.

"But we all knew. We knew what kind of a man Mark Clark was."

I asked Tibbets what sort of mail he got from the Pentagon these days. Was he still given the courtesy of being informed about various goings-on in the military?

"Not really," he said. "I get mail from the

Pentagon, but it's the same kind of mail that all ex-servicemen get. Mass mailings."

"How's it addressed?" I said.

"On a label," he said. " 'General Paul Tibbets.' Some of it I read, some of it I know just to throw away without opening it."

"So no one makes any special effort to make you feel as if you're still a part of things?" I said.

"Hardly," he said. "I'm not a part of what they're doing. I'm on the outside looking in."

I knew that Tibbets had left the service with mixed feelings at best—after the war he had held a number of desk jobs, each of which filled him with increasing frustration about the military bureaucracy. He had risen as far as he was going to rise—brigadier general, never being promoted to two-star or three-star—and he had hated the idea of being evaluated by men he hardly knew, and of, in a peacetime military, becoming a half-forgotten cog in the machine.

He didn't like to talk much about it, but he said:

"You don't have to live under that kind of question mark. They would tell me something today, then change what they said tomorrow. . . ."

He shook his head.

"Anyway," he said, not wanting to dwell on the subject. "The mail I get from the Pentagon is no big deal. I'm on a mailing list. Guys who once served."

• • •

While he was talking about guys who once served, he said that he feels strongly that every guy should have to. Meaning: Bring back the draft.

"Yes," Tibbets said. "Every man ought to pay the price to live in this country. And that means helping to defend it. Discipline comes along with having to do that—and if you're going to grow up with the benefits of being an American, you should have to pay for it."

I told him that the draft must have disappeared from the American scene for some pretty good reasons—otherwise it would still be in place.

"You know what the reason is that the draft is gone?" he said. "It's very simple. People don't like the draft because they don't want to be told what to do.

"And to that I say, 'Show me how you can live without being told what to do.' It's the way the world has always worked, and not liking that fact doesn't change it."

"Do you think the draft is better for the person who is drafted, or just that it's better for the country and for the armed services?" I said.

"It's better for the person *and* it's better for the country," Tibbets said. "But don't assume that it's better for the armed services—it's not necessarily better for any of the branches of the service to have draftees.

"The services might very well be better off with

men who choose to enlist. But the *country*—the country is better off when the draft is in place, because the young men who are drafted become disciplined. And they come out of the service—at least most of them—carrying that discipline inside of them. You don't think that's a good thing—in a country that right now has all these young men in gangs going around killing each other? You don't think we could use the discipline of the draft—for the good of the young men, and for the good of the country?"

"Well, speaking of that, one of the things that people always talk about is 'wanting to leave the country in good hands,'" I said. "Do you think that your generation feels you're leaving the country in good hands?"

"I don't know," Tibbets said. "There are times when I think I'd rather not know the answer to that one. But if you're asking me to think about it: If the ideal situation is to leave the country better, then I think my generation has lost the war."

"Why?" I said.

"My father's generation fought a war to save democracy," Tibbets said. "My generation fought to preserve our freedom from oppression. And sometimes I look around at what the United States has become, and I have to reach the sad conclusion that we may have won the battle—we may have won a lot of battles—but we haven't won the war."

"Because?" I said.

"Because of all the things you and I have been talking about," he said. "Because of the utter lack of discipline in every area of society. Anything goes. There is no center. . . ."

"And assuming that you're right, how do you think that can be changed?" I said.

"I would like to see determined and iron-assed people get into positions of influence in this country," he said. "Some people who wouldn't be afraid to say that there is a difference between right and wrong. I would like to see some standards set that we can be proud of."

"There was no television when you were growing up," I said. "I think it would be kind of hard for any political leaders to really be effective in setting the tone in a society where television is a fact of daily life. That's the difference between when you were growing up and when I grew up—and it's even more so today. The tone of society is set by what is broadcast into every home in the country every day. It has nothing to do with politicians—it's just there, out of the air and into the houses."

"I don't think television did us any good, I'll tell you that," Tibbets said. "And I'm not even talking about the same thing you're talking about—I'm not talking about the programs they put on the air."

"Then what do you mean?" I said.

"The main way television has changed the country is that it has kept people inside their houses," he said.

"It used to be, you knew all your neighbors. Now, people consider the people they see on television as their neighbors—they know the people on TV better than they know the people on their own blocks, or at least they think they do.

"I'm no different from anyone else—I've been as affected by it as anyone. I don't even know who lives three doors away from me."

"I'll bet that's quite a change from the way it was in the neighborhood you grew up in as a boy," I said.

"Of course," he said. "You would knock on any door in your neighborhood without giving it a second thought. That's what being a neighbor meant. Not necessarily that you were the greatest friends in the world—but that you were *neighbors*."

"You might be able to do that now," I said.

"What?" Tibbets said.

"Knock on the door of someone down the street from you, or on the next block," I said. "Tell them who you are and that you just wanted to introduce yourself."

"I wouldn't do that," he said.

"Why?" I said.

"Because whoever's door I knocked on, I would assume that they didn't want to be bothered."

I told Tibbets about the sign I'd seen as I was leaving the Doolittle Raiders reunion—the AIRPORT TOYOTA billboard near the air base in Dayton.

"So?" he said.

"You don't think that's kind of odd?" I said. "The Doolittle Raiders are meeting for the dedication of the memorial to their raid on Japan, and down the street the Toyota dealership is busy selling cars to the people of Dayton?"

"No," Tibbets said.

"Why?" I said.

"Because I drive a Toyota myself," he said.

It was one of those moments when I couldn't do anything but sit there and stare at him.

"But if that's the case," I said after a few seconds had passed, "then what was it all for?"

"What was what all for?" Tibbets said.

"What the Doolittle Raiders did when they flew off the *Hornet* toward Tokyo," I said. "What you and your crew did when you flew to Hiroshima. . . ."

"It's purely commerce," he said. "It's a competitive thing. I bought a Toyota because at the time I bought it I was looking at cars, and I thought it was the best one out there for me. I looked around and I decided that American carmakers were giving you what *they* wanted to give you, not what *you* wanted to drive."

"And you didn't think twice before you bought the Toyota?" I said.

"I like my Toyota," he said. "I don't hold any grudges. It was a good product, it was what I needed, so I bought it."

"Did it make you feel funny at all?" I asked.

"Not in the least," he said. "I have never held a thing in the world against a Japanese man or a Japanese woman. It was the system we were fighting against—what the government of Japan had put in place.

"But the people of Japan? I've never had a bad thought about them."

So here he was, at eighty-four, driving his Toyota around the freeways of central Ohio.

"Which is harder for you?" I said. "Driving the freeways here today, or flying a B-29 back when you were younger?"

"Driving the freeways is definitely harder," Tibbets said. "I have to be much more alert driving the freeways than I did flying an airplane."

"Just because of your age?" I said.

"No," he said. "Because we've got people driving cars that have no business being behind the wheel."

"Like who?" I asked.

"A lot of older people have no business driving," he said. "They can't see. Their eyesight is poor."

"You're not including yourself in that group, I assume."

"No," he said. "I'm a good driver.

"But on the road, I see so many aggressive drivers, and then I see these people driving with their telephones to their ears—they don't know what they'd do if they suddenly had to make a decision on the road while they're talking on the phone. It tears me up to see that."

"So compared to the flight of the *Enola Gay* . . ." I began.

"It is much more nerve-wracking for me on the freeways of Columbus than it was flying the *Enola Gay* to Hiroshima," he said. "Too many people make up their own rules of driving. It's like everything else you see today—people just think they have the right to make up their own rules, on the road just like anywhere else.

"I'm driving the right way, at the right speed. And they honk at me—like I'm impeding their progress."

"Do you think you're going too slow for them?" I said.

"I drive the limit," he said. "I don't set the speed rules—I obey them. I'm watching everything around me as I drive. Every curve on the road has a groove—people don't know that. But they're out there, driving any way they want."

"Still, though," I said. "You're probably exaggerating about the flight to Hiroshima being easier. Right?"

"No, I'm not exaggerating," he said. "Between Tinian and Hiroshima, there wasn't any traffic for me to have to deal with."

SEVENTEEN

My father felt the same way about drivers on the central Ohio freeways—and not just in his later years. When my sister and brother and I were children, sitting in the back seat as he drove somewhere with my mother in front next to him, he had a phrase that we turned into a family joke:

"These are treacherous driving conditions!"

He said it so often—he used it in so many road situations—that it lost just about all meaning. "Treacherous driving conditions" could refer to anything from a slight drizzle to a severe thunderstorm; from a lost-her-way woman slowing up the lane of traffic in front of him to teenagers passing him at eighty miles per hour and then cutting him off. "Treacherous driving conditions" could mean that the sun was too bright—but what it really meant was: Quit fidgeting back there.

He liked us to be quiet and still as we rode in that back seat. And I don't think he even noticed that, as the years passed, the driving conditions really did become treacherous for anyone riding in the car, and anyone in the vicinity of the car—not because of the weather, not because of speeders in adjacent lanes, but because of him.

He was too old. He had become a bad driver. Yet no one could tell him that—he insisted on driving wherever he went. This is something that millions upon millions of men and women in middle age must almost certainly go through with their suddenly elderly parents—the knowledge, on the part of the children, that the parents really should not be on the road anymore. And the great reluctance of the parents to even discuss this, much less give up the independence that driving represents.

So as Tibbets told me about his experiences on the freeways—he didn't use the phrase "treacherous driving conditions," but that was the message he was delivering—I thought about my father, and there was one difference:

I never knew Tibbets as a younger man. He was a man of eighty-four telling me about the freeways, just as he was a man of eighty-four telling me about World War II. With my father, my memories went all the way back to when he was in his thirties, when I was a small boy. Whatever the freeways eventually became for him, I could put that in the context of what the roads and highways—in the days when I was first in his sedan with him, before there had even been freeways— had been for him. I could, in my mind—for I seldom said this out loud to him—picture the roads as they were in his and my younger days, when the treachery had come exclusively from outside his car, and then picture him in his eighties, backing out of the driveway on nights when I knew that he shouldn't do it.

If there was one good thing about him getting so infirm in the end—and there weren't many good things—it was the relief that came with the knowledge that he wasn't going to be getting behind the wheel of a car. I imagined him and Tibbets driving alongside of each other on I-70, heading downtown, each of them wary of the other—each of them distrusting of the old man in the next lane.

Inside of a man, it must seem to happen so quickly—to go from vitality to something less. To go from complete confidence in what you can do . . .

On the tape of his life, his voice told of those initial days in North Africa, as the 91st Infantry waited to find out what was coming next. Treacherous conditions indeed.

The minefields were still there, and the booby traps were still there, which was a constant source of danger to everybody. . . .

There were all kinds of rumors about when the invasion of *Festung Europa* would begin. That phrase meant Fortress of Europe, and Hitler had really prepared the west coast of France and all the other contiguous countries to repel the invaders when they did come. And as each day went by, the rumblings and rumors continued. . . .

• • •

Sometimes, when we went on family vacations when I was a child, I would hear my father and mother discussing whatever hotel in which we were staying, and commenting on whether it was "American Plan" or "European Plan."

I didn't know precisely what those two things meant—I still don't—but from the way my parents talked about them, it was clear that the words referred to whether some of your meals came with the price of the room. When you're a kid, though, you pick up certain messages underneath the words—and the message I got from the American Plan/European Plan conversations was that my father must be a pretty worldly fellow.

How else would he know these things—the hotel plan that was used in Europe, the hotel plan that was used in the United States? He had to have an awfully sophisticated understanding of the ways of the world—at least to the ears of his son, that's the way it sounded.

And of course whatever worldliness he really did have—knowledge of the way things were done in Europe, knowledge of the way things were done in Africa—came almost entirely courtesy of a long trip that his employer, the United States Army, once sent him on.

It's a little-noticed aspect of what happened to the men of my father's generation and Tibbets' generation—but they were boys who grew up during the Depression, when there was absolutely no hope of going on any kind of a long vacation anywhere, much less across the Atlantic Ocean. And then, because of history's violent jog in the road, these small-town Depression boys were seeing places that even the most fabulously wealthy international travelers of previous generations never got to. These children of the Depression were—under the worst possible circumstances—cast to the most far-flung corners of the globe, to countries and cities that only a few years before they had been looking at on color-plate maps in their public-school geography books.

The man-made globes—the little globes, the ones that spun in the dens of American homes—must have looked so different to them when they got home from the war. Italy, Africa, Germany, France . . . Japan . . . these impossibly distant places were now a part of their lives forever. These young men had gotten out of town, all right—they had gotten about as far out of town as they ever might have dared to dream.

With a twist that even O. Henry might not have been able to come up with. See the world? You want to see the world, young man? All right, if you insist . . .

There were earlier twists, too—twists that transpired not at the end of the story, but at the beginning.

I had long been curious about how my father became an officer in the Army. He went in as a private
and came out as a major; how had that happened?

It turned out to be one more instance of life's
abrupt and unplanned detours. Because his family
had not been able to send him out of Akron to go to
college—because the working man's school up the
hill was all that he could afford—he had followed
the curriculum that Akron University required. He
wouldn't make it all the way through school—his
father's illness, and the need for him to help support
the family, precluded that—but during his brief
time at that commuter college, one of the classes
that the school insisted all male students take had a
ripple effect more powerful than almost anything
else in his lifetime.

**Let me digress just a bit, I have to go back to
my Akron University days, which were not particularly fruitful as far as my education was
concerned, but one thing happened that con-
ceivably could have changed my life. One thing
I do know, it sure changed my military career.**

**ROTC (Reserve Officers' Training Corps) was
a required course at Akron U., and I took it and
did well in it. One thing that I did was obey the
orders given from a certain Sergeant Gee, and I
got to be a pretty good cadet. Well, after I arrived in Camp Shelby and started basic training, I seemed to be about the only one in our
training company who knew his right foot from**

his left foot and knew close-order drill. As a result of this I made buck sergeant after three weeks in the Army, which was some kind of a record in those days, and I attribute it all to ROTC because, as I said before, it taught me my left foot from my right foot—obviously very important in the Army. . . .

The continuum of a man's self-regard: from a boy who thinks that he has no command over life's vagaries, to a soldier who begins to understand that confidence is something that can be attained, to an older man who senses things starting to shift inexorably back in the other direction. . . .

In the early 1980s, when my brother got married in Colorado, the family gathered at a hotel complex in Keystone for the ceremony. My father had rented a car—he was still in his sixties, driving had not yet become a problem for him, even in our eyes—and one afternoon he and my mother took a ride down the mountain road to pick up some things at a grocery store.

When they returned, there was a sound in his voice I hadn't often heard before. Apparently as they were driving on the narrow road their car had been passed by some raucous young local guys who thought my dad had been holding them up.

Never one to hide his opinion of people—especially people who annoyed him—he had given them an angry stare out the open window of his rented car. He wanted them to know that he thought they were driving like jerks.

And one of the guys in the car had rolled the window down and shouted at my father: "What are you looking at, you son of a bitch?"

Mountain road, sparsely populated part of Colorado, my mother in the passenger seat, outnumbered by young men he knew nothing about. . . .

"I just gave them a little nod and rolled the window up," he reported to us. "And I slowed down and let them go on."

He hadn't liked the cut of their jib—and it had turned out that they didn't much like the cut of *his* jib, either, and appeared ready to do something about it if he pushed things.

Discretion won out—as it undoubtedly should have. And the sound of his voice that day . . . it wasn't exactly that he sounded defeated, it was more a concession that he was reluctantly resigned to something. There are some battles not worth fighting; there comes a time in your life when you defer to people you once wouldn't have even wasted your spit on. There are wars and there are wars . . . and a man reaches a juncture in his days when he must realize that he's no longer a fighter.

He didn't say he was scared that day; it's not a word he would have chosen to use. But in his voice was the acknowledgment that he was glad the face-off had ended where it had—and maybe regretful that, with my mother in the car, he had initiated the incident with that first disapproving stare out the window.

Being afraid, at one time, was something he evidently used as fuel—being afraid was something he depended upon to propel him. In recording his personal history, he talked about the emotions that filled him in the months before he was sent overseas when, unexpectedly, he was selected to be trained as an infantry officer and sent to Fort Benning, Georgia, to see if he could make the grade.

. . . When I got there I was full of trepidation, because this was major league stuff, and the stories about the guys who busted out were legion. And I was just hoping and praying that it would not happen to me. . . .

One of the things I dreaded was the obstacle course, which we had to run every Saturday morning. I was never a particularly athletic guy, as you all know—I could hold my own in physical training and boxing and that sort of thing, but I really wasn't such a jock that I would break any records, and the obstacle course was a big fear of mine.

Well, I was very, very pleased when I found that I was far from being the last in the class as far as scoring in the obstacle course was concerned. As a matter of fact I was about in the top 15 percent, which was good enough for me.

And so as I went through this obstacle course and the combat course, week after week, I eventually got stronger and stronger and had much more confidence in myself.

One of the things in the combat course was we had to crawl under barbed wire with live machine gun bullets being fired above our heads. This was very frightening, but it was all a part of training. . . .

When the last week rolled around, which was the most important week, I was named to command the whole class of potential officers at Fort Benning. And on July 14, 1942—what a feeling that was, not only to survive the thirteen weeks and to be called a ninety-day wonder, which is what we were called, but to realize that from that day on we would be officers. . . .

For all that had happened to the men and women of his generation—for all the places he had been, for all that he had been through—my father, and, I think, many of his contemporaries, regarded the world with a constant sense of distance.

"It's Akron calling," he would say when I was a child and his father or mother would phone Columbus on the weekend to say hello. The words themselves, and his phrasing of them—"It's Akron calling"—made it sound as if this was the most momentous, stop-the-presses telephone call that anyone had ever placed. The implicit sense of scale went way beyond the importance the call really carried.

And this was from a man who had been to Africa, to Italy, this was from a man whose country had sent him across the ocean. Maybe it was because he and the men of that generation returned from the war to a United States that was still mainly local—to cities with invisible walls around them in the years before the interstates opened. It remained relatively difficult to get from one place to another in the U.S. in the first years after the war—the roads and highways were still the old kind, the freeway entrance and exit ramps had not been constructed, even a car trip to another part of Ohio required planning in advance.

But later—after the interstates, after network television, after the worldwide computer network—he still spoke that way. I would telephone Columbus on a weekend to check in with my mom and dad, and if they had people over I could hear him put his hand over the mouthpiece of the phone and say to their visitors: "It's Chicago calling."

As if to silence them; as if, because the phone call was coming from a few states away, everything should stop, become hushed. It was long distance—it wasn't a call from right there in town. The world—or so his words and his tone of voice said—was very large.

I never quite understood the ever-present surprise in that tone. The world was, in fact, large—and no one had a right to know that any better than he. It certainly wasn't large because Akron was calling, or Chicago was calling; it was large in a manner that he and his friends and division mates had been shown ample evidence of when they were very young men.

His voice, speaking not of a long-distance phone call from the Midwestern United States to a house in Columbus, but of his first impressions of Naples, Italy, after the 91st had gotten its orders to march:

. . . There was no sanitation, and the Germans had taken everything with them, including the food the Italians had left, and there was very little clothing, furniture, everything you can imagine. The once beautiful city of Naples was a complete shambles.

We stayed there a few days, and then early one morning we loaded up on trucks and started the long trek northward to where, nobody knew. We got into the same situation that we found ourselves in in Africa. We had a chance to get off the trucks to rest. Some of the men were careless and wandered off into the bushes and that's where they were booby-trapped and stepped on mines and were terribly maimed or killed.

It was really war at this time. . . .

In the days after my father's death—the days leading up to the funeral, and then the days after he was buried—there were times when I was away from my mother's house for a few hours, and I picked up a phone to call her.

Usually she answered. But sometimes—if people were in her house making condolence visits, if she was busy doing something else—the answering machine clicked on to take the call.

And there was something I didn't really know how to tell her:

My father's voice was the one on the greeting tape.

"You have reached the Greenes. Neither Phyllis or I are available to take your call right now. . . ."

It was hearty, energetic, full of welcoming enthusiasm; he was always a pretty theatrical guy in his daily dealings with others, and it extended to the answering-machine tape.

But it was more than a little spooky. He was dead, and here was his voice, and if it was unsettling to me, his son, at least I understood that my mom had obviously not gotten around to taking care of certain things, which was why his voice was still there. But I thought of other people who might call—friends, relatives, his former business associates—and I really didn't want them to have to hear this. It was quite a shock—people call the house to say how sorry they are to learn of his death, and there his happy voice is, telling them to leave a message until he can get back to them.

My supposition was that my mom didn't know

about it; I thought that she would be mortified if she knew that callers were hearing him greeting them. But I wasn't sure if I should bring it up to her, not only because it was one more thing I didn't want her to worry about—but because, in a strange way, I thought part of her might resist the impulse to change the tape.

It was one of the few things that remained from the way life had been in that house only a few days before. It had always been a house that belonged to the both of them, in every way—they thought of themselves as a couple, full-time, inseparable. *You have reached the Greenes. . . .* That's who they were, every bit as much as they were an individual man and an individual woman.

Getting rid of his voice on the tape might be a small detail, in the context of what she had just lost—but I knew that it would matter to her. His voice would no longer be speaking for them, in any way. I told my sister about it, and I'm not sure what she said to my mom, but within a day or two my father's voice had been erased and replaced by my mother's.

Not that I wasn't hearing his voice all the time, telling stories about a once-young man very far from home:

We continued the trek northward and found ourselves going through Rome, which had re-

cently been liberated by part of the Fifth Army commanded by General Mark Clark.

We did receive quite an acclamation from the Italians, they just thought we were wonderful, but of course that's what they thought the Germans were when they first came in. So there we were on the way up what was to become Highway 65, but it had a different number at that particular point, and . . . again, this sounds like a storybook, but we were going to engage the Germans in battle. . . .

Sometimes I would hear young businessmen— usually white-collar types, stock traders and the like—speak of their jobs in terms of warfare.

"He's a killer," they might say admiringly of a colleague. "This is going to be a real battle," they might say as the deadline for a deal approached. "Hey, this is a war—don't forget it."

I never heard my father talk about business that way. He always—no matter what was going on at his office—spoke of business as just that: business. A job. He didn't pump it up into something like combat.

It made me think about whether the men of his generation—the men who had come back from the war in Europe, the men who had come back from the war in the Pacific—just instinctively knew better than to use those kinds of terms to describe something that was not even close to a war. Whether—out of respect not only for themselves and the men they had left behind, but out of dark respect for the very concept of war—they would have felt foolish using that kind of language to refer to the safe venue of the officeplace.

He was gone, and I couldn't ask him about it. But I made a note to ask Tibbets. I was doing that a lot now—the questions I had never asked my dad about the world in which he had lived, I was taking to Tibbets, to see what he might have to say.

EIGHTEEN

Business is not a war and it never has been," Tibbets said. "Your job may not be a lot of fun at
times, and you may not like the people you're com-
peting with—both outside your company, and *inside*
your company—but war? That demeans the word."

I had come to see him again in Columbus, and we
were having lunch at a casual place just a few blocks
from the apartment house where my father and
mother had lived right after I was born. Tibbets told
me that work was not the only part of contemporary
life that is wrongly compared to warfare; he said
there is another of life's aspects that is even more frequently placed falsely in that category:

"Look at sports," he said. "All the talk about how
football is a war, how the football field is a battlefield. It's so ridiculous. You say that your father used
to go to the Ohio State football games?"

"For fifty years," I said.

"I can almost guarantee you that he never acted
like those people who paint their faces and their
chests," Tibbets said. "Am I right?"

Of course he was—but then, in his later years,
there was obviously no way a man my father's age
was going to do that. I understood Tibbets' broader
point—that even when my father was a younger
man and just back from the war, he and the mem-

bers of his generation likely accepted sports events, including the seemingly most crucial ones, as what they were: colorful entertainment.

"Your father knew, and I know, the difference between reality and fiction," Tibbets said. "Fiction is fine—as long as you don't get it mixed up with the things in life that are real.

"I don't think that any of us who came home from World War II made the mistake of confusing what happened there with what happens at a sports contest. Look, your dad probably hated to see Ohio State lose—he liked the team.

"But he was a realist—he knew that *he* wasn't playing. He wasn't down on the field, and he couldn't do anything about what was going on down on the field. Whether the team won or not, he was still going to get in his car and go home when the game was over—and then be back in the stands for the next game.

"It was a relief for us, to come back after the war and be able to attend the games. We didn't whoop and holler—we'd give our teams a good hand, but we understood that it was a game that we weren't playing in, that everyone, including the people on the field, was going to get to go home safely from it. It would have been sort of stupid to put the same kind of emotions into that that we'd put into the situation overseas that we'd recently been actual participants in."

• • •

I had brought a list with me—things about my father's life that I had been thinking about lately, things that I had never gotten around to asking him directly. I was looking for Tibbets' help in understanding some of them.

The importance my father had placed on being a major, for example. He had gone into the Army as a private—drafted—and when he left as a major, that had seemed to be one of the accomplishments in his life of which he was the very proudest. It was a running joke with my dad and his friends—they would call him "the major" ("Is the major home?" his friend Harry Hofheimer would ask my mom when he would call our house, all during the years of my growing up); they were kidding, but kidding on the straight. They knew that the rank mattered to him.

But why so much?

"Think of the Army as a company, as a business," Tibbets said. "Think of your father going in as a person at the most menial level—as a person sent down to the basement to work, sweeping the damn floor.

"That's what it was like when he was drafted into the Army. He was sent to the basement—he was a private, in the basement.

"And when he left the Army after the war, he was an executive. That's not something a young man ever forgets, even when he's no longer young. Why did it mean so much to him? Because at the first time during his life that it really mattered, he was recognized by the people he worked with. They recognized his talent and his ability."

"And what was the meaning of the rank?" I asked.

"The meaning was that the Army trusted him to tell other men what to do," Tibbets said. "They put that kind of trust in him.

"You only knew him when you knew him—after you were born. But he was someone before you were born—in the Army, he was a young man who went in with several million others. Was being a major a big deal to him? You're damn right it was. It ought to have been. Those millions of others didn't make it to major. He did."

Yet for all that pride in what he had become in the Army, my father was not an openly patriotic man—not in the sense that he was a flag-waver, or a maker of I-love-America speeches. That had always struck me as curious—that he and so many men like him, who had risked so much for their country, seldom talked about the affection they held for the United States. It just wasn't a subject that came up much.

Why?

"We didn't talk about it because we didn't see any reason to talk about it," Tibbets said. "Love our country? We were taught that, by our parents, and in our schools, and in our churches and synagogues.

We grew up knowing that it was expected of us—
to love this country and to treat it with loyalty and
respect.

"Talk about it? That would be like talking about
the air that we breathed."

"But the experiences that all of you had in de-
fending the country . . ." I began.

"Look, I didn't know what my father did during
his war," Tibbets said. "He was a captain. In World
War I. But that's about all I knew, because it would
have been ridiculous to say it out loud—to say that
you had done a lot to help defend your country."

"Why ridiculous?" I said.

"Because everyone felt the same way that your father did and that I did," Tibbets said. "To love your
country didn't make you something special—of
course you loved your country, of course you would
give your life for it if it came to that. You didn't
need to tell people that—it was just the way things
were."

"Was that the only reason?" I said.

"When we came home from the war, we were in
the midst of millions of men who had just come
home from the same war," Tibbets said. "And even
if a man wanted to talk about what he had been
through, he usually had enough sense to know that
there were other men around him who had had experiences they did *not* want to talk about. So we usually made the choice not to bring it up.

" 'Patriotism' is a general word. It's vague. When

you're fighting a war it is not a matter of patriotism in the general sense. It's about the death of friends.

"You watch friends get blown to pieces. And that is not a patriotic feeling. It's a revolting feeling.

"It's revolting to watch anyone die, and it hurts when the person is a friend of yours. You're talking to a guy one minute, and the next minute he's body parts and dead.

"It's shocking. It is a shock that doesn't leave you, and when you come back home you may not want to bring those things out. So you don't."

Once, when I was a young adult and my father was in his fifties or his early sixties, I was back in Columbus and I had lunch with him downtown.

We were walking down Broad Street, and at the southeast corner of Broad and Third my dad saw a man he knew—a business associate of some kind. He stopped the man and said that he wanted to introduce his son to him.

"Bob," my father said to me, "this is my old friend Johnny Johnson."

And the man corrected him. He said what his last name really was.

It was close—I don't recall now whether the man's name was Johnny Jackson or Johnny Jones, but I know that it wasn't all that far off from Johnny Johnson. But my father, I could tell, was mortified. He had committed a blunder, and quite publicly—

and the next thirty seconds were uncomfortable for
him, much more so than they were for me or for the
man whose name he had gotten slightly wrong.

In the grand scheme of things, what had it
meant? Nothing. A blown name on a busy city
street. But when I thought about it in the years that
followed—and I thought about it every time I
passed Broad and Third—I tried to envision the
battlefields of Europe, and then to juxtapose that visual image with the safe and civil streetscape of
downtown Columbus. A mistake on the battlefield
could cost a man his life—or the life of a friend. A
little slip at Broad and Third? Gone with the next
changing of the traffic light.

But was it? Or, to the men who came home, did
the downtown streets sometimes seem as foreign
as the hills of Africa and Italy? Had the war in
Europe, the war in the Pacific, become, in a certain
sense, these men's real hometowns? Had the war become their point of truest reference—the place they
knew best?

And if it had, what was it like for them when
they returned to city streets, and found the combat-
ants wearing business suits instead of uniforms, in a
different kind of conflict?

"Boy, you've been thinking about all of this a lot,
haven't you?" Tibbets said.

"More than I would have expected," I said.

"Don't spend a lot of time thinking that part of
us would have preferred to be back in the war," he

said. "You're right that the war started to feel more real to us than our memories of what we had left back home. It was just like that—you've got it right.

"But it wasn't a reality that we wanted to keep alive. It never was that. Most of the guys wanted only one thing—to get out. To go back home and to start our lives over again."

"It just would seem to be such a harsh shift," I said. "To go from a place where the rules are the rules of warfare, to a place where your enemies—or at least your adversaries—are dressed the same way you are, and you have to relearn a whole new set of rules."

"It's like I was telling you before," he said. "Business was never war to us. We knew the difference, and we never confused the two.

"And no matter how annoying business could become, it was never an annoyance that we would trade in for what we faced during warfare."

I told him that story of my dad and the man whose name wasn't Johnny Johnson. It had felt, to me, like a lost skirmish played under rules of engagement that were at the same time stringently meaningful and totally irrelevant—rules of engagement my father had returned to after taking part in something that had been governed by a set of regulations quite separate.

I guessed that whenever I recalled that moment at the corner of Broad and Third, I had this twinge of a suspicion that the man in the oil painting back in our house—the young soldier in uniform—may have, at least on occasion, been surer of his footing in Italy in 1945 than on the concrete sidewalks of central Ohio thirty years later.

"I wouldn't give that too much thought," Tibbets said.

"I don't know why it sticks with me," I said. "And it's not like I think about it all the time."

"I'll guarantee you one thing," Tibbets said. "You've thought about it a lot more than your dad or that other guy ever did."

"Maybe it's not all that complicated a thought," I said. "Maybe it just comes down to the hunch that, given the choice, he would rather have been a soldier than a businessman."

"On that one, I can't tell you you're wrong," Tibbets said.

A nd I wanted to know about my father's music. He liked Les and Larry Elgart; he liked Si Zentner; he liked Doc Severinsen in the days before Severinsen was on the *Tonight Show*, in the days when Severinsen was known as a great jazzman instead of a fellow in loud sport coats who, from the bandstand, traded jokes with Johnny Carson. He liked grown-up musicians with grown-up talent who made grown-up music.

And I got the impression that he had liked them

even as a very young man—he had liked them on the day he had come out of the Army. It seemed to me to be symbolic of something that went well beyond music: It seemed to emblemize once again the notion that it was just about impossible to come home from World War II and seem like a kid. Prolonged adolescence—which became almost a way of life for generations born after the war—was a concept that would have had a hard time making it past years of fighting the Nazis.

Or so it had always seemed to me—and the music of my father's generation was a part of that. The men and women of that generation loved music that was older than their years.

"I think it was because there were changes going on at home while we were away at war," Tibbets told me when I asked him about it. "Rock and roll, the way I understand it, came along in the years after we came home and started raising our families. I think that rock and roll music was the outgrowth of the changes in society that were taking place while the men were away.

"After rock and roll, there was no going back to the music that was there before. We found that out quick enough. Speaking just for myself, rock and roll always disturbed the hell out of me. I couldn't stand it."

I told him that my father—who had despised Elvis Presley from the moment he had laid eyes on him—always appeared a little confused about Elvis after Elvis had joined the Army. All the terrible things my father had said about Presley—but how could he believe those things about a man who suddenly wore the same uniform that he had worn? How could he say that Presley represented everything that was wrong about American life, when Presley, just as my father had, answered the call of his country and served in the United States Army?

"When we went into the service, we matured in a hurry," Tibbets said. "The transition period was very short. During World War II, if you didn't mature fast, you were dead.

"It wasn't a choice we made—it just happened, because of where we were. In most societies, the maturing process takes place over a period of years. We didn't have that. I went from a twenty-three-year-old kid to a person who felt like a forty-year-old serviceman in a big hurry.

"So of course it was hard for your dad to stay mad at Presley after Presley was in the Army. Presley was being put into the same situation that your dad and I were in—although Presley didn't have a war to fight. But by going in, he was growing up. And any man who has done it understands that."

And was that why—when my father and Tibbets and all those men came back from the war—they seemed so solid? Was that why their music was the music of adults, and all that followed seemed designed for the ears of children and adolescents?

"Let me put it to you this way," Tibbets said. "Where we were—during the years that we were serving—there was not much time for levity. You grew up so fast precisely because you weren't given any time to grow up.

"We came to maturity quickly. We didn't do it because we had sat down and made the choice. We did it because our lives depended on it."

And their lives had depended on one another—both in matters that could kill them if someone did something wrong, or matters that would merely inconvenience them if someone declined to do a little thing right.

It's something else I had been thinking about when moments from my father's life came back to me. And I decided to tell Tibbets one small story, from a Christmas Eve long ago.

"We were in the house," I said. "All of us were still little kids. And there was this huge sound from the garage, like an explosion or something, and then the sound of water gushing.

"It was freezing outside. We opened this side door that led into the garage—and a water pipe had burst. It must have been a pipe that extended across the ceiling of the garage, because the water was just pouring onto my father's and my mother's cars. I mean, more water than you've ever seen come out of a pipe.

"And you could tell that it was very hot water—it was really steaming as it came out of the ceiling of the garage. And we stood there—I can see my father looking at it—and what were we supposed to do? It was Christmas Eve—late in the evening on Christmas Eve, if I'm remembering right. Who are you going to find on Christmas Eve to come fix a burst water pipe?"

"What did your father do?" Tibbets asked.

"Well, I remember him going to the phone in the back hallway, and calling all these plumbing services," I said. "But of course, no one was there. So he looked up the home numbers of some plumbers who lived near us, and he told them what had happened. But they didn't want to go out on Christmas Eve. I couldn't blame them—but the water was just gushing into our garage.

"I guess what I think about when I think about that is: In the Army, you always must have had all these people to do every job with you. You had been asked to save the world—but even on the little things, there were millions of you, always doing everything together. However tedious it might have been, however hurry-up-and-wait it might have been, at least you were all there. You know that old line: 'Yeah? You and what army?' You had the answer, back then. You and what army? The United States Army."

"So what's that have to do with the garage on Christmas Eve?" Tibbets said.

"If he'd been back in the Army, there would have been hundreds of guys around to fix the pipe," I said. "Hundreds of pairs of hands. And I remember him standing there with his family, with all the water pouring out . . . and I think about whether life got so much harder for all of you once you got home, and there was no army with you. The pipe blows, the furnace breaks . . . and it's not you and what army anymore. It's just you."

"It's still you and the Army," Tibbets said.

"What do you mean?" I said.

"That's one of the things that the war did for us," he said. "It's an old saying, but it's a true one: There is nothing like American ingenuity. For the GIs during the war, it was a question of coming upon new problems to solve every day. Problems that none of us had ever anticipated before—and we had to figure out ways to solve them every day of the war.

"Yes, we did it together—but I don't think that made it harder once we got home. I think it made it easier. Because we had all those months and years of coming up with solutions when there was no choice but to find a solution. So your friends might not be with you once you got home and were faced with problems—but the experiences you had gone through were with you."

"So you don't think a lot of men didn't know what to do once they didn't have the Army at their side?" I said.

"I think a guy's lost if he feels that way," Tibbets said. "And I don't think a lot of us came home feeling lost. We had our experiences inside of us. That was as good as having our friends from the Army next to us. Or almost as good."

"I don't know," I said. "I keep thinking about the expression on my father's face that Christmas Eve."

"Let me ask you something," Tibbets said. "What finally happened?"

"What do you mean?" I said.

"What happened with the burst water pipe in the garage?" he said. "Did it just keep pouring the water out all night long?"

"No," I said. "He got it shut off."

"I'm not surprised," Tibbets said. "Did a plumber come over?"

"No," I said.

"Then how did he fix the pipe?" Tibbets asked.

"I don't know," I said. "I don't remember what he did."

"He did something," Tibbets said. "And whatever he did, it worked."

"It must have," I said.

"That's my point," Tibbets said.

In the last days of my father's life, the tree trimmers were next door.

It's a sound I will never forget. He had lost the battle; he was going to die.

And there it was, just out the bedroom window: the sound of power saws revving up, the high whine of the motorized blades cutting into wood, the throaty rumble as the teeth did their job—and then that whine again, louder, sharper, a dentist's drill amplified a thousand times.

And my father in his bed. Outside our house, no one knew; it wasn't a question of a neighbor being rude or unfeeling. This was the tree trimmers' day to come to this neighborhood. They had their job to do.

And he lay in his bed, and there was no silence. Only noise, as his life slipped away.

I told Tibbets. And I told him about how quiet the street where I grew up had always been— so quiet that even something as mild as teenagers yelling at each other from their cars late at night was a big event. Even noise like that seldom happened— it was enough to make us all wake up. What's wrong? we would think in those first moments of wakefulness. What's that noise?

Teenagers calling out to each other. That broke the peace and the quiet.

I asked Tibbets about the noise of war—what it had been like to leave a country where there was usually quiet, and enter a world where the sounds were like nothing they had ever heard before.

"That's something that no one ever thinks about," he said to me. "The sounds of war. I haven't even thought about it for a long time.

"But it was a big part of it. The war was not quiet. We were all raised to respect our neighbors' privacy—to keep things quiet in the neighborhoods where we grew up.

"And then we went to the war, and the noise wasn't like anything else we ever experienced before, or like anything we would ever experience again.

"There was no mistaking it. The gunfire, and the tank noises, and the sirens and the aircraft overhead all the time. It never really stopped. It became part of the background of our lives—sometimes it was louder than other times, but it never completely went away. We even got used to it. That war sound."

I asked him if it was difficult adjusting to the quiet once the soldiers came home to the United States.

"No," he said. "It was a pretty easy adjustment. We liked the silence of home. It meant something to us."

"What did it mean?" I asked.

"The silence?" Tibbets said. "It meant that we weren't going to get killed the next minute.

"Think about it," he said. "What does silence indicate?

"Tranquility."

NINETEEN

I don't know if my father even heard the power saws cutting into those trees. His face was filled with sporadic flashes of pain, but that had been happening for a while; the noise may have contributed to his discomfort or it may not have, but in any event we finally went out to speak to the neighbors and to the tree crew, and they were kind enough to give my father some quiet.

Even if he was aware of the noise, though, it couldn't have been anything close to the level to which he had once had to train himself to become accustomed. The tranquility of which Tibbets had spoken was homefront tranquility—it was the tranquility that awaited those men once they returned to the American towns they had left.

The places to where their country had sent them were a different matter entirely. My father's voice:

. . . The Bay of Naples was something that I shall never forget as long as I live. The harbor was absolutely jammed with the wreckage of all kinds of Italian warships, French warships, and it had been practically impossible to thread our way into the bay. But it was accomplished. We had to pick our way over the decks of these sunken ships. . . .

. . . . I was all pumped up with the glory needle and everything, and I thought, this was it. If ever I was going to be a hero it was going to be right now, because we were closing in on the Germans who were retreating very, very rapidly, but we were proceeding rapidly, right on their tail.

They made good use of their 88s—they were called 88 howitzers, and they actually used them to pick off trucks and even individual soldiers. One night we were bivouacked at a little place called Piombino. And it was in this little village that we got our first taste of an air raid and an attitudinal change.

During the night, as was really necessary, we slept beneath the trucks because we didn't know when we would be hit by incoming artillery or what. To our great surprise and horror we received an air raid that night, and the shell fragments were flying all around, injuring and killing more guys. And I can only imagine what the front line troops were receiving. . . .

One day toward the end when I was visiting him in Columbus, and my mother, my sister and I were in the bedroom with him, I walked out to get something in the kitchen.

As I left the room, my mom and my sister shifted chairs, so that he could see them from the bed.

I could hear him say to them:

"You girls stay here, now."

And then:

"Don't leave me."

Two simple declarative sentences. Yet the plaintiveness of them. . . .

I don't think I had ever heard him ask for something that directly before—at least not ask for something that important.

I stopped where I was, and looked back into the room.

"We're not going anywhere," my mother said, holding his hand.

"We're not leaving," my sister said, with the smile I was seeing on her face so often during those months—a smile that didn't match the wetness of her eyes. The smile was for him to see; I think she was hoping he didn't notice the tears.

Don't leave me. I knew that those were words he never would have said out loud during the years when he was younger and stronger. Would he have thought them to himself? I didn't really know. There was no way for anyone but him to know the answer to that.

But as my mother and sister sat with him that day, I asked myself a question that I knew I would never ask my mother:

If the circumstances had been reversed—if my

mother had been the one whose health and life were slipping away, and my father had been the one who was still vital—would he have been this good with her?

Would he have had the fortitude and the patience and the singlemindedness to do for her what she, over all these months, was doing for him?

I knew one thing: No one could ever do this better.

"We're not going anywhere," she said, moving her chair closer to the bed. "We're right here."

His voice, telling about the sunrise after the German howitzer attack:

. . . The next morning we saddled up as if nothing had happened and proceeded northward. We finally learned that our goal was to go through Florence, which was right across the Arno River, and occupy the slopes to the north of the city.

This was really a beautiful part. . . . we went through Tuscany and saw all the beautiful old Italian towns, and it was an experience that no one will ever forget—and it was very peaceful at that time. . . . We went across the Arno River on pontoon bridges and saw the most beautiful city you can ever imagine.

Florence was declared an open city, which meant that while the bridges would be bombed and taken out, none of the city was to be touched. This was an arrangement that had been made by the Axis and the Allies, so it was really something to see.

We went through the city very, very fast. Oh, I meant to tell you that the only remaining bridge was the Ponte Vecchio, which was a bridge that was made up of small shops, silversmiths, jewelers and everything like that—a beautiful bridge.

Up we came to the slopes to the north of the city, and there we bivouacked to wait the next phase. . . .

There was a drive-in on East Main Street where he always used to take us for hamburgers and milkshakes. The Eastmoor, it was called—car hops and cruising convertibles and warm summer nights. The men who had come home from the war would bring their young families out for burgers and fries and Cokes—the Eastmoor felt like fun and freedom, it felt like the kind of place they must have dreamed of during those months and years in Europe and the Pacific.

Come to think of it, the Eastmoor wasn't all that far from the Top. If the men home from the war would take their wives to the Top for adult nights out—steaks and martinis—then the Eastmoor was the place where the children were welcome. Both a part of Main Street; both a part of what, in central

Ohio, made the post-war years feel as good as they did.

Once, I remember, we ate inside at the East-moor—we were headed somewhere on a car trip (maybe to see his parents in Akron), and we stopped off at the Eastmoor and went to a booth. There was loud music playing in the restaurant—not jukebox music, just music coming out of the ceiling.

He called the waitress over and asked her to turn it down.

"We can't turn it down," she said. "It comes from downtown."

I thought his eyes were going to turn to icicles and steam was going to come puffing out of his ears. "The music comes from downtown," he said, each word an accusation.

"It does," she said.

"*Where* downtown?" my father said.

"I don't know," the waitress said. "It just comes from downtown."

My guess is that it was Muzak; my guess is that this is what she meant. And even with Muzak, or so I assume, there must be a way for an individual place of business to control the volume. If there's not, then there should be.

Which is what my father seemed to believe, too. "You're telling me that we have to sit here and have this music blast into our ears because someone downtown is controlling the volume?" he said.

I wanted to sink into the cushion. He was probably right; why should he have to eat his meal with high-volume music blaring right over his head? But when you're a kid, you don't want to be around any public confrontation in which your parents are involved. It doesn't matter who's right or who's wrong; you just want things to go along on a smooth path.

"Do your *hamburgers* come from downtown?" he said. "Because if they do, maybe you can tell the person who brings them to turn the music down on his way."

I was telling my brother that story as we looked for the medical supply store. It was on East Main Street, too; it probably had been there for years—maybe going back to the early years of the Eastmoor and the Top—but we'd never seen it. At least we'd never noticed it.

You don't see places like that until you need them. A sickroom supply store—that's what it was. As he lay dying, there were all kinds of things that suddenly became necessary. Things you don't have around your house until your life turns downward.

Items needed for the basic functions of daily living when you can't get out of your bed—items that, by their existence, speak of the new unpleasantness of your mornings and nights. Products and devices designed to help you accomplish those functions you never had to even think about needing help with before.

"I think it's that place, right there," my brother said, and we turned into the parking lot.

And so we went shopping. The place wasn't glitzy

or inviting; this was not some Wal-Mart designed to lure its customers into impulse purchases. The people who came in here to shop knew what they wanted before they walked through the door, and in most cases they weren't shopping for their own needs. They were doing it for someone who couldn't come here himself or herself. Anyone who could come in here himself probably wouldn't.

So we went through the aisles like kids in an old 5-and-10, looking for articles to buy. Except no one would enter this particular version of a 5-and-10 unless they had to. We found some of the things our mother had said that our father needed, and the ones we couldn't find we asked the man at the counter, and he bagged everything up for us—all the things made of plastic, all the things made of glass, all the things made of cloth—and as we left he said, "Have a good weekend."

"Those words have a different sound, in there," I said to my brother as we got back into the car.

"What, 'Have a good weekend?'" he said.

"Yeah," I said. "That's not exactly a good-weekend kind of place."

"It's Saturday," he said. "He's just being nice."

"And he probably knows that he'll see us again next week," I said.

"Until we stop coming," my brother said.

I didn't have to ask what he meant.

We drove onto Main Street, on our way back to our father.

"Where was the Eastmoor Drive-In?" I asked my brother.

"One of these blocks," he said. "It's been gone for years."

Main Street must have seemed like such a blithe piece of roadway to him, after where he had been:

   . . . We sat on the northern hills of Florence for a few days or maybe a week or so, and then the order came to saddle up and get going up Highway 65.

   You kids have heard me talk about Highway 65 many, many times, and are probably sick of it, but as I am recounting my experiences now, it really flashes back very clearly. What we knew, and what was rumored, didn't sound very good. As we were going up Highway 65, you must remember that it was barely sixty or sixty-five miles from where we left, to Bologna, which was to be our phase line and our goal.

   This ordinarily could have been done in a couple of hours, but believe it or not it took us over six months to get up that sixty or sixty-five miles of road to accomplish our objective. . . .

When I was in high school I'd had some summer jobs—including some in the factory of the company where he worked—but things changed the summer I got a job as a copyboy at the *Columbus Citizen-Journal*.

I was seventeen; it was a morning paper. I would ride the bus downtown and start my shift at noon, or sometimes at two o'clock in the afternoon. I'd get off at nine, or at eleven.

This was different from anything with which he had ever been familiar. Factory work, he knew; cutting lawns and painting street addresses on curbs, he could understand. I'd done those things, without taking much of an interest in them. They were what you were supposed to do: work during the summer to make a little money.

The job at the newspaper seemed to interest him, in the sense that for the first time I was doing something that had absolutely no connection with anything that he had been involved with in his lifetime. It's not that he asked a lot of questions about it. He didn't.

But there was something in the tone of his voice, and in the way he would look at me on weekend mornings. Our lives suddenly had fewer intersections—I would still be asleep when he left for his office in the morning, and in the evening the family would have dinner without me, and by the time I got home from the *Citizen-Journal* often everyone would be in bed. So there were weekend mornings when several whole days had passed since I had seen him.

And he would look at me as if he knew I was doing something special. Not just the fact that it was newspaper work—the look on his face had more to do with me finding something that I liked, not something that he liked or that my mother liked or that any of my friends liked, but that I liked, on my own, and then going out and pursuing it. Without very many words being exchanged, it was clear to me that he thought this was good.

There was something else in the air, too, something beyond the fact of my discovering at a young age a kind of work that I was falling in love with. There was the parallel idea that our lives were beginning to diverge—that by finding this kind of work, and devoting myself to it, I was setting a course that would send us off in different directions forevermore. It was not that he minded this; I think that he kind of liked it. It was just that, as a father, he was seeing something for the first time—his child, his oldest child, becoming a different person than the boy from all those thousands of dinner table evenings.

I would ride the bus downtown in the off-hours, hours when few other people were commuting to work, and I would do my job in the city room. There wasn't much grandeur to it—running copy and filling pastepots and going to Paoletti's restaurant next door to get coffee and sandwiches for the editorial staff—but the world in that city room was a world he had never seen, never been a part of. Everything else in my life, up to that point, had been in the context of our family. This was mine alone.

There were nights when he and my mom would drive downtown to pick me up. Most nights I took the bus home, but if I was working late, or if they had been out with friends, they might offer to give me a ride.

So at nine o'clock or eleven o'clock, I would grab an early copy of the morning paper from the first press run—a seven-cent newspaper that we who worked there got for free—and I would take the stairs down to the newspaper building's front entrance on Third Street, and they'd be waiting in the car, he behind the wheel, my mother next to him.

I'd show him the paper—this was all done very casually, we didn't make a ceremony out of it or act as if it really mattered, I'd just hand it to him, with tomorrow morning's headlines on it—and he'd glance at it, seeing on the night before what all his friends wouldn't see until breakfast. And he'd always say the same thing to me:

"How was work, Scoop?"

It was a joke, of course; by then newspapermen weren't called Scoop anymore, he was making fun in the gentlest of ways. But joking or not, that word—*Scoop*—meant a lot. It was shorthand for: You're doing something on your own. You're doing something exciting. You're doing something that I think is all right.

And at seventeen, it was exciting—to be a young man starting off in a line of work that seemed like so much fun. I look back on those nights now, and it seems most generous of him, to be so quietly happy to see his son doing something like this. I often ask myself now whether he ever wished that as a young man he had been able to lead a life like that one.

Because through no fault of his own the nights of his young manhood had turned into something very different.

. . . It started to get cold and it started to rain and the hills began to get steeper, and lo and behold they turned into mountains, which were the Apennines. And up and up we went, and in the far distance we could hear artillery fire, and we knew that the Germans were just waiting for us to come around a bend.

But still we kept going, making a few miles a day and then bivouacking in any place that seemed good. In the meantime the front line troops up a few miles ahead of us were engaging the Germans and we started to take many, many casualties, and this is where I first got a real taste of seeing dead soldiers, both American and German.

It was a very, very pitiful sight, because the grave registration people would gather these bodies up, put them in white mattress covers, and stack them neatly, if you will, at a road junction. . . .

The white mattress covers, of course, had turned color, and that color was red blood, and the stench was something that one would never forget. But that was part of the cost of that awful war, and still we continued going up and up, maybe a few yards at a time.

The day before he was supposed to be buried there was a telephone call at my mother's house. It was from a woman at the cemetery.

The house was full of people making condolence calls. The woman from the cemetery asked to whom she was speaking, and said, "Honey, I think there may be a problem with the burial plot."

She asked to speak with my mother. I said no. I said to tell me what she meant.

She said, "Honey, I'm confused about which plot your family thinks your father is supposed to be buried in. I think we may have it reserved for someone else."

My mother, having heard the phone ring, came into the room where I was talking. She asked me what the call was.

I said it was nothing.

After she had left the room, I told the woman that I was quite certain she was wrong about there being any misunderstanding. My parents were very precise in all of their dealings, I said, right up to getting the arrangements for their burials taken care of years in advance.

And I told her that I could not believe she was making this phone call on this day.

She said, "Sweetheart, I know it's hard."

My brother came into the room. I put my hand over the receiver and told him what was going on. I thought his face was going to turn purple.

I asked for the woman's name and I told her I would call her back in five minutes.

My brother and I made an excuse to have my mother let us take a look at the paperwork from the cemetery—the paperwork she and my father had taken pains to have completed years before. As I expected, everything was in order, in a file folder, with no detail unrecorded or left to chance. They wouldn't have let it be any other way.

With my parents' friends and loved ones all over our house, I called back the cemetery. I was told that the woman was unavailable—she was involved in a sales meeting with other prospective clients. Could she call me back?

I said no. I said to get her.

Five minutes passed. I was told that she was still in her sales meeting.

I said to get her.

She came to the phone. I read to her from the paperwork that the cemetery had given to my parents.

"All right, sweetheart," she said. "Then the burial plot is your father's."

My father always had quite a temper. I have always tried to keep mine in check.

On this day, I thought a combination of the two might be in order.

In a voice so soft that I could barely hear it myself, I asked her for the name of the director of the cemetery. She told me.

I said, "First of all, you and I have never met. I am not honey. I am not sweetheart."

There was a silence. "I'm sorry," she said.

"Second of all, I'd like you to find the director of the cemetery right now. As soon as we get off the phone. Can you do that?"

She said that she could.

"I want you to tell him exactly what our conversations have been about," I said. "I want you to tell him that you have made this call to my mother as she is getting ready to bury her husband.

"And then I want you to tell him that I don't want to see either of your faces tomorrow at the cemetery. I don't ever want to hear your voice again.

"And please tell him that if there are any complications like this at the cemetery tomorrow—any complications at all, anything my mother is asked to deal with—then he should make plans for two more funerals, too."

"Why two more funerals?" she said.

"Because both of you are going to wish that you were dead," I said.

I looked across the room, where he used to sit at his desk. That one was for you, I thought. They may not have been able to turn down the music over your head at the Eastmoor Drive-In, but they're going to get your burial right. Hope you thought I did OK.

A few minutes later, when I was back with the people in the house, my mother said, "What was that call all about?"

"Just someone making sure that you have everything you need for tomorrow," I said.

TWENTY

That day went smoothly—and later, when I told Tibbets about what had happened, I had a question for him:

Because my father had always been so careful to have every detail buttoned up and taken care of, because he always planned everything out in advance, I had long half-assumed that this was a quality of all men with his background: all men who had served in the armed forces and who had come of age imbued with military discipline.

Thus, when something happened where someone was sloppy, where someone was not attentive to detail, I often found myself writing it off to the person not being part of the same generation of Americans he and Tibbets were a part of. But was I right?

Or even in the Army had there been people who were just plain bad at what they did? Even in the victorious American Army of World War II, had there been guys who were total screwups?

I think I knew the answer before I asked the question—which is why I asked it. And when Tibbets started laughing before he talked, I had a good idea of what he was going to say.

"Were there guys who were no good?" he said. "Hell, yes. They were all over the place."

"And what happened to them?" I said.

"Most of them made out all right," he said. "Listen, we were surrounded in our own units with some of the worst fuckups in the world. It's just the way mankind is."

"Your unit?" I said. "In Wendover? And on Tinian?"

"Well, that unit was a little different from most," he said. "As I have explained to you. But we had our guys who could never quite get with the program, and who were always messing up. If you're thinking that your dad's close attention to detail was because of the Army, give him a little more credit than that. There were a lot of guys in the Army who never got anything right."

"And they didn't end up being tossed out?" I said.

"No," Tibbets said. "But whenever there was something difficult or important that needed doing, you knew where you could find them. Showing up at sick call, running to the infirmary."

"So the people who screw everything up today are nothing new?" I said.

"They don't wear uniforms," Tibbets said. "Our fuckups did."

Maybe that was why the rank of major meant so much to my father—maybe that was why, even though it was a joke with his friends, they often good-naturedly used that rank when they spoke to him. The more I thought about it—the "Is-the-major-home?" kidding that went on for so many years—the more I wanted to understand its significance to him.

"He and his friends may have joked about it, but there are a lot of things you can joke about," Tibbets said. "The idea that they picked 'major' out, all those years after he came home from the war—of course the rank meant a lot to him. And it should have."

"But why all that time later?" I said. "Fifty years had passed since he had left the Army, and the 'major' references were still there from his friends."

"He was entitled to be called 'major,'" Tibbets said. "The rank of major was not taken away from him. Look—I know that you tell me he kidded about it, I know he must have made fun of himself about it, but there are certain things that a man can't wash out of his mind.

"Military service will change the personalities of most people who serve. If they're lucky, they will change for the better. You *think* differently when you come out of the military. If you're lucky, you come out changed for the good.

"So if you come out as a major . . . it's like I told you before. Certain decisions have been made about the kind of man you are. The decisions may be made when you're a young soldier—but even when you grow old, the fact that those decisions were made means something to you. And it ought to."

"And yet he wasn't a member of the VFW," I said. "There were no VFW magazines around the house, no American Legion magazines. He must have had the chance to join—and he didn't."

"Neither did I," Tibbets said. "It's quite understandable."

"Why?" I said.

"For me, I guess more than anything else, I didn't want to be a has-been," Tibbets said. "I'm not knocking those who did join. But I stayed in the military for a long while after the war, and when I finally did get out I made the decision not to join the VFW and not to join the American Legion." He later was made an honorary life member of both organizations.

"Did you have something against them?" I asked.

"No," he said. "I'm just not a joiner. I never joined the Boy Scouts when I was a kid. So joining the American Legion or the VFW would have been very much against the way I have always been.

"That's not a comment on their members—it's a comment on me, on how I feel about joining up. To go down to the American Legion hall, in my opinion, is too often an excuse to go in and get stinking drunk and talk about the good old days.

"They weren't so good, a lot of those days—they were days of warfare. So, yes, I can understand why your father was proud of what he did, but why he also chose not to join any of the organizations. It makes perfect sense to me."

And there was that lingering thought I could not escape—the thought of how my father, as he grew older, viewed so much of the world with increasing disdain. As he looked upon the things he didn't like—the carelessness of contemporary society, the lack of respect for institutions, the every-man-for-himself mentality that made millionaires and cultural heroes of go-for-broke financial flim-flam artists, and consigned people who played by the old rules and followed the chain of command to lives of modest means and subdued anonymity—I could tell that there were days when he questioned what he and his fellow soldiers had fought and won the war for. If this was the country that resulted from the victory, then what was all the bloodshed and heartache for?

At least that was what I had for many years read into his outlook. Maybe I was wrong.

"You're not wrong," Tibbets said. "I'm not saying that your father and I were right for feeling that way—but you're not wrong in the accuracy of your observation. Yes, there are a lot of times that I feel that way—so I can understand why your father would feel that way too."

"What is that like?" I said. "To have that anger

toward the way things are in the country you fought for?"

"Oh, it comes and goes," Tibbets said. "It's not an all-the-time thing. But you see little things— how undignified people purposely are in their conduct and mannerisms, how people's behavior when they are in public shows a complete lack of a proper upbringing—and you find yourself asking yourself: Why did I do it all? Was it just for this?"

"So it's not politics?" I said.

"Politics has nothing to do with it," Tibbets said. "It's just . . . you know, what really bothers me, and I'm not even sure why, is how many loud-mouths there are walking around, not caring who they are offending, not caring when they use certain words in front of ladies and their elders. It's disgusting.

"And the reason they can get away with it is that we have freedom of speech in this country. Which is as it should be. But you know, someone fought to preserve that freedom for them. And it's like they never stop to think about that—as they're walking through a store using language that you should never use in public, at the top of their voices, they never stop to think that some of the older people they are offending are the people who fought as hard as human beings can fight to save those rights for future generations.

"Is it an old man's viewpoint?" Tibbets said. "Is

this how old men think? Maybe it is. But you know
something? That doesn't make it wrong."

There was a moment—when Tibbets was trying
to explain something to me—when I failed to
understand what he meant at first.

He ended up raising his voice. The matter at
hand was that important.

I had told him that I was struggling with the
question of why my father—and, apparently, so
many men his age—thought that on some level the
war was the best experience of their lives.

Not that it was fun; not that it was enjoyable.
But as terrible as the war was, there was nothing
else in my dad's entire life that meant quite as much
to him. Nothing that came before, nothing that
came after, ever seemed to contain the same power.

And although I understood some of the reasons
for this, I didn't understand them all. I asked Tibbets if he did.

"It was because your father was a man among
men," he said.

That sentence stopped me. Tibbets had never
known my dad—the two had never met. I thought,
just for a second, that Tibbets might be patronizing
me—might be saying something he knew would
please me by praising my father to an extent that was
not possible from someone who had never set eyes on

him. I thought that he was calling my dad a man's man—giving him a macho, dagger-between-the-teeth, pistol-swinging-from-the-belt stature.

And I said so: "How do you know that he was a man among men? It's a very nice thing for you to say—but my dad was just another soldier."

That's when Tibbets' voice got louder.

"I don't mean it that way!" he said. "What I mean is that the war was the one time in a man's life that he got to be a man surrounded by men, all of them working for the same thing, no one better than the person next to him, regardless of rank.

"A time like that comes along only once in a lifetime—if that. You are literally risking your life every day, and you're doing it with the men who are next to you. You form friendships during days and nights like those that nothing and no one in your entire life will ever match.

"Please pay attention: The reason those years mean so much to so many of us is that it is the one time in your life that you are absolutely proud of what you are doing, and you are absolutely proud of your friends and what they are doing. It's a relationship of man to man.

"It is your ass and his—your ass and the guy next to you and the guy next to him. And the people back home can't see you, and they don't know what you're doing, and they don't know who you're doing it with. These men are your friends, and you are depending on them to live.

"Men among men! Men among men! And when you come back home after the war, it is never the same. You faced odds, and you made it back, and you faced down your worst fears. And all of a sudden you're back in a country where things are quieter, things are safer, and the people around you on the streets are not all working for the same goal.

"And you go on, and the war is over, and you become the person you will be for the rest of your life. But inside of you, the time when you were men among men will never go away. That's all I was trying to tell you.

"You had asked me a question. Why it all meant so much to your dad. I was trying to explain. It's no big secret. I think it was probably the same for all of us. We would be fools to think that anything that ever came along later in our lives could affect us like the war did. The best experience of our lives? 'Best' is a funny word. But there is nothing we could ever do that could ever measure up to what we found in each other's company when our country sent us off to do what we did."

One day when I was with Tibbets I saw the most unexpected, most moving thing:

A yearbook.

It looked like a high school yearbook, the kind that come out each spring. More specifically, it looked like a high school yearbook from the middle

of the twentieth century—blue cover made out of
that hard-yet-slightly-soft material all school annu-
als seemed to use back then, gold lettering meant
to set off a vibrant contrast, pages and pages of
group pictures inside, the feel of young people
doing something together that is short in duration
but will create memories to last forever. . . .

Yet this wasn't a yearbook from a high school,
and the young people whose photos were inside
were not living an Archie-comic-books existence.

It was the yearbook of the 509th Composite
Group—a school annual for young men who were
not in school, a volume of personal memories that
also were history that changed the world.

It's easy to forget that a lot of these soldiers were
little more than kids. Of course it would make sense
that they had a yearbook—if the planet had not been
at war they might have been the recipients of yearbooks from their high schools, or colleges. Instead
there was this.

Pictures with captions identifying the "service
club dance." The "base bowling alley." The "base
swimming pool."

Pictures taken in Wendover. Pictures taken on
Tinian Island.

Photos of the 509th's musical combo—one
young soldier/musician identified only as Shad, one
identified as Flip, one identified as Bill.

Lots of shy, youthful expressions throughout:
guys smiling stiffly for the yearbook photographer.

There were only a few hints that this was a year-book unlike the ones most Americans grew up with.

The photo of a group of young men gathered around a radio, for example—obviously, from the looks on their faces, listening for news of something of great moment.

And before-and-after photos of a city: Hiroshima.

Headlines in the back of the yearbook—newspaper headlines describing the result of the mission that the 509th had worked toward.

There was a letter in the book—a letter of the kind that high school principals write in yearbooks, summing up the school year just past.

There was no principal for the 509th.

The yearbook letter was written by Paul Tibbets.

It was as direct as the man himself.

"On August 6th we dropped our first atomic bomb. Three days later we dropped our second.

"Two days later Japan asked for peace, and three days later she got it.

"That is the significance of the 509th Composite Group."

I don't think I ever saw my father in uniform, except in pictures.

Perhaps, when he was just returned from the war, he would wear his uniform out to dinner, out on the town; perhaps not. But by the time I was old enough that any of my memories stay with me, there was no uniform. Not on him—and, as best as I can recall, not in the house.

I asked Tibbets what the routine was on this. Didn't men, in the years immediately after 1945, wear their uniforms on the streets and in the restaurants of their hometowns? It would be difficult to imagine that they didn't—the country was in love with the soldiers who had won the victory, the soldiers who were rejoining civilian life had to have been a little heady about all the adulation . . . it would only make sense for them to wear their uniforms, even after leaving the service.

"There was some of that," Tibbets said. "It still went on—guys would have left the service, but when they went out with their wives or their girlfriends, they would put on the uniform. It didn't last all that long."

"What happened?" I asked.

"Oh, I suppose they wanted to live with their glory for a while, before they put it away," he said. "Hard to blame them. As fast as I could, I got my uniform off—but it was a matter of personal choice. I can understand that when we came home, a lot of men liked what it felt like to walk the streets of America in their uniforms."

"Did the women have a lot to do with it?" I asked.

Tibbets laughed. "What do you think?" he said.

"Well, I would imagine that a lot of women liked the idea of being out with men in uniform," I said. "They always have—and you had just won the war."

"Yes, of course," he said. "Don't forget—during the war it was very common to see men in uniform on the streets. You saw it everywhere. So when the war ended, it wasn't like men in uniform taking women out to dinner was something new. It had been going on for a long time.

"It was just the fact that now the war was over, and the uniforms meant something different."

"So tell me what the women had to do with it," I said.

"There are women who marry men to present a certain image of themselves in the eyes of society," he said. "At that time, being out with a man in uniform presented a very favorable image for the women who were with the men. Yes, the women liked the uniforms.

"But for some of the men—and I was one of them—it was a feeling that you wanted to relax now that the war was over. You didn't want to have to have that uniform looking spotless every time you got dressed. But sometimes the women got their way—and anyway, the uniforms were the cause of a lot of trouble between men and women."

"What do you mean?" I said.

"There were a lot of women who fell in love with men in uniform, and married men in uniform," he said. "They never knew their men any other way—the men were soldiers when they met, soldiers when they became engaged, soldiers when they got married.

"And then the men came home from the war, and eventually the men started dressing in regular street clothes. The uniform was put away. There was no longer a need for it.

"And in the minds of some of the women—some of the wives—their men became different people."

"Just because they weren't in uniform," I said.

"Yes," Tibbets said. "Because they weren't in uniform. The wife would look at the husband, or the girlfriend would look at the boyfriend, and without the uniform something was missing. In the woman's mind, the man had become something other than what she was used to."

"Not very fair, right?" I said.

"Well . . . maybe not fair," Tibbets said. "But also not entirely inaccurate. In reality, a lot of guys *were* different once they left the service. It wasn't the clothing itself, of course—but a lot of men were one way in the service, and a different way once the war was over. Whatever it was that they were in the Army—whatever they were inside the uniform—out of uniform, it was gone. Happened a lot."

My father, in his last years, walked very slowly. I never said anything to him about it.

But in restaurants—when he would be arriving for a family dinner, when he would be leaving after dessert—his pace was so slow that there were times when it felt as if he was hardly moving at all.

It's not that people stared—there are a lot of older people who go out, and they don't move quickly, and it's part of the landscape—but for my dad it was new, and I didn't know how aware of it he was. Whether he knew just how deliberately he was walking.

I had seen Tibbets the same way.

There wasn't any question about it: He sometimes moved slowly. Not as laboriously as my father had, but in the same category.

I asked him: Were men aware of this when it happened to them? Did they know they were walking so slowly, or did it just seem to them that the rest of the world was too fast?

He smiled.

"Oh, believe me," he said. "We know."

I asked him if he could guess what was going on inside of my dad's head on those occasions when he was leaving public places and taking so much time to get to the door.

"He's hoping he can keep you fooled," Tibbets said. "He's thinking that he doesn't want anyone feeling sorry for him, and hoping that you don't see just how bad he's feeling. I can tell you that this is the way he was thinking—because I've gone through it myself."

Tibbets said that he had been ill recently: "I was shuffling. Did I feel bad that people noticed? Yeah. But what am I going to do about it?

"I was tired, I was making myself move my feet

one after another, and that was hard—just doing that was hard. I was walking like an old man and I knew it.

"I felt like, in sports, like a boxer—when someone hits you and you're unsteady on your feet. I felt like I didn't dare even sneeze or I would lose my balance.

"You get older and your muscles aren't as springy. They're not as capable of carrying the load. So you just tell yourself that there's no hurry. It depends where you are, of course. Everyone wants to be twenty-one, and you don't want to make it so obvious how slow you have become."

I told him some more about walking out of a certain restaurant with my father—about how I had slowed down to walk with him, and he had told me to go on ahead: He didn't want me helping him, and he didn't want me seeing just how difficult this had become for him.

And I hadn't known—not then—that he was aware of it. Or at least to what extent.

"He wasn't walking slow just to walk slow," Tibbets said. "He didn't want to fall on his face.

"That's what is going on in your head—I can tell you that because I know. You watch your footsteps, and you go slow for a reason. You don't want to fall down. If you fall, you know that you will not be able to catch yourself. That's why you walk so slowly. It's not that you can't go any faster—you could if you wanted to. But you're afraid you might fall down and embarrass everyone."

"He never said anything like that," I said.

"Of course you don't say what's in your head," Tibbets said. "Say how afraid you are of falling? Of course you never talk about it."

The science-fiction movies of the 1950s—the films that made their money by scaring the children of the men and women of the World War II generation, children who were delighted to be scared—usually centered on a generic plot device: Monster attacks Earth. Heroes emerge to save the world.

A case can be made that, in a very real sense, the Allied soldiers of World War II really did save the world. But did they see it that way as they were in the midst of doing it—did they see themselves in grand, heroic terms? Or did they, at the time, see their service just as something difficult that their country had asked them to carry out?

"Those sons of bitches—the German leaders, the Japanese leaders—upset my whole life," Tibbets said. "They infuriated me. That's how I thought about it—that they disrupted my damn life.

"That's what it came down to. Not politics—the politics of Germany and Japan had nothing to do with me directly. What did affect me directly was that I was trying to live my life, and because of what their leaders decided, my life changed forever.

"And I was just one of millions and millions of young American men who that was done to. It happened to millions of young American women, too—the lives they had thought they were going to lead became something different, because the men were sent to fight the war. So young wives and mothers and girlfriends said goodbye to their men, and the women went to work in factories for the war effort.

"Our lives were not supposed to be that way. Our lives became what they became because of what the Germans and the Japanese decided to do. We who fought the war were not trying to 'defeat the enemy's way of life.' It wasn't anything like that. We were trying to kill the sons of bitches. That's the level where we were—we were put into a position of basing our every waking moment on trying to kill the other guy.

"We did it for each other. We did it because if we didn't, we knew the other side would be just as serious about killing us. So, no, we weren't trying to save the world. We were trying to kill people, because that is the position we were put into. It doesn't sound very nice, but it's true, and it's not a decision that any of us made. It was made for us."

It seemed that, in so many ways, their boyhoods were stolen from them. They never had a chance to be very young. Was that how Tibbets saw it? Was something irreplaceable—their youth—taken from them? Or was it a question of something better—solid adulthood—being given to them under the hardest possible circumstances?

"My father put me in military school when I was thirteen years old," Tibbets said. "So in a way, I think my boyhood was taken from me then. I was in military school for five years. When I got out my boyhood was over.

"Was military school good for me? Probably. Would I do it again, if the decision were mine to make? I would not do it again.

"But I look back on my young life, and on going into the war, and I think that I am glad that I did grow up quickly. There's something to be said for growing up in a hurry. So many temptations are out there in the world to get you in trouble. I became cautious very young. And I'm glad I've been cautious."

"So you don't think that any part of your life has been stolen from you?" I said.

"If it has, it probably doesn't matter," he said.

One day he had left his car in the parking lot of the Park Towers, the apartment building where his friend Gerry Newhouse had his office.

We'd had lunch. Tibbets was going to go home.

It was an extremely cold and windy afternoon, with ice on the ground; people were bent over against the gusts, trying to keep their balance.

A woman was getting out of her car in the little driveway in front of the main entrance to the building. She must have been twenty years younger than Tibbets, but she was having trouble in the weather, so he stood by her car as she stepped out and he helped her to the front door.

Then he walked off toward his own car.

I was in the lobby talking to Jesse Harrell—the doorman who had been there all those years, the young man I had first met when I was just a teenager and he was not all that much older. Now, at sixty, he as usual was at his post.

Security cameras had been installed in the building and in the parking lots in the years since I was a boy; Jesse had a television monitor in front of him, and a console to control the camera selections and angles.

After Tibbets had walked off, I asked Jesse, "Where's his car?"

"It's in the side lot," Jesse said.

"The outdoor lot?" I said.

"Yes," Jesse said.

The lot was west of the building—a hundred feet or more from the door, down a sloping sidewalk.

"Is he OK getting there?" I said. "In this weather?"

"He hates people trying to help him," Jesse said. "He likes to take care of himself."

"But you see how windy it is," I said.

"He would hate it if either of us came after him

to help him out," Jesse said. "It would make him angry."

Jesse hit a button on his security console. We could see a grainy black-and-white picture of the parking lot.

An elderly man was leaning forward against the wind.

"There he is," Jesse said.

"That's him?" I said.

Jesse hit another button and the camera showed a closer shot. It was Tibbets, all right. He had his hands on top of the roof of a car, steadying himself.

"Is that his car?" I said.

"No," Jesse said. "It's the next one. He'll be there in a second."

Tibbets was the only person in the parking lot. The man who brought World War II to an end.

"There he goes," Jesse said.

The figure on the screen opened the door to a car, and got inside. We watched on the screen as the car pulled away.

"He's fine," Jesse said, and then we lost sight of the automobile.

TWENTY-ONE

Tibbets wasn't the only one who seemed almost constitutionally incapable of accepting help from anyone.

When it became apparent that my father's dying was not going to be quick—that it was going to transpire painfully over a period of months, if not longer—we hired someone to assist my mom with the things she simply could not do.

Lifting my father from the bed, getting him into the shower (before even that became impossible), helping him across the room into a chair during the weeks when he was still able to sit . . . my mother did not have the strength.

So Andre Frazier entered my father's life.

My father hated the idea of anyone having to carry him, to bathe him, to shave him. Andre—physically strong, full of vitality, an African-American man who had grown up in Columbus—was a daily reminder to my father of everything that he had lost. Here would arrive this stranger to assist my father with the tasks he had never had to think twice about. It made him despondent. It made him fully understand that things would never be the same.

And Andre overcame that. He made his relationship with my father work.

Because in the months when my father could do virtually nothing for himself, Andre made sure that he still knew he was a man. "Good morning, Mr. Greene," he would say in a bright, upbeat voice every day as he arrived. And then—small gesture— he would extend his hand for my father to shake.

I'm not sure if Andre had any idea what an enormous effect that daily handshake had on my father's self-regard. My dad was in bed, he could hardly move, yet Andre would approach him—in the minutes before he would begin assisting my dad with the most private and potentially humiliating bodily necessities—and would greet him like one businessman greeting another. "Good morning, Mr. Greene"—that sound, those words, were so reassuring. He was being treated with respect. He was being treated as a full person.

There was an almost military precision to Andre's routine. My dad liked that—he liked the cut of Andre's jib. When Andre sensed that my mother and father wanted to be alone, just the two of them together, he would quietly disappear from the bedroom and give them their time. When the moments came that he would have to lift my father to take him into the bathroom, he would approach it with great decorum and an unwavering sense of the humanity of all of this, allowing my father his dignity.

And they would talk. Andre was studying to try to get a degree that would help him do well in the world; he would explain to my father what he was aspiring to, and my father would talk to him about his own start in business, but much of the time my father would tell Andre about the Army. He would—in the last months of his life—explain to Andre about his time in the war.

Andre would ask him questions—about the people my father had known back then, about the places he had gone—and it was a gift, those questions that Andre asked him. They were two men who might have been thought to have almost nothing in common, but in Andre's curiosity about my father's life my father found a kind of confirmation that he still mattered. Someone was interested.

Who would have thought it—these two men, separated by so many years, and by two lifetimes of utterly different experiences, yet the connection that they established was one of the most precious things to help my father keep his sense of who he was. Two men, talking.

One day—this was at the very end—Andre helped my father into a wheelchair and took him from the bedroom to the front door of the house. It was the first such trip out of the bedroom my dad had taken in days. My mother, and Andre, wanted my dad to see the street on which he lived.

So they went to the front door and opened it to the winter's cold, and my dad looked out. The vistas of a man's life—after all the places he had traveled, all the roads he had walked, it had come to this: this one view.

My father's voice, telling of that long journey with the 91st Infantry up into Italy:

Finally we reached the Futa Pass, which was a pass through the mountain peaks. And then we were going to approach the north side with the road going downward.

Well, it was going downward for a while, but then it would go up some. In the meantime, more cold, more rain, more deaths and more fear. We lived with fear all the time on that terrible trip up Highway 65. . . .

One of the things about which he became confused concerned his father's death.

His father had been dead for well over thirty years, but during my father's dying there were days when he seemed to believe that it was his own father who was departing the Earth. He would talk to my mother and my sister about a memorial service for his father; he would ask, "Are the people from Cleveland here yet? Have they arrived for Dad's memorial service?"

I remember when his father really was dying. I was a boy, my sister and brother and I were growing up in Columbus, and in Akron my father's father was slowly nearing the end. My dad would drive up to Akron to sit with him, then, the next day, drive back to Columbus to be with us.

It must have been a very solitary time for him— those long hours on the road, back and forth between his two families. Once when he came back at the end of a weekend—weariness all over his face— I asked him what he and my grandfather had done.

"We listened to a baseball game," he said. "We listened to the Indians game."

"Who won?" I said, really wanting to know—I had no idea just how bad off my grandfather was, I suppose I sort of liked the picture of the two of them listening to a ballgame on the radio, so I asked him who had won.

"The Indians," he said distractedly.

Later I went to the sports page and I looked. There had been a game the day before, all right. The Indians had lost.

And I pointed it out to him. I was that young— I told my father that he had said the Indians won, when in fact the Indians had lost.

To his great credit, he did not blow up. On some level he understood that I did not know what he and his father were going through, that I could not comprehend that as the radio played neither man was hearing a word.

He didn't get angry. He merely said that he had been mistaken. No, he said, I was right—the Indians had not won.

Now—on one Saturday afternoon during his own dying—I sat with him, and there was an Ohio State football game on the television set in front of his bed. A game in the stadium in whose stands he had sat with my mother on every football Saturday for more than fifty years. His eyes barely saw the screen, and he never asked the score, and I could not tell you—then, or now—who won the game. If someone were to have asked me, I would not have known. Not on a day like this, in this room with my dad.

Once when he kept asking about the memorial service for his father—when he continually wanted to know, from my mother and my sister, the only other people in the house at that time, whether the guests from Cleveland had arrived yet for the service—they did one of the kindest things I have ever heard. They said that the service was just about ready to begin.

They got out three prayer books. One for each of them, and one for him.

And through their tears my mother and my sister held a memorial service. For his father. Afterward, he told them that it was beautiful.

On Highway 65 in Italy, his voice on the tape said, things had become momentarily, and deceptively, calm. It was an illusion.

. . . **We were merrily, if you could use the**

word, on our way to Bologna when something terrible happened.

Unbeknownst to us, the Germans had dug in on a huge mountain called Monte Adone, which straddled Highway 65. And we came up around a curve in a line of trucks when all hell broke loose and the German artillery was being poured down on us.

It was at this point when all forward movement was halted and all the line troops were dispersed laterally to the east and west astride Highway 65, and there we stayed for six months. Beyond a certain point there were no lights at all allowed, so trucks had to move in blackout because the Germans were dug in and had zeroed in every possible road crossing and could hit everything that moved.

All movement, all truck travel, all everything was done at night. In the meantime the poor dogfaces were digging in the best they could along this line with the Germans looking down their throats. . . .

Andre's presence in the house gave my father something he seemed desperately to need: an audience.

With my mother, my brother, my sister and me, the talk was often of the details of his illness, the parameters of his pain. We weren't really an audience; we were his family.

He had always enjoyed getting laughs out of strangers—it always seemed to please him more to evoke an appreciative reaction from people who did not live under his roof.

So when Andre was around, his presence provided a surprising kind of spark in my dad. Andre was someone he could play to.

One afternoon my Uncle Al—my mom's brother—was visiting. He, my mom, my sister and I were talking quietly in the living room.

My dad had allowed none of his friends to see him. He was embarrassed about how he looked, he instinctively knew that if they were to come into his room they would know that he was a dying man. He didn't want it; he gave my mother strict instructions: Keep everyone away.

I knew that his friends wanted to say goodbye. But there was no arguing.

On this day he called out from the bedroom, and in the living room I said to my mom, my sister and my uncle, "I'll go in."

He was sitting with Andre. He said, "Where's Mother?"

"She's in the living room," I said. "Al's over."

"Al's here?" my father said.

"He's with Mom," I said.

"Tell them to come in," he said.

I was shocked.

"Both of them?" I said. "Or just Mom?"

And—out of nowhere—there was this flash of the old cutting, sarcastic, I'll-tell-the-jokes-around-here him.

"What do *you* think?" he said. It was like fifteen years had just dropped away.

"I don't know," I said. And I didn't—if I were to bring Al into the room and it turned out that my father didn't want him there, it could be a very bad moment.

"You don't know," he said. "You don't know." There was no confusion here—he was sharp, he was parrying, he was in charge.

"I don't know," I said. "Do you want just Mom, or do you want Mom and Al?"

And—here was the key moment, here was the reason he was being like this—he turned to Andre. His audience.

My father motioned at me with his thumb and said to Andre, "What the hell is wrong with him?"

Andre started to laugh. "I don't know," he said to my dad.

My father looked at me and said, "It never changes, does it?" And then he looked back at Andre, motioned in my direction again, and said to Andre: "It never changes. My son, the village idiot."

Andre laughed out loud, and my father started to laugh, too, and I was so grateful for that moment. "Yes, *Bob*," my father said, emphasizing the word to make sure Andre understood that the village idiot had a name, "I'd like to see Al, too."

And he meant it. I went to get them—my mother and my sister were startled, they could hardly believe that he was willing to see someone—and Al, who had known my father since the 1930s, when Al's big sister, my mom, first started dating this guy from Akron, came into the bedroom.

He tried to put up a cheery front, but this was too much, seeing my dad this far gone, and he began to cry and said to my father, "You've had a hell of a run." And my father, from his bed, said, "I really have, haven't I?"

Tibbets may have had that high-school-year-book-that-wasn't: the 509th's words-and-photo history. My dad, it turned out, had a book like that, too.

It was a scrapbook, of a kind that by all appearances had been manufactured in large numbers for sale to soldiers and their families. What set it apart from other dime-store scrapbooks was the embossed title on its cover:

HIS SERVICE RECORD

That such books existed makes sense; the sixteen million Americans who served in the armed forces during World War II could have been expected to keep some written and photographic memories of their time in uniform, so there was a ready market

for scrapbooks like this. The pages gave helpful
tips—on this page, fill in the details of basic training; on this page, fill in the names and places that
were a part of going overseas. . . .

The first thing in the scrapbook was the Pledge
of Allegiance— pre-printed by the manufacturer. "I
pledge allegiance to the flag of the United States of
America. . . ."

My dad's scrapbook was completely filled out—
in my mother's handwriting. She had done this for
him—for them. Every step of his time in the military she vigilantly had kept track of; he was fighting the war, she was making sure his scrapbook was
up to date.

Little things: Near the front of the book was a
page on which the birthdates of the father and
mother of the soldier were to be filled in. This book
said—in my mother's blue fountain pen—that my
father's father was born on October 18, 1878; my father's mother was born on April 5, 1888. The sight
of those years on a page: 1878, 1888 . . . it had the
look and feel of once upon a time.

So painstakingly, my mother recorded it all. Training? "Infantry, Camp Shelby, Mississippi, January 28,
1941. Three months Louisiana maneuvers, 1941."

She was writing down what the man she was in
love with was doing. "Left country April 1, 2, 1944.
Arrived April 20, North Africa, near Oran, Algiers.
June 21, approximately, moved to Italy. July 21 in
Naples. May, June, 1945—occupied Trieste."

The idea of it—of "moving to Italy," as if this was a business transfer; of occupying Trieste—of this young man coming from Akron, Ohio, to occupy a city in Europe . . .

And there was this, in her careful penmanship: "June 24, 1945. Bronze Star at Cormons, Italy."

Hers were not the only words in the scrapbook. There was, pasted onto a page, a copy of a letter that apparently had been handed out to the fighting men in Europe on one of the proudest days of their lives, and in the life of their country:

> From the headquarters of the Fifteenth
> Army Group to the soldiers of the Fifteenth
> Army Group:
> With a full and grateful heart I hail and con-
> gratulate you in this hour of complete victory
> over the German enemy and join with you in
> thanks to Almighty God.
> Yours has been a long, hard fight, the
> longest in this war of any Allied troops fighting
> on the continent of Europe.
> (from) Mark W. Clark, General, U.S.A.,
> Commanding

I had found the scrapbook in a back closet of my parents' house. The events in the scrapbook were getting ahead of what my father's voice was telling me on the tape. Victory hadn't come yet, in the words he was saying; he and his fellow infantrymen were still slogging their way up Highway 65:

. . . In basic training we really had gone out of our way to make ourselves miserable—that's what we were training for. But in actual combat we did every possible thing to try to make ourselves comfortable, because there was no other way to live unless you did it that way.

So there were a lot of well dug-in dugouts, which were protected by sandbags and every other possible thing that would deflect incoming ammunition. And as the days and weeks and months dragged on, we actually did get a little more comfortable, which is not very good in combat. It is one of the things that cuts down on the momentum of an infantry division. You get too comfortable and you don't move forward.

Well, that's what happened. Every division that was on the front lines in the Fifth Army was sitting ducks for air raids, all kinds of artillery fire, for weeks on end. . . .

The phrase "television war" was often used to describe Vietnam, but that was before cable, before all-news channels had the airtime available to show endless unedited hours of war coverage, live. And at the beginning of the 1990s, when the Gulf War—"Operation Desert Storm"—was telecast live on CNN, my father seemed more interested in that than in any television show any of the networks had broadcast in years.

I think it was Norman Schwarzkopf—at least that was part of it. Here, again and at last, was a general who got to be admired for being a general. The last time the nation had—with no sarcasm, with no irony—paid respectful attention to a general was . . .

When? William Westmoreland? Not really—he had been at the center of so much controversy that the chaos around him overrode everything else. Probably there hadn't been a time since Eisenhower's day when a general of the armed forces, and the country he represented, looked each other directly in the eye and admitted how much they were counting on each other.

So my father watched General Schwarzkopf with considerable approval—this was a man he could understand, this was a man, or so I sensed, that my father felt would understand *him* if they were ever to meet.

But the telecast of the Gulf War had confused him in ways he could not quite elucidate. There was no sprawl, no distance—you could see everything all at once, it was packaged with great expertise for the home viewer. It was warfare neatly delivered into your house, with no feeling of anyone being lost or stranded or confused or scared or alone. General Schwarzkopf seemed at times more like a genial master of ceremonies, your friendly host, here in your living room right on schedule to guide you through the evening's proceedings.

My dad had watched every night and when the war ended he found something to watch on another channel.

His voice, telling what happened to the infantry on Highway 65:

. . . The problem was, in back of us there was a battery of 90-millimeter anti-aircraft guns, which fired constantly and were being used as artillery against the Germans.

This meant that while it was fairly peaceful during the day, you couldn't sleep at night because of this constant din of those 90-millimeter shells streaking overhead.

The Germans didn't seem to react to this until one terrible morning when they made a direct hit on us, killing several people and wounding some of my best men. And there but for the grace of God . . . I was not wounded that day, which was a lucky day for me, believe me, one of many, many that I had during my Army career. . . .

Many times toward the end, when my father was sleeping, or my mother wanted to be in the bedroom alone with him, Andre would pick up a book he found around the house to pass the time until he was needed.

I had written a couple of books based upon time I spent with Michael Jordan, and my parents had those books in their home, and often Andre would read a chapter or two from them while he waited for my father to wake up. When I would come to town he would ask me questions about the books: what Jordan was like, what Scottie Pippen was like, what it was like to be in all of those NBA arenas.

The context of this was so discordant. Here Andre was—doing work that was, to me, more vital and moving than anything I could imagine, helping my father die with decency, with a sense of still being a man, and he would ask me about Jordan's and Pippen's and Dennis Rodman's food preferences and training routines, as if even those famous athletes' most mundane activities were worthy of notice and praise, endlessly compelling.

I understood, of course—a lot of people found those things compelling, and I was happy to talk with Andre about them, but every time I did so I asked myself whether he fully understood just what a magnificent thing he was doing—whether he knew what an unforgettable gift he was giving to our family, to take such tender care, to pay such close attention, to our father. "He has five or six of them, if I'm remembering right," I said, answering a question about Jordan's cars, thinking the whole while: Thank you so much for being here with my parents every day.

On the day of my father's funeral Andre came to the services, and then came back to the house to help out when the people arrived to pay their final condolences. He waited until the last visitors had left, helped straighten up, and then told my mother that unless she needed anything else he guessed he would be going home.

This would be it—his time in our house was over. Had my father hung on for a little longer, Andre would have had this job a little longer; my dad was dead and so this particular employment was ended. Soon enough, if someone called, he would be in the home of another man or woman nearing the end of life. This is how he made his living: helping families help their loved ones die gently.

I walked him to his car. It was a cold December afternoon; it was just the two of us out there, and he said to me, "You know, I could tell that your dad was tough on you sometimes, but he really loved you."

It was not what I had expected to hear.

"He was very proud of you," Andre said. "He would tell me that, when you weren't there. When you were around, he was always making fun of you—I think he was trying to get a laugh out of me. But he told me how proud he was of you when you weren't there to hear."

I just nodded my head in thanks. Andre opened the door of his car, and I said:

"I have to tell you something."

He stopped.

"You know that I've written some books about people who are the best in the world at their jobs," I said.

"Mr. Jordan," Andre said.

"Right," I said. "But I want you to know something. I have never in my life met anyone who is better at what they do than you are."

We stood there together for a few moments and then Andre said, "I'd like to ask you one favor."

"What is it?" I said.

"If you ever write anything about your father's life, and about his death, I'd appreciate it if you would put something in there," he said.

"What would you like me to say?" I said.

"I'd like you to put that your father and I became very good friends," he said.

Back at the house, I could see that my mother was standing in the front doorway, looking to see where I'd gone. Andre and I stood there together for a little bit longer and then I watched his car head down the block and around the corner and disappear from view.

TWENTY-TWO

Sometimes when I was a kid, I'd make those model airplanes," I said to Tibbets. "The ones that were made out of plastic, and you'd glue them together."

"I know what kind you're talking about," he said.

"You'd have to dip the decals into warm water," I said. "And the water would soak the paper the decals were attached to, and when the paper got wet enough you'd slip the decals off, and put them on the airplane."

"I never put one of those things together," he said. "I'd see them in stores, but I never worked on one."

"That's what I was going to ask you about," I said. "The way I remember it, those model airplanes weren't all American planes. Some of them were German Messerschmitts. Some of them were Japanese Zeros. And we—all of us kids, all of the sons of the men who came home from World War II—were putting them together like toys. We were having fun doing it. And this was less than ten years after the war was over."

"So what's your question?" Tibbets said.

"Well, I remember my dad coming into my room a few times when I was putting the planes together," I said. "And I'd be working on this Nazi plane, or this Japanese plane, and he'd stand there and look at what I was doing, but he wouldn't say anything. I don't know what was going on in his mind while I put together the planes that all of you had just risked your lives against."

"He was probably just glad that you were having a good time," Tibbets said.

"But what must he have thought when he saw the planes?" I said.

"If he saw a Nazi plane or a Japanese plane, most likely he was thinking that plane was no toy," Tibbets said. "That was a real thing, in his experience. That was an enemy. If you ever saw one with your own eyes, you never for the rest of your life forgot that that thing was up there to hurt you."

The more questions, in the months after my father's death, that Tibbets answered for me, the more questions I seemed to come up with. About what those men had been through, and what they came home to, and what they thought when they saw things that their sons and daughters grew up taking for granted.

The Army fatigues that young people used to wear in the Sixties and Seventies, for example—the surplus military uniforms that became fashionable for young male and female civilians to walk around in on the streets of the United States. The fatigues certainly hadn't been worn in an attempt to honor the military—the intent, it had often seemed, was the opposite.

My father, when he would see young people walking down the sidewalks in the faded, torn fatigues, would usually stare for a second, then turn his gaze somewhere else. Clearly the sight bothered him. I asked Tibbets if he knew what I was referring to.

"Of course," he said. "Sure, it bothers you. You see some kid in Army fatigues and combat boots, slouching around, and you know for damn sure that he's never seen a shot fired, that he has never bled for his country, never had sore feet from marching. And you look at him and you can tell that he's making a joke out of the idea of wearing military clothing.

"I suppose the people who did it wanted to attract attention," he said. "They wore the combat clothes so that it would have just the effect that it did—to make people look at them."

"My dad never said anything when he saw people in the fatigues," I said.

"Of course not," Tibbets said. "I never did either. I'd take two looks at them, and then look away. What they were doing was a disgrace to the uniform, yes—but what were we supposed to do? Make a scene?

"You couldn't fight it, so you just kept your mouth shut. Thinking back on it, do you think it would have done your dad any good to create a scene? The best thing to do was just keep walking."

"He did," I said. "But I remember the expression on his face so well. Like he'd bitten down on something that had a terrible taste. This complete disdain. Like, 'Is this what we fought the war for?' "

"I do that same thing," Tibbets said. "I know I probably shouldn't, and I know that we've talked about this before—but so often you see the way that people choose to conduct themselves, their total lack of manners and courtesy toward others, and you do find yourself thinking: 'Why did I do all that I did, and risk all that I risked?'

"We came home from the war, and somehow the way that our parents brought us up—where your parents' word was a command—all changed. And we must have been the ones to make things change—we must have decided to raise our families differently than our parents raised us.

"Like I say, you just see it, and you walk on. It's a fight you can never win. Not anymore."

Listening to Tibbets say something like that—remembering my father's growing disenchantment for some of the everyday aspects of the America he saw around him—I kept coming back to *The Best Years of Our Lives*, and to that movie's message that the greatest years for the men and women of World War II were supposed to be the years right after their homecoming, as they rejoined the way of life for which they had fought all those battles, and spent all those months and years away.

The movie notwithstanding, there were many times when I asked myself again the question that had been so much on my mind lately: whether the real best years of my dad's life were the war years themselves. I couldn't shake it.

"Could be," Tibbets said. "He was very satisfied with what he was doing. He told himself that he was in the war for his family and for his country, and he was surrounded by men who were telling themselves the same thing. It wasn't comfortable and it wasn't fun, but there was never a day when you thought that what you were doing didn't matter."

"Was that how it was for you?" I said.

"This was so *different* for me," Tibbets said. "From what my life would have been like otherwise. Being in the service—being in the war—gave me some experiences to build on that I couldn't have gotten any other way."

"I keep coming back to that, too," I said. "The idea of all you boys who grew up during the Depression, and you thought you had no prospects of going anywhere. And then you ended up going places that you had only read about, or seen on a map of the world. Do you think you ever in your life would have seen those places, if there hadn't been a war?"

"Unlikely," he said. "The places that I ended up

going . . . they were, literally, a world away. Africa? It was just a word that people talked about, a shape on someone's globe. What were the people like there? What went on there? What was the climate like? It never even occurred to me. And then I was there.

"Germany and France would probably have always remained for me what they were when I was a boy—places that were portrayed certain ways in the movies, places I would never have a perception or knowledge of myself. Certainly places I would never be."

"And then there was Japan," I said.

"I can't remember even thinking about Japan when I was a boy," Tibbets said. "Japan? What ever would I possibly go there for?"

Whenever I came to see Tibbets and our meeting place was the Park Towers, I couldn't help but notice something as I said hello to Jesse Harrell, manning the front door:

Jesse kept a baseball bat next to his chair.

It was for protection, I assumed; it was for him to put up a defense if some criminal came bursting into the lobby. Older man, baseball bat that is not meant for baseball—I had seen it somewhere else:

At my father's house.

He had kept a baseball bat in the bedroom. After my sister and my brother and I had moved out of the house—after it was just my mom and my dad, alone—he had begun to keep that ball bat in the room. For the same reason Jesse did: to give himself at least the illusion of being ready for anything. My father didn't like guns, but he lived in a world where many people did. His answer was the baseball bat.

It was such a melancholy sight that I never brought it up. But after I had noticed Jesse's ball bat once again, I pointed it out to Tibbets. I asked him—one more older man in central Ohio—if he kept a baseball bat in his house, too.

"I don't have a baseball bat," he said. "I have a 12-gauge shotgun."

"So you can . . ." I began.

"I have a 12-gauge shotgun," he said again.

It shouldn't have surprised me. He once armed himself with the atomic bomb; it shouldn't have come as startling information that now he kept a gun in his home.

"My father raised me around guns," he said. "One night—our family was living in Des Moines at the time—my dad heard someone fiddling around with our front door. My dad came to the stairs with a .45 in his hand."

"You were there?" I said.

"Yes," Tibbets said. "I was five or six years old. My dad stood on the stairs and the person kept fiddling outside our front door, and my dad took aim and put seven bullets through the front door."

"Come on," I said.

"Yes, he did," Tibbets said. "He had me sit still and he shot the front door seven times."

"What happened?" I asked.

"The person must have gotten away, but he got hit," Tibbets said. "There was blood on the bricks outside our door."

"But what if it was someone you knew?" I said.

"It wasn't," Tibbets said. "This was at midnight, one A.M. No one we knew—or at least no one we wanted to know—would have been fiddling with our front door at that time of the night."

"What did you think, that young, looking at the blood from where your father had shot the person through the door?" I said.

"I felt glad that my dad had the gun," he said. "There was nothing but wood and glass between whoever was trying to get in, and our family."

"So that's why you have a gun in your house?" I said.

"I had a nephew living with us once," he said. "I told him, make noise when you come in the house at night. Make noise to let me know it's you. Because if I hear someone coming in the house late at night, I'll shoot."

"No baseball bat at all in your house," I said.

"I couldn't swing a baseball bat," Tibbets said. "Not in my house, not so that it would do any good. There's not enough room downstairs in my house.

Not enough room to swing it. It would be the same as having nothing."

Just when I thought that he had told me every-thing there was to tell—just when I thought there was no more for me to learn about him—it happened.

I had been thinking about my dad's last months—about how unbearable some of those days had been, about how he had been alive but less than alive, in a living state that seemed worse than death. I knew that, given the choice, he would rather have been gone. But he didn't have that choice; his body would not give out, not completely.

I told Tibbets a little about that, and I said to him: "How long do you want to live? If it comes to something like that, how long do you want to be here?"

"As soon as I lose the mobility that I've got, as soon as I lose the energy that I have left now—or as soon as my mind goes—then I'm going," he said.

"But what if you don't?" I said. "What if you don't want to be here, but you are?" I said.

"I just told you," he said. "I'm going."

He stopped for a moment, as if deciding whether to tell me something. And then he did.

"My old man had cancer of the throat," he said. "I saw him after he was declared 'cured.' He would start to cough, and he would be choking on whatever was in there, and he would have to stick his finger into his throat.

"And he would pull out this long string of stuff, and that was the only way he could stop coughing.

"He told me, 'I will not go through the radiation again. If they say that I need it, I will not do it.' I asked him what he meant, and he said, 'I will commit suicide before I go through that again.'"

"Did you believe him?" I said.

Tibbets stared at me. "Of course," he said. "And he did it."

"Did what?" I said.

"He killed himself," Tibbets said. "He shot himself right through the center of his heart."

I had this momentary half-feeling that Tibbets was pulling some bizarre joke on me, saying something just to shock me. But it was no joke.

"I was in business at the time," he said. "I was over in Switzerland. I got a telephone call at one or two in the morning—it was my brother-in-law. He said that my old man had just shot himself."

"What did you do?" I said.

"I got ready to come back to the United States," he said.

"Were you beside yourself with grief that he had done it?" I said.

"No," Tibbets said. "I didn't feel sorry for him at all. That's what he wanted, and that's what he did. What I was trying to tell you was that I hope I would do the same thing."

"Kill yourself," I said.

"I hope I would have the courage," he said. "I wouldn't want any of my kids to go through seeing me the way I saw my dad. I wouldn't want any of them to go through seeing me the way you say you saw your dad.

"I wouldn't want to be a burden on anybody, and I don't intend to."

"And what do you think your family would think after you did it?" I said.

"I want to be cremated as fast as the law allows it," he said. "No services. No announcement."

"What do you mean, no announcement?" I said.

"I don't want anyone telling people that I'm dead," he said. "I don't want my friends fretting over me. Memorial services are to pacify the survivors. I don't need to pacify anyone. They can think nice things about me if they want. They don't need a guy in a cloak standing there."

"You've got to have a funeral service," I said.

"No, I don't," he said. "I've listened to too many of them. They're upsetting to me. That weeping wailing attitude."

"People cry at funerals for a reason," I said. "They cry because they're going to miss the person who has died."

"Not for me," he said. "I won't have one."

"Well, you know there's going to be an announcement," I said. "You're not a person who's going to die without anyone noticing it."

"I've had enough notice during my lifetime as it is," he said. "I've had enough hoorah, and enough of the opposite."

"So what do you want to happen?" I said.

"Cremate me and take my ashes out over the North Atlantic before anyone finds out that I'm gone," Tibbets said. "Dump the ashes into the ocean."

"Why the North Atlantic?" I said.

"Because that's where I've had some of the most peaceful moments of my life," he said. "Flying in a plane alone, over the North Atlantic. That's where I want to finish up. With no one knowing."

If what he had told me stopped me cold, what happened next was just as unanticipated, but in a different way.

It had started simply enough. I had asked him how many members of the crew of the *Enola Gay* were still alive, and if he still kept in touch with them.

"We're almost all gone," he said. "I've gone to reunions of our crew over the years, seen certain people, and at the next one they're dead."

His two closest colleagues on the flight—navigator Theodore "Dutch" Van Kirk and bombardier Tom Ferebee—were still living and in good health, he said; the only other survivor from the flight, radio operator Dick Nelson, was in such poor medical shape that the others virtually never saw him.

"It was a close group," he said. "It really was. The ones of us who are left don't talk about who's going to be the last, and we don't talk about the others who have gone."

Trying to change the subject to something lighter—and not realizing at the time where this would lead—I made a little meaningless conversation, and then, in an attempt to steer his mind elsewhere, asked him what made him laugh.

"All kinds of things strike my funny bone," he said. "I like Bob Hope's humor. But what's funny now is not funny to me. It's the separation of generations. I don't understand why people think some things are funny."

"Were you ever a fan of *Saturday Night Live?*" I asked.

"No," he said.

"Leno?" I said.

"No," he said. "Don't get me wrong—I don't think I'm necessarily a complete sourpuss. But there's all this *innuendo*. I hate that. *Alluding* to something. That kind of thing doesn't appeal to me at all. Don't allude. I like a straight pitch."

"Give me an example," I said.

"Well," Tibbets said, with genuine delight in his voice and on his face, "last year Dutch and Tom and I went to Branson, Missouri. . . ."

"Dutch Van Kirk and Tom Ferebee?" I said, trying to imagine the three of them on the town.

"Yes," Tibbets said. "And we went to see the Andy Williams show—he has his own theater there—and he had this acrobat act as part of his show. They were acrobats, and they were comedians too. They had me laughing out loud."

It occurred to me, as he told me about the acrobats, that the humor was probably mostly visual. With his hearing as close to gone as it was, Tibbets didn't have to strain to understand the acrobats—he could see the humor.

I still didn't know what was coming. I told him that when my father used to go out to have a good time—whether just for the evening with my mother, or on a vacation with my sister, my brother and me—he had done it with the same military-style planning that had defined his life. If we were supposed to leave the house at 7:30, that didn't mean 7:25 and it didn't mean 7:35. If he had planned to have us home by 11, then no matter how good a time we were having, 11 it was going to be. It was just a part of who he was.

"I sometimes think about whether that's such a good idea," I said to Tibbets. "If all that planning—even making a timetable for having fun—takes away the happiness. If you're so devoted to your timetable that the timetable replaces the fun."

"It does not," Tibbets said.

"How can you be certain?" I said.

"Your father was organized," he said. "So am I. That doesn't mean that you miss anything."

"It just seems that it might rob you of the joy," I said.

"You don't rob yourself of anything by making a plan," he said. "You don't rob yourself of any joy."

And then he said it:

"Dutch and Tom and I are going back to Branson over Memorial Day. You're welcome to come with us."

I looked at him. He was looking straight back.

"I could come?" I said. "With you and your crew?"

"Those acrobats are the funniest thing you've ever seen," he said.

"Are you sure you'd want me?" I said. "It sounds like it's supposed to be your reunion."

"We've known each other since before you were born," he said. "We've said just about everything to each other that there is to say. If you'd like to come, I'd like you to meet them."

TWENTY-THREE

My father's best friends—the men with whom he had been closest for all of his adult life, friends he had made as a young man, men who, with their wives, had remained the people he and my mother saw constantly during the half-century after the war—sensed increasingly, in his final months, how badly he was doing, and wanted very much to visit him.

He continued to resist it. My mother would tell him that they had called; he would say "maybe in a few days," but it was clear to us that he had made the decision: He did not want their final memories of him to be of a weakened, disoriented man. If they were to come into his bedroom—or so he seemed to fear—then forever their impression of him would be the impression of how he looked and sounded as death approached.

But forever would not be all that long, at least for them; they were old men too, they would almost certainly be in a bed like this one before very much more time had passed. A former FBI agent, a leading merchant of the town—these were men who were exactly his age, and I found myself wishing that he felt differently about this, because not only would it be good for him to look them in the eyes one last time, but it would be good for them to be able to look back and say goodbye. He didn't want it.

When he and my mother were a young married couple, they had a name they called their group of friends: the Saturday Night Crowd. Each weekend one couple would serve as host and hostess, and everyone would gather for cocktails and a light dinner and conversation. The Saturday Night Crowd— men and women celebrating Saturday nights, celebrating friendships and a seemingly cloudless peacetime future in the years after the war.

On Saturday nights now, the only crowd with my father was us: my mother, my sister, my brother or me when we could get to town. My father's parents were long dead, as was his only brother; he had never had a sister. So we were it, on Saturday nights that had become no more special than any other night of the week. If he knew it was Saturday, it made no difference to him. The scenery was the same as it was every day and every night—his bedroom and the trees outside his windows—and the crowd was small.

I found myself hoping against hope that he would relent and let his friends in. On Saturday night, or Tuesday afternoon, or Sunday morning— any time. But they would bring cookies, or books for him to read (they didn't know that he wasn't reading), and he would ask my mother not to allow them to come past the front hallway.

In the winter of his dying I thought about another lonely winter of his, far away from here, when he had counted on the nearness of friends.

Winter came and the snow started piling up. It was at least thirty to thirty-six inches deep in some places, and nothing moved, nothing at all.

Try to imagine the troops in the front line enduring the bitter cold and all this snow, with very little relief in sight.

Finally Christmas came, and Bill Ehrman and another guy and I were in our quarters, and it became midnight, and all of a sudden, along the whole perimeter of the front, the Germans started shooting tracer bullets straight up into the sky.

If it wasn't such a horrible thing, it would have been a beautiful sight. I shall never forget this as long as I live. The curtain of bright points of light lasted about three minutes, which was just about a minute and a half before the stroke of midnight and a minute and a half afterwards. The tracers suddenly ceased and it was all quiet on the Italian front.

Several months after my father died, my mother said—almost in a panic—that his friend Bill Ehrman had been scheduled to have surgery on his back, and that she had forgotten to call and see how he was doing. It was almost as if she had neglected to take care of some vitally important, the-world-is-counting-on-this, task.

But Bill Ehrman didn't live in our town, or even in the continental United States. He lived in Hawaii. I had never met him. He was not a part of our lives; he had been a part of my father's.

So many years before, they had stood together in the first minutes of Christmas, and watched as the German tracers flared in the wartime sky of Europe. Now—with my father so recently gone, with my mother having so many new things on her mind—she could have been excused for not remembering that this man was going to have an operation. And excused for not getting in touch even if she had re-membered—he was somewhere off in the Pacific Ocean.

"Daddy would have called," she said. "He always called his friends at times like this."

And so she went to the phone. And did what he would have done.

H is voice, from a time when he was able to take care of all his responsibilities himself:

. . . **About this time the Battle of the Bulge was taking place in the Ardennes Forest in Germany, and the whole Italian front was de-moralized because rumor had it that the para-**

troopers were going to drop on us, and we weren't prepared for it.

So the whole division was alerted to repel the paratroopers that never came. All the cooks and bakers and truck drivers, armed to the teeth and put on red alert, awaiting the paratroop drop which, thank God, never came.

December ended, January arrived, February, March, and all this time we were stuck below Bologna. We knew that very shortly, things would start happening that would permit all the divisions on this Italian line to go forward, and that day came—I believe it was April nineteenth—when our division got the go-ahead to jump off and start attacking up Highway 65. . . .

One winter day, not long after his death, I had to travel through southern Illinois and beyond for my job, and a blizzard hit Chicago, closing O'Hare International Airport.

I got to Union Station as quickly as I could to try to get a seat on the only train that might get me to my destination on time. I just made it; I found myself sitting next to a woman who also was on her way southward—she was going to St. Louis.

She seemed a little distracted, a little unsure of herself; she was about my mother's age, maybe a year or two younger, and I could sense something in her demeanor: that she wasn't used to doing this.

The conductor came to collect our tickets, and when he asked her for hers she hesitated a second before reaching into her purse. She gave her ticket to him, and after we were a good way down the tracks she told me that she was on her way to grandparents' day at her daughter's children's school.

"My husband and I never missed a grandparents' day, and I decided that I'm not going to start now," she said. "But this is hard."

Her husband, she said, had died five months before. They had been married for forty-eight years. This was her first trip out of town since his death.

"We would always drive down to St. Louis," she said. "We liked the long drive, just talking on the way."

Outside our window, to the right of the train, was a highway. She asked me if it was Interstate 55. I said it was.

"I thought it was," she said. "We used to drive I-55 on the way to St. Louis—well, he did the driving—and we would look at the trains as they went by."

From the train window she looked at the cars. She didn't say anything for a few miles.

She was wearing a pair of shoes she said she had bought to make walking easier during her trip; she read a hardback novel and put it down every so often to stare back out at the highway where she had ridden with her husband not so long ago.

In her face I saw my mother's face; in her face I

saw the faces of all the women who have to learn this so late in their lives: how to be alone.

"I'm really looking forward to this trip," she said. "My daughter says it will be good for me."

The blizzard was whipping the winds around the train and blowing snow up past our window, and there were entire minutes when you could not see the highway and when the whole world seemed to be inside this railroad car.

O n that trip up Highway 65 in Italy, my father's voice said, there were sights for which his young life up to that point had not prepared him.

. . . We rolled northward, rolled through Bologna before you knew it, debouched into the Po River Valley and turned eastward toward Yugoslavia. At last we were out of those horrible Apennine Mountains, and we could just smell victory coming. We knew we had them on the run.

And sure enough, after several days we saw columns of hundreds of trucks bringing German prisoners back from the front so that they could be put in prison camps, which were merely big fields surrounded by barbed wire.

We knew that the war in Italy was going to draw to a close. . . .

• • •

His place in the world was measured by his place in the hearts and the memories of the people he knew—both those who knew him the best, and those who knew him only a little. And, in small moments, I kept being reminded of that.

Early in the spring after he died, I was in Florida and I ran into Bud Collins, the NBC television tennis commentator and writer for the *Boston Globe*. Bud and I have known each other for years, and there had been occasions when—out to dinner with my parents—I had seen him and all of us had talked. Bud is one of the friendliest and most gregarious men you could ever be lucky enough to meet, and he always went out of his way to be welcoming to my mom and dad, both when I was with them and when he occasionally encountered them by themselves.

So he didn't know my father well at all—but he knew him. And that spring after my father's death, when I saw Bud I told him the news.

"Oh, I'm so sorry," he said. "Your dad was such a lively guy."

When I spoke with my mother on the phone the next day, I told her that—told her what Bud had said. She was pleased to hear it.

Then—a day later, when I was speaking with her on the telephone again—she said to me:

"That word that Bud Collins used to describe Daddy—what word did you say it was?"

" 'Lively,' " I said.

"That's it," she said. "I was trying to think of it all last night. 'Lively.' He got it right—Daddy really was lively, wasn't he?"

And I thought to myself: There is love. There is love that lasts a lifetime and more. Her husband is gone, he's not there to hear the compliment, but it means enough to her—he means enough to her, in death as in life—that she stays up at night trying to recall the word that had been used to compliment him. She hadn't been present when the person had said the word—but even getting it secondhand, it was important to her to want to remember it correctly. As if she wanted to pass it on to him, because she knew it would please him.

Love?

Sometimes you can hear it in a question.

What word did you say it was?

There were days when he surprised me, even after his death.

One afternoon I received a letter with a Columbus postmark, and a return address not far from the house where I had grown up.

The letter was from a man named David Hathaway. He wrote:

> A few years ago your dad telephoned me
> after he had received a membership list of the
> 91st Infantry Division Association. He said he

didn't recognize any names on the list, but noticed that I lived just a block from where he used to live in Bexley.

We had a long chat about the 91st in Italy. Later a mutual friend (Walter Kropp, a local retired banker who served with the 4th Infantry at Anzio and later in the invasion of southern France) got us together for an afternoon of reminiscing. . . .

Mr. Hathaway said that the three of them—he, Mr. Kropp and my father—had spent at least three hours at lunch that day, talking about their days with the Army in Italy, drawing word pictures over all the years, of friends and commanders and colleagues from a war that was at the same time global in its span, and achingly personal in the tiny, yet eternal, memories it left in those who were there.

I never knew—not only never knew that he'd had that lunch on that particular day, but never knew that he did such things. That he was moved to pick up the phone—a man in his early eighties—and say to a person, a stranger whose name he had read on a list inside a newsletter:

"I see that you were with the 91st Infantry in Italy. I was in the 91st, too. . . ."

I don't know how I missed it.

I had been listening to those tapes—the tapes

of his voice telling our family about the war—and I must have heard the one passage three or four times and I never understood what it was telling me.

But then I played it again.

Now I knew Tibbets—now I knew the whole story of what he and his crew had done, and why they had done it, and what happened because of their flight.

Perhaps that was it—because I had come to know Tibbets, my father's words on the tape were telling me something completely different than what I had heard in them before.

But there it was—unmistakable.

My father's voice, talking about what was happening as the victory in Europe was finally won:

After a very hot summer we started to retrain, because we knew that the war in Japan was continuing, and we were earmarked to transship to Japan.

When that day came, we all saddled up again—the whole 91st Division—and headed southward down the same route we came. We were bound for Naples and I was a convoy commander leading a huge convoy of trucks down through Florence, through Rome, and south of Rome into Naples. . . .

He had been bound for Japan. The land invasion of Japan—the invasion that was beyond question going to cost so very many American lives, the final push of the war that was going to be paid for in death on a scale like nothing that had been previously seen in the fighting—was ready to be mounted. And he had been scheduled to be on his way.

He was traveling southward through Italy, he and the men who were with him were traveling on a route that would send them eventually to Japan, to shores where the Japanese army would be waiting for their arrival.

I went through that wartime scrapbook again— the one my mother had put together for him.

There was a second letter from General Mark Clark—not the one congratulating and thanking the infantry troops for the victory over Germany, but a different one, with a different tone. This one had been written to the soldiers in May of 1945:

> Men of the Fifteenth Army Group, I know
> you will face the task ahead with the same
> magnificent, generous and indomitable spirit
> you have shown in this long campaign.
> Forward, to final victory. God bless you all.

They were being sent to Japan.

H is voice on the tape:
. . . I believe it was just south of Rome that we were in a bivouac area when somebody

brought the news of a brand new weapon that had been used in Japan. This was the first atomic bomb that had been dropped on Hiroshima, and we had no idea what it was, but from all rumors and intelligence that filtered down to us, we knew it had to be the end of the war because the destruction was so complete. . . .

We got to Naples and there were a lot of ships there, just waiting to take us on. The transshipment of us to Japan was still a field order—and evidently in mid-ocean the plans were changed, because Japan had surrendered.

We were on this huge ocean liner, which was traveling without escort, because the seas had been cleared of submarines and mines, and there were no attacking airplanes. When we finally steamed into Newport News and saw all those welcome banners and bunting and bands playing and people waving and screaming and welcoming us, it was a never-to-be-forgotten sight, and there were lumps in many throats as we finally saw our country, a sight that many of us had really thought we would never see again.

They were home. Tibbets and his crew had flown the *Enola Gay* to Hiroshima, and then the second atomic bomb had been dropped on Nagasaki, and the Japanese government had surrendered. The ship that my father and his fellow soldiers had boarded in Naples had gone straight from Italy to the United States. The war was over. They were home.

He was home.

To rejoin his young wife in an America at peace, to make plans for a future together—a life, a family.

Two years later, I was born; then came my sister, then came my brother.

What would have happened if that ship had sped, either directly or after further training exercises, toward Japan? What would have happened had my father been delivered not to Newport News, Virginia, but to a very different shoreline in the distant Pacific Ocean?

Would he and my mother have had a life? And if they had not . . .

I played the tape one more time.

. . . *We knew that the war in Japan was continuing, and we were earmarked to transship.* . . .

I reread General Clark's letter to the troops.

God bless you all. . . .

And now it was Memorial Day weekend—the first Memorial Day since my father's death.

I was on my way to meet up with three men—Tibbets, Van Kirk, Ferebee. The men who dropped the bomb—the men who ended the war.

TWENTY-FOUR

I flew from Chicago to St. Louis, where I would get a connecting flight to Springfield, Missouri. From there we would drive to Branson.

I was using a pay phone on the TWA concourse in St. Louis, checking in with my office, when, twenty feet away, walking slowly as if looking for the right gate, came Tibbets.

He too had flown to St. Louis en route to Springfield, and I was tempted to call out to him, but I knew that he would not be able to hear me. And besides, I wanted to see this—I wanted to watch the reaction to him in the airport.

There was none, of course. He was an eighty-four-year-old man being brushed past by younger people in a hurry. I followed him with my eyes as he made his way down the noisy hallway, and then I finished my call and followed him in person. He had stopped to greet a big fellow in a baseball cap, and the two were laughing, lighting up in each other's presence.

I approached them. "I wondered whether you'd be here yet!" Tibbets said to me, full of the enthusiasm of a boy. "I've got someone I want you to meet!"

He took my arm and nudged me toward the man with whom he had been speaking.

"Bob, this is Tom Ferebee," Tibbets said.

Ferebee, the bombardier on the *Enola Gay*, was eighty. We shook hands, and in a molasses-Southern voice he said, "This is my wife, Mary Ann." She seemed shy as we said hello to each other.

"I was just telling Paul that I don't know if they'll let me back into Branson," Ferebee said. "Last time we were there, we were at dinner at this restaurant, and I got up from the table to go to the rest room, and I walked right into the ladies' room.

"All the women who were in there turned around, and there I was, standing in front of them. . . ."

Tibbets was laughing out loud. "They've probably got your picture posted all over town," he said to Ferebee. "They're on the lookout for you."

Behind us, two small voices called out: "There she is! There she is!"

A boy and a girl had spotted their grandmother coming off an arriving flight; they had been waiting for her. They excitedly ran to her and she hugged them, a joyful family gathering for the weekend leading up to America's day of memorial for its war dead.

There were tears in the grandmother's eyes as she knelt to embrace the children. Just a few feet away, Paul Tibbets was saying:

"Yeah, Tom walks right into the *ladies'* room, and Dutch and I are cracking up, waiting to see what happens next. . . ."

• • •

Dutch Van Kirk would be meeting Tibbets and Ferebee in Branson; he and his wife were driving to Missouri from their home in California for this reunion of the crew. Tibbets' friend Gerry Newhouse and his wife Judy had flown to St. Louis from Columbus. Newhouse had arranged all the logistics for the trip; he had lined up a public appearance for Tibbets, Ferebee and Van Kirk during the weekend in Branson, where the three men would be available to greet and talk with veterans.

Branson was the ideal place for them to do this; renowned as a wholesome entertainment center, the small southwestern Missouri town liked to picture itself as Las Vegas without the gambling or the risqué shows. Whatever the phrase "middle America" was supposed to mean, Branson aspired to be its capital; the average age of the people who came to Branson in search of good times was much higher than in virtually any similar venue in the country—this was a place for grandparents looking for staid, safe fun.

So if there was anywhere in the land where the crew of the *Enola Gay* was likely to be remembered and treated as celebrities, Branson was it. Tibbets, Ferebee and Van Kirk knew that on this weekend, they probably would be made to feel that they were among their own.

First, though, there was the matter of getting something to eat. A vote was taken; the idea of lunch in Springfield, before the one-hour drive to

Branson, won. A second vote was taken on where exactly to go.

Bob Evans.

Of course.

"Can I have that menu, hon?"

Tom Ferebee had been in the middle of a sentence, telling me—matter-of-factly, with no evidence of rancor—that as far as he was concerned, most people still had no real understanding of why the men of the *Enola Gay* crew were asked to do what they did, or what effect their mission had on hastening the end of World War II—when the waitress interrupted him.

He stopped what he was saying to turn in the direction of her voice.

"You're all done ordering, right?" she said to him.

He handed the shiny Bob Evans menu to her.

"I've always thought that these things are a work of art," I said to him.

"What?" he said.

"Bob Evans menus," I said. "Look at the pictures of the food. How can you look at these things and not want to order everything?"

Ferebee—who had a laconic, there's-a-joke-hidden-behind-every-moment-in-life-if-you-look-hard-enough-but-I'm-not-going-to-tell-you-where-it-is-until-you-find-it-yourself manner I have seen in very few people, one being the sportswriter and novelist Dan Jenkins, whom Ferebee reminded me of the minute I met him—looked at the now-departing waitress.

"So you want to put the menu in a frame?" he said.

We had waited a while for our table to be set up; it was clear as soon as we walked in that this place was accustomed to tour buses full of senior citizens on vacation, and Tibbets and Mr. and Mrs. Ferebee fit the bill. There had been no real sense of urgency in getting their table prepared—these were people, the staff seemed to assume, who were used to waiting, and would not complain—and indeed as the minutes had passed Tibbets and Ferebee had showed no annoyance, even though the restaurant was far from full and other tables were sitting empty.

Tibbets—whose wife had not come on the trip—leaned over to Ferebee and said:

"If you have to go to the rest room, you better double-check to see which one it is."

He leaned back in his chair and laughed at Ferebee's shaking-of-the-head reaction, and in all the time I had spent with Tibbets, this was the most relaxed and happy I had ever seen him.

D avid Bean said to wait by the front door of the restaurant, and he would bring the van.

Bean, an earnest young man with a deep admiration for veterans of World War II, was shepherding the crew around during the trip. He was an employee of an Arkansas-based company known as Cooper Communities; he had met the *Enola Gay* crew during their previous visit to Branson, had taken an immediate liking to them, and had arranged for them to stay at a Cooper time-share property called Stone-Bridge Village, just outside the Branson city limits. He and his wife Rita had been waiting at the Springfield airport when we had arrived.

So on a hot afternoon he pulled the van closer to the entrance of the Bob Evans, and we climbed in, and he started on the drive over to Branson. We passed car dealerships and antique stores and cafeterias, and we crossed a bridge that spanned a small river, and I saw Tibbets just looking out the window at his country, saying nothing.

There was a billboard for a Branson theater, featuring a likeness of an Elvis Presley imitator and the slogan YOU WILL BELIEVE; there was another, promoting a different Branson attraction, with the words FORGET YOUR TROUBLES, COME ON, GET HAPPY. Rocks were being blasted on either side of the road as part of a project to widen the highway; Tibbets gazed at another billboard, this one advertising a show by the Osmond family, and said, "There's something about that name that sounds familiar."

"Marie and Donny," Mary Ann Ferebee said to him.

He nodded, maybe understanding the reference, maybe not.

David Bean called back from the driver's seat:

"Dutch called me the other day and asked, 'What's the best way to get to the village?' I told him that the best way was to wait a day, and I'd send him a map." The navigator—the man who had gotten the *Enola Gay* to Japan and back—had been phoning for directions.

Bulldozers were everywhere as we continued toward Branson; Bean said that the highway improvement program was in high gear in an effort to speed the day when an expressway would stretch all the way into the town. We passed a meandering creek, and Ferebee put his hand on Tibbets' shoulder to get his attention, and when Tibbets turned to him Ferebee said: "Look at that. Good trout water."

Tibbets craned his neck to get a look at the creek, and when he turned back around, a contented expression on his face, he said to me—he was suddenly like an eager, unguarded and giddily energized teenager promoting a New Year's Eve party he's trying to put together—"Once you get home after a weekend with Tom and Dutch and me, you'll never be the same."

I looked at him and then at the creek and then back at him again.

• • •

Dutch Van Kirk—"the baby of the group," he told me (he was seventy-eight)—was waiting for us at the condominium complex.

His wife Jean had suffered a stroke several years before, and Van Kirk said he and she found travel easier by car. This was going to be an extended trip for them; after the crew's reunion weekend, they were going to continue east to spend some time with friends.

I told him I was happy to meet him, and he said, "Yes, but you won't say that once you know me." He smiled and put an arm over my shoulder—his line had been the kind of harmless-old-guy humor you tend to hear a lot around men of his generation (it had reminded me of the jokes my dad's friends used to make).

The condos were low-slung, in a straight line cut out of a piece of the Ozarks, surrounded by rugged forest. David Bean had organized everything, but Tibbets, once the three-man crew was fully assembled, almost imperceptibly took charge. "Now you'll give us all our room assignments," Tibbets said to Bean, and the younger man, as if following an order, handed out photocopied sheets telling us which units were ours.

I have traveled with sports teams and with rock-music groups, where such lists are a part of the daily logistics, but there was something different about this. The names were all neatly typed—Paul Tibbets, Dutch Van Kirk, Tom Ferebee, Gerry

Newhouse, David Bean, myself—and the unit numbers and individual phone numbers were placed next to each one. Yet there was something else on the list, that took me a moment to comprehend: a notation to the right of each name, under the category steps.

It was the number of stair-steps required to get to the front door of each unit from the parking lot. For the men and their wives who had the most trouble getting around, David Bean had made certain that there were no steps to climb—there was a zero in the "Steps" column.

I thought of these three men climbing into the *Enola Gay* for the night flight over the Pacific to Japan to end the world's war. "I'll see you at dinner," Van Kirk said, and I headed with my bag toward Unit 174B; my unit mates Tom and Mary Ann Ferebee, in 174A, were already inside and unpacking. I could hear their television set through the wall.

H ey, Dutch—want to ride a roller coaster?" Tibbets—still in the highest of spirits—was in David Bean's van; we were on our way to dinner, and we passed a little amusement park in Branson that offered a roller coaster ride for children.

Van Kirk, instead of answering, started to tell Tibbets a story about a jelly bean factory in California—a factory that offered tours of its production facilities. Apparently Dutch and Jean Van Kirk had visited the facility, or were planning to.

Mrs. Van Kirk had walked with some difficulty to the van; Dutch had helped her in. The stroke she had suffered had affected her severely, and now, riding next to her husband, she was silent on our way to the restaurant. Tibbets, having abandoned the roller coaster idea, was talking about how, in the late 1950s, an Air Force flight surgeon had given him a choice: Quit smoking, or stop flying.

"You?" I said. "They were going to ground *you?*"

"Damn right," Tibbets said. "I took my physical, and he said it was up to me—smoke or fly."

"How many cigarettes were you smoking a day?" I asked.

"How many hours was I up?" he said.

"So did you stop as soon as he told you to?" I asked.

"I had to," he said. "For a while there, it was so hard that I wanted to bite my hands off."

David Bean pulled into the lot of a restaurant called Shorty Small's—a big, raucous barbecue-and-burgers place. Evidently Bean had called ahead; the sign in front of the place had letters that said:

WELCOME TO ENOLA GAY CREW

"Look at that," Mary Ann Ferebee said.

"Yeah," Van Kirk said. "And look what it says underneath."

In the same size lettering, the sign said:

NOW HIRING

Bean put the van into "Park" and came around to open the side door and put a stool on the ground. Dutch Van Kirk got out first and extended both arms to his wife.

"Come on, honey," the navigator said. "Big step."

Mrs. Van Kirk, doing the best she could, moved toward her husband's arms, and he eased her way to the pavement and made sure she was steady on her feet before releasing his grip.

David Bean went inside to see if a table had been saved as he had requested. A family pulled into the parking lot, and the driver called out his window to Van Kirk: "Do you know how long the wait is here?"

Van Kirk—having no idea at all—said to the man: "You won't have to wait more than twenty-five minutes."

Ferebee shook his head. Van Kirk—who had the look of a retired high school biology teacher, and the voice and demeanor of a 1950s situation-comedy dad, his feigned befuddlement and gentle prankster-ism mixed equally with good intentions—said to Ferebee, "Well, it *could* be twenty-five minutes."

Out the door of Shorty Small's came an older lady with some young children by her side. We were waiting for David Bean to come out and tell us what to do; the woman, encountering our group, said, "Grandma's tired."

"Well, then sit out here with us," Van Kirk said. She declined the invitation and moved on. Van

Kirk began to tell me a story that I could see Tibbets and Ferebee were long familiar with. He mentioned the name of a minister; he said that the minister had inquired of him, "What are Paul's plans for passing on?"

"I asked the guy, 'What do you mean?'" Van Kirk said. "And the guy asked me again: What were Paul Tibbets' plans for passing on?

"I said, 'He doesn't have any plans for passing on.'

"And this minister said, 'Everyone dies sooner or later.'

"I said, 'Paul will take later.'

"It turned out that what he was leading up to was that he was offering to do free eulogies for the crew."

"Come on," I said.

"It's true," Van Kirk said. "He wanted to be the guy who did the funerals for the crew of the *Enola Gay*. He told me that he'd do all of our eulogies on the house."

"What did you tell him?" I asked.

"I told him to practice on Tom and Paul first," Van Kirk said. The three men erupted into laughter, and David Bean came out of the restaurant and said our table was ready, and in we all went.

I never drove through rain like the rain we saw yesterday," Van Kirk said. We were at a long table in the loud, boisterous restaurant; Branson may draw a predominantly older crowd, but there were plenty of younger people here tonight, and most of the waiters and waitresses appeared to be of college age. If the crew had been hoping for something sedate, this wasn't going to be it.

On our way in, some people in their twenties had been leaving the restaurant in a hurry, and had stopped to move aside to let Tibbets, Van Kirk, Ferebee and the women pass by. I heard one of the young people say to another, "It seems like we're in Florida." As far as they were concerned, the crew of the *Enola Gay* was here for the Early Bird Special.

And now Van Kirk was telling about the downpour on his drive to Branson.

"All the way from the border of Colorado to Wichita," he said. "The rain never let up, even for a minute."

A waiter of about twenty-three approached the table and slapped Tibbets on the back without looking at him.

"Good evening, guys, how you doin'?" he said. "Shannon will be coming over in a minute; we'll be taking care of you guys tonight." He handed a menu to Ferebee. "Here you go, buddy," he said to the eighty-year-old bombardier.

Tibbets—who had told a long story during the afternoon about getting drunk on moonshine as a young man—said to me now that it had made him so sick that he still can't stand even the smell of hard liquor. As we were discussing this, the voice of a young restaurant hostess came over the loud-speaker. She obviously was reading from something that either Gerry Newhouse or David Bean had handed her; she said that the crew of the *Enola Gay* was having dinner in the restaurant—she stopped when she got to the name of the airplane, hesitated, then pronounced it "Enolya"—and some of the customers stopped eating to applaud.

"What's going on?" Tibbets asked me. "What are they clapping for?"

I told him about the announcement that had just been made.

"I can't hear, doesn't make a damn bit of difference," he said.

We studied our menus, and the waiter and waitress took our drink orders, and Van Kirk, sitting close to Tibbets and Ferebee, said to them:

"You know that trip when we took Eisenhower down to Gibraltar? . . ."

And of course Tibbets had not been alone on that flight; his friends had been there with him. Now they were in Branson, together more than fifty years later, and Van Kirk went on with his story, as if he were describing a cab ride they had once shared.

"Paul, I remember when you were making up your mind whether to take off," Van Kirk said, and as I sat with them and listened I thought about what my father would have made of this scene, and this meal, and how much he would have loved to be here this weekend with these men.

TWENTY-FIVE

As much as I washed my hands, I couldn't get that smell out of them."

Van Kirk was talking to Ferebee; they were standing outside the row of condominium units, early in the morning, just the two of them. This was on Thursday; we had arrived for the long Memorial Day weekend on Wednesday, and I had awakened early the next morning and had decided to go out for a walk.

I had been alone on the walk, in the hours just after dawn in this isolated part of southwestern Missouri; I had wandered the roads for about an hour and a half, and when I returned the two of them were standing in the early sun talking. Evidently everyone else was still asleep inside their units.

"It was like roast beef," Ferebee said to Van Kirk.

"Oh, I know it," Van Kirk said. "It is a smell I will never forget."

I asked them what they were referring to.

"We were in Algiers," Van Kirk said. "In 1942. We were at the airfield in Maison Blanche, and during the night a German dive bomber had hit one of our planes that had been getting ready to take off—a B-17."

"Every man in that plane was crushed and burned," Ferebee said.

There were birds singing all around us on this beautiful Ozarks morning, and the sound of a dog barking somewhere in the woods behind us.

"Dutch and I were just talking about what it was like to drag those men out of there," Ferebee said.

"You were the ones who had to do it?" I asked.

"Someone had to do it," Ferebee said.

"Who told you?" I said.

"Nobody told us," Ferebee said. "The sun came up the next morning, and there was the wreckage of the plane, and somebody had to get the remains out of there. I think there were only six crews at the base at the time—somebody had to do it. We just went into the plane and did it."

"It was like burned roast beef," Van Kirk said, looking away for a second. "That's what the smell was like."

"It got under your nails," Ferebee said. "You couldn't get the smell of it out of your hands . . . I think it was days before I was finally able to wash away that smell."

A minute or so passed and Van Kirk said:

"We probably ought to go see if the girls are up yet."

They went into their condo units.

I took a shower and when I came out I could hear the Ferebees' television through our common wall.

A news channel was on; the anchorman was talking about a nuclear testing dispute between India
and Pakistan.

The anchorman, finishing the story, continued:
"And a different kind of bomb is expected to be
dropped by the World Court today. . . ."

Someone in Ferebee's room hit the zapper and
changed the television to another channel.

We gathered for a late breakfast in Tibbets'
unit.

The men were talking about the series of raids
that American-led forces had recently been flying
over the former Yugoslavia.

"We brief the whole world every day, telling
them exactly what we're going to do," Ferebee said.
"We announce our flight plans on television."

The others shook their heads. Tibbets passed the
toast.

Around noontime a young visitor burst through
the doorway: Paul Tibbets IV, Tibbets' grandson.

"Well!" Tibbets called out, his face lighting up.
He got off the couch to embrace the younger man.

Paul IV—"P4," he was called by everyone in the
room who knew him—was thirty-two years old, an
Air Force captain assigned to fly the B-2 bomber.
He had that Tom Cruise, I-can-do-anything look to

him; he wore a pair of shorts and a casual shirt, and he had driven to Branson with his wife Angele to spend the weekend with his grandfather and his grandfather's friends.

Angele, a friendly, model-pretty woman who wore a short skirt and a pair of sandals, hurried over to Tibbets to give him a welcoming hug.

Van Kirk, sitting on a couch, said to Ferebee: "Oh, to be young like that."

"I'm not sure we were ever that young," Ferebee said.

Tibbets was in the midst of a story about going fishing when he was a teenager:

". . . I'm telling you, I caught a four-hundred-pound grouper."

"Four hundred pounds," I said, disbelieving.

"Yes," Tibbets said.

"What kind of bait do you use to catch a four-hundred-pound fish?" I said, certain he was putting us all on.

"Well, it's not a worm," he said.

"Then what?" I said.

"You use thirty-five or forty pounds of dead cow or horse," he said.

"Why would you even want to catch a four-hundred-pound fish?" I said.

"To sell," he said. "To get money to buy gas to take girls out."

"And the hook?" I said.

"Iron hook," Tibbets said. "Big iron hook."

But it wasn't a story about catching fish that I was interested in hearing from Tibbets. I had something else I had been wanting to ask him about.

"What happened on that flight your mother took?" I asked.

"Which one?" he said.

"When she was coming to Wendover to visit you," I said.

"Oh," he said, as if dismissing it. "That flight."

I had heard bits and pieces of the story from people who knew him. Tibbets always seemed to pride himself on his lack of emotions, his ability to put his feelings on hold. The trip to Wendover his mother had taken during the war, though . . .

The way I had heard it, he had invited her to come to Wendover in the months he was preparing the 509th for the atomic-bombing mission. She had flown on a commercial airline from her home in Florida to Utah.

And Tibbets—this was the story—had flown a fighter plane alongside the commercial flight. He had been her escort—getting her safely across the country.

"So?" he said.

"So, that was a pretty nice thing to do," I said.

"Well, we were both going to the same place," he said, trying to change the subject.

"There are other ways to get to the same place than flying escort for a commercial plane," I said.

"I had been in Washington," he said.

The way he told it, his mother had been booked on a United Airlines flight that was scheduled to take her from Chicago to Des Moines, and then to Omaha, to Cheyenne, Wyoming, and into Salt Lake City. This was in March of 1945.

And Tibbets decided to fly alongside the flight— to fly off to the side of his mother's plane as it crossed the United States. It struck me as a pretty impressive show of love and concern.

"They could see me from the plane," Tibbets said, as if that was what I was asking him. "The passengers could see me—it wasn't like I was going to scare them. I was talking on the radio to the pilot, so everyone on the plane knew that nothing was wrong."

"I didn't think that anyone thought anything was wrong," I said. "I just think that was an awfully nice thing for a son to do for his mother."

"What was nice about it?" Tibbets said.

"That you flew that whole flight next to her plane, to look out for her."

"I didn't do it to look out for her," he said. "I told you—we were just heading for the same place."

"Well, I think you were looking out for her," I said.

"OK, you do," he said.

• • •

Apresentation to the crew—the key to the city of Branson, by the mayor—had been scheduled at the clubhouse of the condominium complex in the afternoon, so we all got into David Bean's van to go over.

The building felt like a country club—it was located on a golf course—and once we arrived, I talked with Paul Tibbets IV about his relationship with his grandfather.

"We've really become good friends," he said. I knew about the emotional distance that Tibbets had felt with his own sons. Apparently it had taken a generation, but now there seemed to be a genuine closeness in the family—between Tibbets and P4.

"My grandfather and I never really had any conversations about me becoming a flier," the younger man said. "But there's a picture of the two of us when I was three or four years old. And there's a model of a B-29 in the picture.

"He didn't tell me that I should be a flier, but he's the reason that I'm a flier."

Tibbets saw us talking and came over to join us. I asked his grandson how many crew members flew the B-2 with him.

"Just one other guy," he said. "That's the whole point of it—it's so technologically advanced that two pilots can fly it. The two of us *are* the crew—we can fly that plane from the United States to a war zone in Europe, if need be, deploy the bombs ourselves, and fly it back to our base in the U.S. without landing anywhere."

I looked over at Van Kirk and Ferebee, sitting together against the wall across the room. The *Enola Gay* crew had been twelve men; I thought of that crew, and then thought of Captain Paul Tibbets IV flying a bomber with just one other man aboard, and the older Tibbets seemed to be having the same thoughts.

"He won't have the camaraderie that I did," Tibbets said.

"Well, things are different," his grandson said.

"All of us in our crew knew each other as well as you can know a person," Tibbets said. He nodded in the direction of Van Kirk and Ferebee. "I trust those guys with my back turned."

"I know," his grandson said. "But in the B-2, we really don't need a navigator."

"All the money the government spent to build that plane," I said to him. "It's just such an odd thought—two guys having control of the whole mission . . ."

"That's the whole idea," Paul IV said.

"Is your plane much bigger than the plane your grandfather flew to Japan?" I asked.

"The B-2 is all wing," he said.

"The B-29 we flew was actually longer than the plane P4 flies," Tibbets said.

"Is that why you had to use every inch of the runway when you took off from Tinian?" I asked.

"No, no," Tibbets said. He and his grandson looked at each other as if to say: What's the use trying to explain this to a non-pilot.

"Lookit," Tibbets said. "We did not have the thrust back then. We were not flying jets. I needed that whole runway because I needed to have the thrust to get it off the ground."

"Our plane can do a lot more things," his grandson said.

"That may be true, but I grew up fast in the B-17 and the B-29," Tibbets said. "When you get shot at, you mature pretty fast."

"I know you did," the younger man said.

"We had to fly low to the ground," Tibbets said. "You don't. Hell, when I was flying the B-17, they shot at us with *rifles*."

"Big rifles," his grandson said.

"They were just rifles," Tibbets said.

From across the room, someone called to say that the presentation of the key to the city was ready to begin.

Gerry Newhouse pulled Tibbets aside and said that Wayne Newton had wanted to be present for this, but that he was not in town.

"So this is the mayor?" Tibbets said.

"The mayor had to be somewhere," Newhouse said. "You're going to get the key from the head alderman."

Tibbets, Van Kirk and Ferebee lined up and were handed a key that also could be used as a bottle opener, and then we returned to David Bean's van to go back to the condos. On the radio, an announcer was reading a commercial for a Memorial Day weekend sale.

"Memorial Day," Tibbets said. "People drink beer, people play golf."

"Does that bother you?" I said.

"Not at all," he said. "I don't know if 'memorial' is even the right word. War's a mess."

I waited to see if he was going to expand on that.

But he just looked out the window and said, "War is a mess."

Y ou'd have to be a damn idiot not to be able to get to Japan from Tinian."

Van Kirk was talking; it was dinnertime, and we were all back in the van, on our way to a Landry's seafood restaurant in Branson. I had asked him about the difficulty in navigating the *Enola Gay* from the minute Pacific island to the target city in Japan, and he was answering that it was no big deal—to fail, one would have had to be an "idiot."

"You would?" I said.

"Yeah," he said. "You had all kinds of barrier reefs to guide you—once you got to Iwo, it was easy."

He was talking as if the flight had been a stroll in the park—maybe. For I was finding that with Van Kirk, as with all three of them, there was a constant deprecation of the skill the mission had required, but a deprecation cloaked in confidence, almost as a challenge: Yes, it was easy for us. But could *you* do it?

We got to the restaurant and were given a table in a back room, against a window; we were in a hurry tonight, because we had tickets to a show later at the Lawrence Welk Theater. We were looking at the menus, getting ready to order, and a waiter came in and said: "Is one of you named Tibbets?"

"Who wants to know?" Ferebee said.

"There's a man out in the main restaurant who said he heard the crew of the *Enola Gay* was here tonight," the waiter said. If he had any idea what the *Enola Gay* was, it was not obvious. "He wanted to know if a Mr. Tibbets was here, and if he was, which one was he?"

Van Kirk, staring at his menu, said, without looking up: "Tell him it's Tibbets and a bunch of bums."

I had seen a flash of this at dinner the night before, when a woman had approached our table because she wanted an autograph from Tibbets. She had gone up to Ferebee—the biggest of the men—guessing that it might be him, and when she had asked, he'd had to say that, no, Paul Tibbets was the fellow across the table. I had observed this kind of thing before, in a different context: with the Chicago Bulls on the road during the championship years, when people would come up to

Scottie Pippen . . . and ask him if he could get them Michael Jordan's autograph.

So tonight the waiter, a little confused, went back to the diner in the other room with the answer that, yes, he *thought* Mr. Tibbets was in there. We continued our conversation at the table; I told Ferebee how Tibbets, the first day we met, had described the jolt of the plane once the bomb had dropped out—"The seat slapped me on the ass"— and asked if that had been his observation, too. Had the plane's sudden motion felt like a slap, a kick?

"Depends who's kicking," Ferebee said. "We'd felt things before."

Meaning that the atomic bomb was hardly the first bomb that Ferebee had dropped out of a Tibbets-piloted plane during World War II. We talked about it for a minute, and Van Kirk joined in, and I guided the conversation to a more mundane aspect of the flight: It had been such a long one—had they eaten? The history of the world might have been hanging in the balance—but did bomber crews take food along with them?

"He always fed us real well," Van Kirk said, gesturing at Tibbets and rolling his eyes, as if to say: Don't even ask.

Then: "Maybe an apple. Maybe with Paul, we got an apple on the flight."

"Come on," Ferebee said. "That's not true. Paul always fed us halfway through a flight."

They were making fun of the question. They

were saying: This was not a businessman's flight from Chicago to New York. We were trying to win a war. We weren't concerned with having lunch.

Van Kirk said he had heard or read somewhere that a famous New York auction house was going to be selling the "original log" of the *Enola Gay* to the highest bidder.

"I called them up," he said. "I said to them, 'I understand you have the original log from the *Enola Gay*?' And the man said yes. And I said, 'Well, that's very interesting. Because I'm the navigator of the *Enola Gay*. And I have the original log up in my attic.'"

"What did the guy say?" I asked.

"He took whatever it was he had off the auction block," Van Kirk said.

"Do you really have the original log?" I asked.

"Oh, yes," he said. "With my own handwriting."

"What does it say?" I asked.

Van Kirk—trying to get a rise out of Ferebee—said: "I wrote in the log just before we got to Hiroshima: 'Woke Tom up.'"

Ferebee, who had heard it before, said: "Yeah—that's why I missed."

Behind the banter seemed to be two things—a stolid acceptance of the horror and death that followed what they did, and a quiet, enormous pride about the mission and the victory that ensued.

"What did you really write in the log?" I asked Van Kirk.

"At that moment?" he said.

"Yes," I said.

"I wrote 'Bomb away,'" he said. "That's all."

We rushed through our dinner so that we could make it to the show at the Welk Theater; in David Bean's van on the way to the performance it seemed as if we might be lost for a moment, and Ferebee tried to remember directions from the last time the crew had been in Branson.

"Don't listen to him," his wife said to Bean. Then, to me: "Tom still doesn't even know how to fold and unfold a map."

Ferebee—continuing the conversation about the purported flight log at the auction house—said he had heard somewhere that the bombsight from the *Enola Gay* was for sale.

"I called up the Smithsonian," he said. "I told the person who answered the phone who I was, and I said, 'Is my bombsight there?'"

He sounded like a man looking for a lost dog.

"Was it?" I asked.

"Yep," he said. "The man said, 'It's here.' So the bombsight that someone was trying to sell was a phony."

A block of seats had been saved for us at the theater—a big, ornate place—and an usher was waiting in the lobby to take us in. He wanted to ascertain that we were the right party, so he looked at a piece of paper in his hand and said: "Are you the *Enola Gay* group?"

Van Kirk said, "You ever hear of us?"

The usher said, "Of course." Then: "Who flew the plane?"

"Who flew the plane," Van Kirk said softly, more to himself than to the usher. Then, nodding in the direction of Tibbets: "That, over there."

The usher led us in. Well over half of the seats in the theater were empty; this was a weeknight, and there were yawning sections of upholstered chairs with not a soul in them. We were taken to a row near the front; on stage, the master of ceremonies was beginning the show, but he could not stop coughing. It wasn't a put-on—he was hacking away, and he was unable to do anything about it.

Another usher hurried to him with a glass of water. The MC apologized; he said this was his first night back with the show after being sick for six days. His coughing resumed, even worse. "Talk among yourselves," he said, embarrassed, and the audience, understanding and polite, waited until he could compose himself.

"Did I ever tell you about Andy Williams' dressing room?" Tibbets whispered to me. "It was more beautiful than most homes I've ever seen."

The show was billed as "The Welk Resort Center and the Champagne Theater Present This Won-

derful Century of American Music." It commenced
with a marching band parading down two aisles,
playing rousing marches—"You're a Grand Old
Flag" was performed while an enormous American
flag was displayed in the background.

The entertainment centered on re-creations of
events from U.S. history, to the accompaniment of
songs from each era. Over the public address system, Franklin D. Roosevelt's voice on tape boomed
out the "date which will live in infamy" speech; on
the stage, the cast re-enacted the Lawrence Welk
television show, circa 1955.

During a pause in the theatrical tapestry of moments and music, the master of ceremonies read a
list of announcements about people in the audience.
"Mr. and Mrs. Paul Sommerville are celebrating
their fifty-sixth anniversary. Mr. and Mrs. Glenn
Moore are celebrating their fifty-seventh anniversary." There was enthusiastic applause for each anniversary couple; this crowd, for the most part, was
composed of contemporaries of the couples.

But when the MC then announced that the crew
of the *Enola Gay* was in attendance—and when
Tibbets, followed by the other two men, stood up to
wave to the crowd—there were a few moments of
uncertainty.

"Is that really them?" I heard a man behind me
quietly ask his wife. Some in the audience clearly
felt this must be one more re-enactment; after all,
the Sousa-style band had marched right through the

audience, so were these men part of the performance, too? Were they cast members pretending to be the men who had won the war?

Tibbets applauded the crowd—he held his hands up and clapped in their direction—and within seconds they were applauding the crew in return. Most seemed eventually to believe that, yes, these men were combat fliers, not entertainers.

After the long show, ushers approached our group and invited us to come backstage and meet the cast. I walked with Tibbets—he told me he just wanted to go back to the condos—and after we had spent a few minutes with the singers and musicians, David Bean said he would bring the van around.

Jean Van Kirk—who had appeared filled with delight to meet the actors and actresses—was moving with great difficulty, the effects of her stroke the most evident they had been on the trip.

"That's OK," I heard Dutch say to her as he helped her. "If they're going too fast for us, we'll just let them walk past us." And he got her to the van and eased her into a seat near the front.

It was after 11 P.M. as we began the drive down unlighted roads to the condominium complex, back in the woods. There wasn't much conversation; a few of the people appeared to be sleeping.

I looked at Tibbets, I looked at Van Kirk, I looked

at Ferebee. The strains of the old-time music were still ringing in my ears from the performance we had just seen, but it was another song that I was hearing—a song from a much more recent era.

It had been playing on the background tape at the seafood restaurant during dinner. I had been struck by it then—it's a famous song, written and performed by Bob Seger—and now, in the silence of our ride home, I looked at the men and I heard Seger's words anew:

> MY HANDS WERE STEADY,
> MY EYES WERE CLEAR AND BRIGHT.
> MY WALK HAD PURPOSE,
> MY STEPS WERE QUICK AND LIGHT.
> AND I HELD FIRMLY
> TO WHAT I FELT WAS RIGHT
> LIKE A ROCK.

I thought again of a man who wasn't with us tonight, and I wanted to tell someone about it, but no one was speaking, so I remained quiet.

> LIKE A ROCK,
> I WAS STRONG AS I COULD BE,
> LIKE A ROCK,
> NOTHING EVER GOT TO ME. . . .

We rode through the darkness, at times the only vehicle on the two-lane roads.

TWENTY-SIX

Friday morning was the time that had been set for the public appearance Gerry Newhouse had arranged for the crew; they were scheduled to go back to the same theater where we had watched the Welk show the night before, and to sit at a table in the lobby to greet people who wished to meet them.

The way the table was set up, Van Kirk sat on the left, with Ferebee next to him and Tibbets on the right. But the line of people who had come to see the crew—it wasn't long, but it was respectable— was forming on the right wall of the lobby. So the first man they encountered at the table was Tibbets.

"Thank you for what you did," a woman said.

"Good morning," Tibbets said.

"I just want to shake his hand," a man said to me, as if permission were needed. Tibbets seemed slightly uncomfortable today—later he would tell me that the acoustics in the lobby were making it very difficult for him to understand what the people were saying—and when the man did extend his hand to Tibbets, Tibbets took it and the man asked a question about the war.

"Good morning," Tibbets said.

Gerry Newhouse and Paul IV were at another table about twenty feet away, where they had unpacked from boxes items available for purchase, for the crew to autograph. There were photographs of the crew from World War II, there were lithographs, there were copies of a career-retrospective book that Tibbets had first had privately printed some thirty years before, and that Newhouse kept updated and in stock at his office back in Ohio. Throughout the year, on occasions when Tibbets visited military bases and air shows around the country, Newhouse would accompany him and arrange signing sessions such as this one; sometimes there would be good crowds, sometimes it would be less than successful, but this visit to Branson was the only time that Tibbets' crew would join him to meet the public.

"Good morning, General, sir." "Such an honor to meet you." Some men and women who had come to the Welk theater to purchase advance tickets for the stage show, or to buy Branson souvenirs in the gift shop, or to have lunch in the restaurant, appeared puzzled by the sight of the three elderly men at the table, but those who did know who Tibbets, Van Kirk and Ferebee were seemed genuinely thrilled to be able to have a few words with them.

In the line, I saw a man in a wheelchair, accompanied by his wife. I introduced myself to them; he was Howard Casle, seventy-seven, she was Lilli Casle, seventy-four. Mrs. Casle nodded toward Tibbets and said to me: "He's still a looker, isn't he?"

I glanced over at Tibbets. "Are you talking about General Tibbets?" I said.

"Yum yum," Mrs. Casle said.

She told me that her husband had cried when he heard that Tibbets was going to be in Branson.

"He was an MP with the 509th in Wendover and on Tinian," she said. "You have no idea what these men mean to him."

Mr. Casle held something in his hands; I could see that it was a 509th yearbook—the same kind that Tibbets had shown me in Columbus.

When it was Mr. Casle's turn to speak to Tibbets his eyes teared up, and he said, "They said that what we did was going to end all wars. They lied to us. We worked so hard . . ."

Tibbets, instinctively recoiling from any out-pouring of sentiment, said a few words to Casle and then introduced him to Ferebee. Ferebee seemed almost amused at this setup—the three of them sitting shoulder-to-shoulder, as if in a receiving line—and he knew that Van Kirk was the gregarious one of the bunch, that Van Kirk would be the one to spend the time and listen to the stories.

Which he did.

"You were an MP with the 509th, were you?" Van Kirk said to Casle. "Well, then you must have arrested Ferebee. . . ." Within seconds he had Casle smiling and then laughing; he asked Casle if he knew about the reunions that the 509th held from time to time, and when Casle said he didn't Van

Kirk wrote down an address and handed it to him. "You ought to come," he said. "We have a lot of fun."

I stood with Mrs. Casle and asked her what was tougher duty for her husband—serving with the 509th during the war, or getting around in a wheelchair today.

"He was twenty-three," she said. "Nothing was tough duty for him back then."

The morning passed and the pattern did not change. Sometimes the line was steady, sometimes it winnowed down to nothing, always the people were almost awestruck to have their few moments with Tibbets, were uncertain how to deal with Ferebee's taciturn, if pleasant, demeanor, and were warmed by Van Kirk's chamber-of-commerce-style openness. "These your children?" Van Kirk would say. "Great, great, now tell me what their names are. . . ."

One man got to the front of the line and said to Tibbets: "You ever know a bombardier named O.K. Graves?"

Tibbets nodded toward Ferebee and said, present tense, "He's the bombardier. He'd know."

To Van Kirk, a man said, "So you're the fellow who found the way across the blue Pacific." To which Van Kirk responded by launching into a detailed discussion of the coral reefs he could see from the plane en route to Japan.

I saw a man put his three-year-old daughter up on the table so that she was sitting right in front of Tibbets' chair; the father snapped a picture. He was Jimmy Dolan, thirty-two, of Sherwood, Arkansas; he said that he had brought his little girl Abbie to the theater lobby today because "I know my history. I had a grandfather in World War II. Not enough attention is paid."

Another man with a child—Lamar Steiger was the father, his nine-year-old son was Eli—told me that they had driven to Branson from Bentonville, Arkansas. "These three men helped to save my father's life," Steiger said. "Once Eli heard they were going to be here, he wanted to come."

Steiger's own father, Don, had been stationed with the Army in California toward the end of World War II, he said. "They were practicing hitting beaches in California. They were going to be sent to Japan for the land invasion."

The little boy came back from the table, where he had said something to Tibbets.

"What did you tell him?" Steiger said.

"I thanked him for saving Daddy Don's life," the child said.

There was a show going on inside the theater; I walked in, to find even fewer people in attendance than had seen the Welk production the night before. This daytime performance featured the Lennon

Brothers (the Lennon Sisters were saved for prime time, in the evenings); I stood in the back for a few minutes and watched a skit based on old-time college football weekends.

When I returned to the lobby, Tibbets was being approached by a man named Fred Jones, who was seventy-four. With him was his wife, Marilyn.

"Sir, you saved my life," he said to Tibbets.

"Well, we thought that might happen," Tibbets said.

After Jones had spoken with Tibbets and had said hello to the other men, I asked him what he had meant.

"I was a paratrooper in Europe," he said. "We knew we were on our way to Japan. I had a friend in high school who went to the South Pacific. He died within six weeks."

He said that he had grown up in Oakley, Kansas, a town with a population of approximately 1,500. His father owned a farm on which he raised wheat and milo. "Dad died when I was seven," he said. "He was only forty-three years old. My mom managed to keep the farm—I don't know how she did it. I went off to the war.

"I got to come home because of those three men who are sitting there. I still live in Oakley—I still work that farm. My wife and I have been married for fifty-two years. And I know in my heart why I have had the chance to do it. Because of what those men did. That's why I came here today. I just wanted to thank Paul Tibbets for letting me live my life."

Things slowed down, and the crew said that they thought they'd break early for lunch. I went back to where we were staying, and walked around the area for a few hours; afterward I walked over to Tibbets' unit, and he was sitting in the living room.

Something had been on my mind since the night before—and it had only been reenforced by what I had seen on stage at the Lennon Brothers' performance this morning.

The G-rated nature of the entertainment—it was what older people are expected to enjoy, I supposed, but when you thought about it, it didn't necessarily make sense. These men had seen things during warfare that no person should ever have to see—the carnage they witnessed on a daily basis had to be indelibly branded on their psyches.

But they were part of a generation that grew up seeing no nudity in movies, hearing no foul language and seeing no explicit violence in their popular entertainment—yes, they were the target audience for the Lennon Sisters and the Lennon Brothers, they had been raised in an American society where forbidden things were just that: forbidden. Their children and grandchildren came of age in a culture that laughed at the concept of the forbidden, that did not understand or honor the idea of anything being out-of-bounds.

And that's what I wanted to know. Did my father, and Tibbets, and the men and women of their generation, go through their adult lives feeling that they had been unnecessarily sheltered because there were so many things they had not been permitted to see? And did it all ring false with them—having been eyewitnesses to the death and bloodshed of warfare in their young adult lives, did it now feel faintly ridiculous that the entertainment they were allowed to see when they were young had been cleaned up, sanitized?

"If your dad and I had grown up with the nudity and the language and the violence that young people see on TV and in the movies now, I don't think it would have had an effect on us one way or the other," he said.

"You really don't think so?" I said. "You don't think it would have changed you—to grow up seeing the things that people see in entertainment today?"

"I think it would have certainly been better for the country, if the violence and the nudity and the foul language hadn't taken over," he said. "But you asked about us—about your father, about me. And I don't think we would have been any different as men, even if we had seen all those things when we were growing up."

"Why not?" I said.

"Because it's not like we didn't know it was out there," he said. "Sex was all hush-hush—you couldn't see it everywhere like you see it on cable TV today. But it was there—the world just didn't serve it up to us on a silver platter. The entertainment when we were boys was based on the thought that sex was a sin—but no matter what we weren't allowed to see, we knew about it."

"I was sitting with you at that show last night," I said, "and I was thinking about how wholesome the performance was, and then I thought of all the killing and gore that you got used to when you were a young man. . . ."

"So what?" Tibbets said. "We were better served, being protected from the kinds of things that kids see now as they're growing up. By the time we got to the war, we were ready to look the hard side of life right in the face—and if we weren't ready, we got ready, real quick. I do not feel deprived that when I was a boy the entertainment was clean and happy."

"Would you have said so at the time?" I asked.

"I don't know," Tibbets said. "I was a boy. But if you're asking me to look back and guess how I would have felt about having sex and violence all around me in entertainment when I was young . . .

"I suppose I feel that seeing all of that would have put a pretty heavy burden on me when I was a kid. Having to pretend that I understood it all. I suppose I'm glad that it was kept away from me, that I was allowed to wait a while before I saw some of those things."

"And you enjoyed the show last night?" I said.

"It was fine," he said. "I'm just sorry Andy Williams isn't in town, so I could show you those funny acrobats."

I went back to my place and Ferebee's door was open. His wife was in the bedroom; he said he thought she might be taking a nap. He waved me inside; I was pleased, because I had been hoping to get some time alone with him and with Van Kirk.

"So I take it they were kidding last night when they said they had to wake you up when you got to Hiroshima," I said.

"Yes, but the fact was, there wasn't a lot for me to do until we got there," he said. "You look at your film in advance to pick out the target area—you decide what the best aiming point will be. In Hiroshima, it was pretty clear to me that it had to be the T-shaped bridge.

"And then you talk about whether you want to come in upwind or downwind. I wanted to approach upwind—I would be more sure that I would hit the target. Downwind would have given us the chance for a faster getaway. But I wanted to hit the target, that's all, and Tibbets agreed."

"The bombardier flies the plane in the last minutes?" I said.

"Yes," Ferebee said. "But it's not the way you're probably thinking—the bombardier doesn't climb into the pilot's seat. The pilot turns it over to the bombardier, so that the plane is being controlled mechanically through the bombsight. You're steering the plane toward your target."

"When Tibbets turned the *Enola Gay* over to you, did you tense up?" I asked.

"No," he said. "The only thing I was nervous about was that I didn't want the bomb hanging up in there—I wanted to make sure it left the plane.

"I could see the bridge from more than sixty miles away—it wasn't a case of having to find it visually at the last moment."

"And when you released the atomic bomb?"

"I knew I didn't screw up," he said.

Tibbets took the controls back as soon as the bomb was released, Ferebee said: "I couldn't see the bomb anymore after he started turning. But then, as we flew away . . . it was like something I'd never seen before. Parts of *buildings* were coming up the stem of the bomb—you could tell that something strange was going on, because you could see parts of the city, pieces of the buildings, like they were being sucked up toward us.

"I had forgotten to put my goggles on. It was the brightest thing you've ever seen, underneath us."

And when the *Enola Gay* landed back on Tinian?

"I was just thankful that it worked," he said. "It was just another mission, and it was over."

A preposterous notion, of course—"just another mission"—but I was beginning to understand that this was Ferebee's style: low key, understated, not overly interested in explaining a lot. He was born in Mocksville, North Carolina, in 1918; he had stayed in the Air Force until 1970. His forearms were enormous, like a lumberjack's, or a professional arm wrestler's; of the three men, he was the one who, even at his age, had the look of a person who could intimidate strangers if he was of a mind to. He wore a baseball cap most of the time, and his drawl was so thick that there were moments when it was difficult to understand every word.

I asked him if he recalled the first time he had met Paul Tibbets.

"I was reporting to Sarasota in April of 1942," he said. "I was walking down this dirt road to the tents. I was supposed to be picking up a .45, for some reason, and I ran into this guy. Tibbets.

"You could tell right away that he was a real competent person. We weren't buddies—not then. We were just in the service together."

And now?

"I know him like a book and he knows me like a book. He is one of the most *loyal* men in the world . . ."

His voice kind of trailed off, and I asked the question: What's it going to be like when there are not three of them, but two? When the first of the three goes?

"It'll hurt bad," he said. "If Dutch or me goes first, it'll hurt Paul, but he'll keep it inside. He won't show it."

"And if he or Dutch are the first to go?" I asked.

"I'll try to do it like Paul would," Ferebee said. "I'll try to keep it inside. But I don't know if I'll be able to."

I asked him his thoughts about the people beneath his bomb—the people who lived in the houses and the buildings that he saw being sucked up the bomb's stem toward the plane.

"I would hate to think about someone in my family being down there," Ferebee said. "But it's just a part of war. If you let those kinds of thoughts get to you . . . This is a war. If you let yourselves think those kinds of thoughts, you might end up going nuts."

"Is that how you got through it?" I asked. "Not just the Hiroshima flight, but the whole war up to that point? By trying not to think about it?"

"I always told myself, never get close to anyone," he said. "Never get close to anyone, because you might lose them."

"But you did lose them," I said. "In Europe, you lost people in your unit all the time. People you knew really well."

"I told myself, when you lose someone, treat it like they've gone on vacation," he said. "Tell yourself that they're on vacation, and they're not back yet."

· · ·

I was afraid that our talking might be disturbing his wife in the next room, but Ferebee said that she, like Tibbets, had significant hearing loss—hers was just in her right ear—and that there was no way, with the door closed, that she could hear us. I asked him if he was really as matter-of-fact about the Hiroshima flight as he seemed. Not only about the death—but about what he seemed to feel was the routine nature of it.

"It was just another flight," he said. "Another mission in that war. We'd flown a lot of them together."

"But this . . ." I began.

"Paul tells me it was a boring flight," he said. "I know what he means. At least on a B-17 flight, there was a little shooting going on. This was just like a cross-country flight in an airplane. Basically uneventful, except for what happened when we got there. You're trying to win a war."

"And you did," I said. "Is that what you dreamed about when you were a kid—being a soldier and winning a war for your country?"

"I wanted to play baseball," he said. "That was my dream. I went down to Florida with the St. Louis Cardinals for spring training in 1939. That's the dream I was after."

"What happened?" I asked.

"I wasn't good enough yet," he said. "And then the war came."

"Well, you helped to win it," I said.

"I would rather have helped the Cardinals win a World Series," he said. "That's all I ever wanted."

Tibbets seemed in a somewhat pensive mood as we got ready to go out to dinner—when I had come to visit him in his unit I had picked up from a table a piece of historical literature about World War II that he had been reading, and I noticed he had left it open to a passage that listed the number of casualties among bomber crewmen from the Eighth Air Force in Europe during the war: 44,786. Whether that was on his mind, or if it was something else, I wasn't certain. But he was quiet this evening.

When some people who were joining us for dinner were late showing up at David Bean's van, Tibbets said to me, "If they had been on my crew, I would have taken off without them. Left them behind." We had reservations at a restaurant called the Outback—not part of the national chain, but a hometown steakhouse of the same name in Branson—and when we arrived we found that a table for twenty-one had been set up in a private room.

Some owners of the restaurant were joining us, and some executives of the company that ran the condominium complex, and some Branson civic leaders—this seemed to catch Tibbets by surprise. He said nothing—just looked at the long table, then chose a chair on one side near the end.

The noise level was high, and he didn't seem eager to join in the conversations all around him. A young man stood behind him and said to some of the people at the dinner table, "I fly some—I don't have a pilot's license, but I do some flying anyway." To Tibbets it seemed to be part of a great wash of noise; Mary Ann Ferebee said to me, "This is difficult for me, and I only have bad hearing in one ear. It must be so hard for Paul—you feel so isolated in a setting like this, and you have to work so hard to try to hear what everyone is saying. It's just . . . tiring."

Dutch Van Kirk was expressing some opinions—"Well, if you can't get a job now, in *this* economy, then you can probably never get a job"—and Ferebee was telling some war stories, perhaps apocryphal, perhaps real: "I offered to sell one of our planes to some Arabs for twelve eggs. . . ." Van Kirk and Ferebee were exchanging reminiscences about an old gunner they referred to as Horizontal Hague, and waiters were passing big platters of appetizers, and Tibbets turned to me and said:

"This will be the last big blowout for me."

I wasn't certain what he meant, but he looked up and down the long table.

"No more of having all these people at dinner this trip," he said. "I don't like it. It's just too damn noisy."

Wanting to remind him of the small lunches that he, Gerry Newhouse and I had eaten at his favorite hangout in Columbus, I said, "For me, a table for three at B.J. Young's is the maximum size."

"I know it," Tibbets said.

A few minutes passed, and he seemed lost in thought, and I could see something in his eyes. He got up in a big hurry, and started off for the rest room alone.

The conversation at the table was loud and lively, and no one appeared aware of his absence. I looked into the main restaurant—jammed, high-decibel, with ramps leading from one level to the next, and music playing, and a surprisingly young crowd standing shoulder to shoulder, waiting for tables to open up—and I stood and followed him.

He seemed a little confused in the midst of all the people. "You don't have to do this," he said when he saw me next to him. "Go back and have your dinner."

"That's OK," I said.

I asked someone for directions to the men's room, and I got us there, and walked in with him. "Something just hit me in the belly, Bob," he said. "I'm not feeling so hot."

"Well, I've got to use the rest room, too, so we can just walk back together when you're finished," I said.

I did not, in fact, have to use the rest room, but I waited until he had gone into a stall before I went back outside for a moment. I was going to wait for him and pretend that I had just finished up, too, so that I could make sure he got back to the table all right. I stood there outside the rest room, and I thought about this being the first Memorial Day since my dad had been gone, and I picked up the receiver of a pay telephone and I called my mom.

She was at home tonight. "Where are you?" she said. "It sounds like you're at a party."

"No, I'm just out to dinner," I said. I didn't tell her where; I didn't say that I was in Branson, or who I was with.

"You're having dinner in a bar, from the sounds of it," she said.

Sort of, I told her; the place was sort of a bar.

We talked for a few minutes, and she seemed as if she was doing all right, and two young guys talking at high volume, with beer bottles in their hands, came past me and into the men's room, and after a while Tibbets came out by himself.

I told my mom goodbye; I told her I'd be coming to see her soon.

"You must have finished before I did," Tibbets said, and I said, yes, I had. I asked him if he was ready to go back to the table.

"I suppose," he said. "You know . . . one of the things I've lost is my taste for things. I just don't have the same taste for food that I used to."

I put my hand on one of his arms, as softly as I could so that he would not realize that I was guiding him, and we walked onto one of the wooden ramps that would take us back to the others. When we got there everyone was in full conversation and no one seemed to have noticed that he had been gone.

TWENTY-SEVEN

On my walk the next morning I found myself in a part of the complex that was just being constructed; a man and a woman were being shown a model unit, and as they were coming out they saw me and called hello.

I didn't recognize them; at first I thought they might be greeting someone else. But they walked over and said that they were in Branson for the weekend from their home in Iowa, and that they had seen me in the lobby of the Welk Theater the day before with Tibbets and the crew.

"We were really surprised at how few people were there to say hello to those men," the woman, a second-grade teacher, said.

Her husband said, "I was a senior in high school when the bomb was dropped. I went into the Navy after I graduated, and I served Stateside. I've always thought that if Colonel Tibbets and his crew hadn't flown their mission, I probably would have been on my way to Japan."

I asked the couple if they had overheard anything that the other people in the theater lobby—not the ones in line to meet the crew, but the people who were just passing through—were saying about Tibbets, Van Kirk and Ferebee.

"Nothing much," the husband said. "To tell you the truth, there was a lot of confusion. No one really knew who the three guys were."

When I got back to the development where we were staying I thought I saw that Tibbets' door was ajar, so I walked up to find out. I knocked; I heard him say "Come in," and I stepped inside. . . .

To find him sitting in a pair of boxer shorts and a T-shirt, working on something as he sat at a table. I was embarrassed to be walking in on him like this: He was all but undressed. I apologized and began to leave.

"No, no," Tibbets said. He motioned for me to come in. "That's all right—this is how I am around the house in the morning." I saw what he was doing: trying to load new batteries into his hearing aids.

"This may help," he said. "I was having a lot of trouble last night."

We talked for a while, and I told him that I had heard a few people during our trip—not many, but some—discussing him and the crew in disparaging terms. Saying that when they flew the mission in 1945, the war was going to end soon anyway—that had the crew, and the country, been patient, the flight of the *Enola Gay* would have been rendered unnecessary.

He finished inserting the batteries. Then—looking, at the same moment, all of his eighty-four years and like a seventeen-year-old kid gearing up for a street fight—he turned to face me.

"Those people never had their balls on that cold, hard anvil," he said. "They can say anything they want."

I asked him the same thing I had asked Ferebee the day before—I asked him whether he ever thought about a trip like this when there would be only two of them, instead of three. And of how he would feel once that one of them was gone.

"If I'm the one to go first, I hope to hell that the other two don't shed any tears over me," he said. "Because I'm not going to shed any over them."

I was stunned.

"Why do you say that?" I asked.

"Because I don't shed tears," Tibbets said.

"Come on," I said.

"What good do tears do?" he said.

"Even in private?" I said. "Even for these two men? I don't believe you."

"Maybe I'll wipe my nose," he said, and grinned at me, meaning: Change the subject.

I ran into Ferebee a little later. He asked me what I had been talking to Tibbets about, and I hesitated for a few seconds and then I repeated what he had told me.

"It's probably the truth," Ferebee said. "Paul probably won't shed a single tear. It's just his way."

Van Kirk had invited me to come by sometime during the day, and I had been looking forward to it. Wry, constantly observant, seemingly filled with a full sense of life's dark absurdities, and of blessings disguised as disappointments, he appeared to me to be both of the crew and outside it—he, more than Tibbets or Ferebee, had the air of looking at the three of them, including himself, from a certain remove.

When I arrived at his place, he told me that he was in no hurry—that he had all afternoon to talk. I looked at him—this pleasant-faced man who had been born in Northumberland, Pennsylvania, in 1921, who had navigated the *Enola Gay* to Japan at the age of twenty-four, who had earned a degree in chemical engineering from Bucknell University and who had gone on to work for DuPont for thirty-six years, finishing his career as a district manager on the West Coast—and I tried to envision him on that August midnight in 1945. What must have been going through his mind—being in charge of getting that plane to a place no one on board had ever flown before?

"We took off from Tinian at 2:45 A.M.," he said. "Total darkness, of course—we knew it was going to be about two and a half hours to Iwo Jima."

"Where were you physically?" I said.

"In the B-29, when you're the navigator you sit up in the end of a tunnel across the top of the bomb bays," he said. "So you're sitting there alone, and you look around, and you've pretty much already made up your mind about which stars you're going to use to set your course."

"And it was all done by hand back then?" I asked.

"A hand-held bubble sextant," Van Kirk said. "You select your star, and you get it in the middle of the bubble . . ."

There were books on board, he said—a series of them—to translate the positioning of the aircraft in relation to the stars: to let the navigator know whether his airplane was on course.

"How many times back then—not just on that flight, but on your B-17 flights in Europe—did you ask yourself, 'What am I doing here? How did I get here?'" I asked him.

"You know, I don't think I ever asked myself that question," he said. "Not then."

The dawn, he said, was lovely to behold. "That morning was just a beautiful sunrise morning," he said. "The colors . . . The sun came up just before we got to Iwo."

And once he had daylight, getting the airplane to Japan on schedule was no problem. The *Enola Gay* arrived on time, Tibbets turned the controls over to Ferebee, Ferebee guided it through his bombsight . . .

And then?

"What I probably saw was kind of a flash in the airplane," Van Kirk said. "Sort of like a photographer's bulb. And the sound . . . the best way I can describe it to you is that it sounded like a piece of sheet metal rolling. That *snapping* sound.

"At first I thought that they were shooting at us from the ground. But it was the shock waves. With the shock waves and that rolling metal sound from the bomb, it felt and sounded very much like a bunch of flak used to sound when we were flying the B-17s over Europe. And there was that white cloud."

"Do you recall being able to put any thoughts together?" I said.

"A sense of relief," he said. "You've been training for this for six or seven months—all of the training for this one flight—and you've carried it out, and there was just this sense of relief. It had happened.

"It had happened, and even though you were still up there in the air and no one else in the world knew what had happened, you just sort of had a sense that the war was over, or would be soon. And that you could go home."

"You all knew that?" I asked.

"I think so," he said. "I think we knew."

"Did you show it?" I said.

"Do you mean celebrate?" Van Kirk said. "No.

There was no celebration. You were trained not to do something like that. I don't think that people back then were as demonstrative as they are today—and we certainly were trained not to be that way on our missions. Think about the era we grew up in. Babe Ruth would hit a home run and he would run around the bases and that would be it.

"You didn't show much. You took pride in being disciplined."

I asked him if, when he had first met Tibbets, he had sensed that they would end up as lifelong friends.

"Well . . ." Van Kirk said. "I think, number one, he was a captain and I was a brand-new second lieutenant. I regarded him as very exacting and capable—but as a friend? Not at first. He was twenty-seven when I met him, but if you'd asked me at the time, I would have thought he was sixty years old.

"The way he carried himself, the experience he had . . . compared to other squadron commanders, Paul Tibbets was so consistently no-nonsense. . . .

"For a long time, our relationship was one where he was our commanding officer, which was really not the same thing as being our friend. We flew with him—and it's hard to even explain to you just what an excellent pilot Paul was. He could do things with an airplane that I never saw anyone do in my life.

"I've looked at Paul over the years, and I've listened to him talk to other pilots. I think he just understands the dynamics of an airplane, how they fly, more than other people. I'm not even sure if *he* is aware of how far above other people's feel for airplanes his feel is.

"But you were asking about when the real friendship started. I think that we started getting closer to each other on a flight when we took Mark Clark to Gibraltar, and then when we took Eisenhower to Gibraltar. You're together so much, you're washing your clothes together, you become friends.

"But it wasn't until after I'd left the service that I called him 'Paul.' "

"You didn't call him by his first name?" I said.

"Oh, no," Van Kirk said. "Never in the service, and not for years after I was out of the service. Even when I had been out for a while, and I would see him, I would address him by his rank."

"And would he do the same with you?" I asked.

"No," he said. "I was always 'Dutch' to him."

"What about on the airplane?" I said. "What would you call him on a mission, when you were on the intercom?"

"It was always 'Navigator to pilot,' " Van Kirk said. "That's who we were, on that airplane."

Tibbets, it seemed to me, always operated under the assumption that the world did not really understand what he and his crew had done on the Hiroshima mission, and why they had done it; Ferebee seemed almost not to care what the world thought.

And Van Kirk?

"I think that if people take the time to research it, and think about it, then they do understand the mission," he said. "The majority of the world will not do that—but the people who do look into the history of it, I think, will at least have some understanding of what we were trying to do, and why we were sent to do it.

"Paul says he has had some pretty bad reactions from people over the years, but I personally have never had any venomous phone calls or anything like that. Oh, you'll get questions—one girl one time asked me, 'Don't you feel bad?,' and that pretty much sums up what is on people's minds who disagree with the mission. And yes, if you were a resident of Hiroshima, you would have a very different feeling about the mission than if you were a member of the family of a person whose life we saved by hastening the end of the war."

"So you don't resent people who have doubts about what you and the crew did?" I asked.

"Of course not," Van Kirk said. "It's reasonable to have doubts about what we did. There are pros and cons to what we did—and I don't think anyone, in good conscience, can say that it's wrong to have doubts."

"How about you?" I asked.

"Do I have doubts?" he said.

"Yes," I said.

"I don't," he said. "I never have. It's never bothered me any. I really think it was a necessary act."

"The most violent act in the history of the world," I said.

"But I don't think we were violent people," he said. "I was twenty-four when I flew the mission, and to the best of my memory, I had never had a fistfight in my life.

"You can ask yourself, 'Gee, why did this happen, gee, why did that happen?' I've asked myself that. And I always come up with the same answer: that what we did was for the overall good."

I asked him—as I knew I would—the question I had asked Ferebee and Tibbets. The question about what he envisioned it would be like when there would no longer be three of them.

"When the first of us dies?" he said. "That'll hit me pretty hard. I've lost a fair number of friends. Some in the last few years. That's what happens when you get to be our age.

"But if it's Paul or Tom? I like to think that I handle things pretty well."

I told him what Tibbets had said. I told him that Tibbets had vowed that he would not shed a tear.

"I'm sure he did say that," Van Kirk said. "Paul

will never let on. That doesn't mean that it won't be doing the same thing inside to him that it would do to Tom or me. It just means that he'll never let on. He's telling you the truth."

"And you?" I said.

"I'll feel it a lot," he said. "I won't be able to hide it, but then, I won't want to hide it. That's how Paul and I are different. For whatever reason, he'll choose to hide it."

Before I left Van Kirk's room, I asked him if he ever thought about how he and the crew would be remembered two hundred or three hundred years from now.

"You tell me how the world's going to be at that period of time," he said. "And I'll tell you how the people will think of us."

"What do you mean?" I said.

"I hope the world two hundred years from now is a peaceful world," he said. "If it is, then I think people will look back at the atomic bomb and think of it as something that helped the world evolve toward a lasting peace."

"And if the world isn't peaceful?" I said.

"If it isn't," he said, "people will be tossing atomic bombs around like they're going out of style."

• • •

Just before we sat down to dinner that night in the clubhouse of the condo development, I saw Gerry Newhouse and David Bean whispering to one of the waiters.

I walked over. Bean was saying, in the softest of voices, "Please clear his plate as soon as he finishes his food. Right away."

I asked him what was going on. "General Tibbets is a real stickler about dirty plates," he said. "He doesn't want the plate in front of him once he's done with what's on it."

Newhouse said that at one restaurant on one trip, "The waiter was slow coming around to clear the plates, so Paul got up and cleared the table himself. Every plate—he removed them from the table and walked them over to a tray."

I found myself smiling, and thinking about my father in restaurants—how sensitive he was to what he perceived as even the slightest inattentiveness or lack of diligence in service. Organize, delegate, supervise, check—and, in Tibbets' case, if, when you checked, everything didn't check out just right, the next step was to bus the dirty plates yourself.

Dinner was quieter tonight—the group was smaller, even with the inclusion of the Lennon Brothers, who had accepted an invitation to join us (the Lennon Sisters were said to be working and unavailable). And after the meal, there was to be a presentation of sorts.

Tibbets—for the edification of the Lennon Brothers—was going to speak about the *Enola Gay* mission. Gerry Newhouse had brought along a videotape—an educational documentary about the flight—and Tibbets had asked him to show it following dinner. He would answer questions afterward.

So we went to a small meeting room, and Tibbets—appearing a little keyed up—entered first, and said with some concern to Newhouse: "Where's the projector?"

Newhouse explained that a VCR was hooked up to a television set in the room; no movie projector would be necessary.

"We'll take a count," Tibbets said, meaning that Newhouse was not to start the videotape until everyone from dinner was present and accounted for.

There weren't many of us—beside the crew and their wives, there was Paul IV and Angele, there were some relatives of Angele, there was an aunt of Gerry Newhouse's wife, there were a few executives from the development company that owned the condos. And there were the Lennon Brothers.

Tibbets made sure that everyone was in the room and seated, and then—to an audience of fifteen—began to explain the end of World War II.

"We're not quite as bad as some people have depicted us," he said, standing at the front. "In fact, we think that we're pretty good citizens."

Van Kirk and Ferebee looked as if they might be here under duress—not only had they seen this video before, but they had been on the flight of the *Enola Gay*, this wasn't exactly new to them—yet they did not stir from their chairs; Tibbets was the commanding officer, and this was a command performance. The video played, and then the lights came up, and Tibbets said he was available to answer questions.

Someone asked him if he had ever had any doubt that the mission would succeed. He cleared his throat; even though he had been with these people all through dinner, and with some of them all through the weekend, he had assigned himself the role of orator tonight, and spoke formally.

"I was so confident," he said. "There was no question, it would be done. I can fly an airplane from Point A to Point B."

Had he ever given any thought to entering politics?

"They wanted me to run for governor of Florida after I came back from the war," he said. "But I said no. I wanted to fly airplanes."

He was briefing—briefing these fifteen people, briefing the Lennon Brothers. Someone asked him what he thought of Paul IV as a pilot, and Tibbets said, "My grandson knows more than I ever knew or will ever know about the operation of airplanes. But I'll tell you one thing: He'll never have as much fun flying an airplane as I did."

There weren't many questions, and within a few minutes we headed back to our units. I ended the evening in Van Kirk's room; someone had brought a bottle of wine, and Ferebee was trying to get it open, but couldn't quite figure the cork out. Fifteen minutes into trying, the bottle still stayed shut tight, and there they were, on a warm Missouri night fifty years and more after their war, and I saw Van Kirk shoot an amused look at Ferebee, and Ferebee shake his head in frustration as he kept twisting at the bottle's neck.

TWENTY-EIGHT

For our last day in Branson, Tibbets had planned a cookout lunch with hamburgers, hot dogs and cold soda pop, but it rained in the morning, so we gathered in his living room and had cold cuts inside. This would be it for the trip; the three men would be going their separate ways at the end of the weekend.

That Thing You Do!, the Tom Hanks–directed movie about a one-hit rock band in 1964, played silently on a cable channel on the television set against one wall, while the men fixed themselves sandwiches and talked of an even earlier time. Ferebee was telling the others about an occasion just after the Bay of Pigs—he was still in the service then—when he had met President John F. Kennedy at an air base. I asked him if there had been the feeling of electricity around Kennedy that we have read and heard about for so long—that special quality that people still analyze and reminisce over.

"No," Ferebee said. "He looked sick. When you saw his face up close, he looked like a sick person who had been under a sun lamp."

There was nothing much planned for the day, and the weather was unpromising. After lunch everyone drifted off on their own, with plans to get together early in the evening for the one event that had been scheduled: The Shoji Tabuchi Show.

Shoji Tabuchi had become the entertainment phenomenon of Branson. Born in the Japanese city of Daishoji, raised in Osaka, he had begun taking violin lessons at the age of seven. When Tabuchi was in college in Osaka, American country-and-western musician Roy Acuff, famed for his appearances on *The Grand Ole Opry*, was visiting Japan, and performed in a show that Tabuchi attended. The young man was mesmerized, especially by the song "Listen to the Mockingbird."

He told his parents that he wanted to become a country-and-western musician. He moved to the United States, got a job as a waiter in Japanese restaurants and worked part-time polishing cars. He eventually was hired to play fiddle in a country band at the Starlite Club in Riverside, Missouri, and in 1968 ran into Roy Acuff again. He told Acuff about the time he had seen him perform in Japan; Acuff invited him to come to Nashville and look him up, and Tabuchi did just that. Acuff arranged for Tabuchi to perform a song on stage at the old Ryman Auditorium, home of the Opry, where audience members greeted him warmly.

He moved to Kansas, where during the days he worked in a hospital's X-ray laboratory and at night played in a country music club. By the mid-1970s he was touring as a backup musician for a country singer, and eventually ended up in Branson. He set a goal for himself: to become so popular in the town that he could some day be the featured performer in his own theater. The tourists who came to Branson fell in love with the Japanese violinist who put on the country show, and in 1990 he built his 2,000-seat Shoji Tabuchi Theatre.

It became the hottest ticket in Branson; the word-of-mouth was like nothing anyone in the city of 3,700 had ever encountered, and soon enough Tabuchi was selling out almost 400 shows a year. People would return to their hometowns and would give their neighbors a two-word piece of advice about what to do when they took their own trips to Branson: "See Shoji."

The recommendation had gotten to Tibbets, Ferebee and Van Kirk: No visit to Branson would be complete unless they saw the Shoji show.

And so they had made their plans for the evening: dinner at a steakhouse, followed by Shoji Tabuchi's performance.

We ate hurriedly, and then David Bean drove his van to the front of the Shoji Tabuchi Theatre—where staff members were waiting outside to greet Tibbets and the crew, to guide Bean's van to a special roped-off area of the pavement within steps of the theater entrance, to escort us to a private room where we could wait before going into the auditorium itself. Three steps into the theater building and we all knew that this was a different Branson than anything we had seen before.

The lobby was breathtaking, elegant, like a new version of one of the movie palaces of the 1930s—a place designed to make its customers feel like royalty for a few hours. There was a hush; the men and women who were finding their way to their seats spoke softly, reverentially, as if by instinct. Women were telling their husbands to please wait for just a minute—they wanted to get a look at the famous rest rooms (word around town was that each rest room, men's and women's, had been decorated at a cost of $250,000, although a Tabuchi Theatre staff member told us that figure was low). The capacity crowd that was arriving was treating the edifice as if it were an art museum.

Which seemed to be the point—the people who were running this place clearly understood that separating the Tabuchi Theatre, and the Shoji show, from everything else in Branson could only be good for business. We were taken to the private waiting area, so that we could go to our seats inside the theater at the very last minute; chairs had been reserved for Tibbets, Van Kirk and Ferebee so they would not have to stand. Tibbets sat down, and a woman— she appeared to be a relative of a theater staff member, and, like everyone we had seen so far, was not Japanese or Japanese-American—approached him

and said she would be honored if he would hold
her baby.

She handed the baby to Tibbets. Tibbets looked
the baby in the face; the baby looked Tibbets in the
face.

Lights blinked in the lobby, and we were told
that it was time for us to go to our seats.

A staff member said to me that the management
of the Tabuchi Theatre would be grateful if Tibbets,
Van Kirk and Ferebee could sit together, right next
to each other.

I told this to Ferebee as we were walking down
the aisle toward our row.

"Why?" he said to me. "So they can shoot us?"

The show was . . .
Well, it was Las Vegas minus the drinks and
sex and dirty jokes, but it was more than that. There
were lasers, there was smoke and mist, there were
fireworks and dancers and computer-timed stage-
craft. There were musicians all over the place—the
theater, we were told, employs two hundred people—and above all there was a sense of unending
bigness. And into this—the lights, the colors, the
pyrotechnics, the coming-at-you-from-every-corner
sound—strode Shoji Tabuchi.

He was a tall man dressed in combination Elvis/
Liberace; before he was two feet onto the stage the
crowd was standing and shouting. He carried his

violin in one hand, he wore a broad smile that registered even in the back rows of the cavernous theater, and his first words—heavily accented, much more so than you would expect from a man who had been living in the United States for so many years—were:

"How many people are first time in this theater?"

He waited for the show of hands.

"Whoa!" he called out. "Where you been?"

And lifted the violin to his shoulder and began to sing a spirited rendition of the old Louisiana-Texas rouser "Jambalaya."

Hank Williams and Bob Wills by way of Osaka, and at one point balloons and confetti came drifting down from the ceiling—there was never a second during the Shoji show when something wasn't going on—and I looked over at the crew, and their eyes were riveted on the stage, and it was much too loud for me to say anything to them.

There was everything—show tunes, classical, bluegrass, Cajun, rock and roll, gospel, polka—and the show barely stopped to exhale. During a section of the performance devoted to nostalgia for the 1950s there was a big replica of an I LIKE IKE button on the wall, and before one part of the show in which Japanese music was played, Shoji said to the cheering audience, "We thought you'd like to see a little different culture."

Then: "And now we'll take you to Hawaii. I wonder how many of you folks have been to Hawaii?"

Dutch Van Kirk raised his hand.

He had told me before of visiting the memorial at Pearl Harbor, but I had no idea whether that was what was on his mind at this moment, or if he was merely responding to the I-ask-it-every-night question of the show's star.

As I looked around at the people in the audience, there was no escaping what was going on here: In a contemporary American culture built on the new concepts of "edge" and "attitude" and "in-your-face," a culture that seemed to constantly devalue the literal in favor of the jabbingly off-angle, here, in Branson, Shoji Tabuchi had discovered, and was prospering from, something quite basic:

There was a huge, largely uncatered-to American audience—many of them from the World War II generation—who were starving for an old form of entertainment: welcoming, courteous, based on the assumption that the people in the seats were ladies and gentlemen. Earlier in the day I had spoken with my mother on the phone; she had said that she and a friend were planning to go to a movie in Columbus this night, and that she was trying to select "a nice one—not upsetting."

I understood. And so, clearly, although he had never met her, did Shoji Tabuchi. He treated his audience with unending respect—not just during the performance, but from the moment they walked into his building. Much of the rest of American society these days—everything from MTV to crudely suggestive situation comedies to the sardonic, dizzying, rapid-cut nature of many television commercials—might have seemed foreign to many members of this audience, but Tabuchi's stage show felt like home. Like a place with which they had somehow lost touch, a place they missed.

"Are you having a good time tonight?" Shoji called from the stage.

They answered with applause.

"Good!" he called, beaming, and picked up his violin to give them more.

At intermission I went out to see the rest room. It was everything I had heard. In the men's room there was a pool table, there were leather armchairs, there was a spectator section in case anyone wanted to watch the pool players. There was marble everywhere, and fresh flowers, and a long line outside—not because there was a paucity of facilities inside for the guests to use, but because once the men arrived, they tended to stay a while to absorb it all, as if at an exhibit of some sort. Many men talked animatedly to friends about the lavishness of the room; some were taking snapshots.

When I left—intending to walk over to observe the line in front of the ladies' room—I noticed someone midway back in the long line waiting to get into the Shoji Tabuchi men's room:

Tibbets.

He was by himself, and remained so as the line moved slowly forward.

Following intermission the pace of the Shoji show intensified—there was one part in which gigantic Japanese ceremonial Taiko drums were played, one of them weighing a ton and having been purchased at a cost of more than $200,000—and then Tabuchi himself stepped to the front of the stage and the music stopped.

"Thank you," he said to the audience. "We have some very, very special guests here with us in the theater tonight."

The customers in their seats looked around, as did the musicians with Tabuchi on the stage, not knowing to whom he was referring.

"They are the original flight crew of the *Enola Gay*," Tabuchi said.

There was applause, tentative at first—as if the audience was surprised—and then building in volume and in duration.

"They have been in town for the last several days," Tabuchi said, "and we are very honored to have them here tonight."

He gestured from the stage to the row in which we were sitting.

"Would you mind standing up, please?" he said.

The three crewmen did; this is why the theater personnel had wanted them to sit together.

"Brigadier General Paul Tibbets," Tabuchi said, with great flourish, into the microphone. "General Tibbets served our country for twenty-nine years in the military. . . ."

And it was, indeed, "our country" for Tabuchi. He had become a United States citizen in recent years; when Tibbets and the crew had dropped the atomic bomb on Hiroshima, Tabuchi had been a child in Japan, but now he was an American.

"Major Dutch Van Kirk. . . ." Tabuchi said.

As he read the names, staff members of the theater came up the aisle with gifts and flowers for the crew and the women in the party.

"Also, Colonel Tom Ferebee. . . ." Tabuchi announced.

The crewmen were on their feet, accepting the presents and letting the applause wash over them.

"These men have served our country with great loyalty and honor," Tabuchi told his audience. And then, directly to the three crewmen:

"We are so glad to have you here."

There was one more sustained ovation, and then the show continued. At the end, Tabuchi said to the packed house:

"America will always be the place where every one of your dreams can come true. Thank you for being with us tonight."

He raised his violin and began to play "The Impossible Dream," as the audience stood and cheered him.

We had been invited to meet Tabuchi after the show. Ushers came to our row and led us to a flight of stairs, which we climbed until we were in a lounge area near his dressing room.

There were snacks and beverages and a cake; Tabuchi was taking a few minutes to rest after his performance, so for a while it was just us in the room, standing around, not quite sure what was expected. There was some small talk between the crew and the theater staff, and then Shoji entered and walked from person to person, shaking hands.

We had been sitting far enough back in the theater that I wasn't sure whether Tabuchi, on stage with the spotlights in his eyes, had been able to see the faces of the men he was introducing to the audience; now, as he circulated through the room, he seemed to be trying to determine who was who. He approached Tom Ferebee, who extended his hand and said to Tabuchi:

"I'm one of 'em."

The two men spoke briefly, and then a theater employee took Tabuchi over to meet Tibbets. "This is my grandson, Paul," Tibbets said. "He flies the B-2."

"Glad to meet you," Tabuchi said to the young aviator.

There was a small silence, and Tabuchi said to Tibbets, "How long will you be in town for?"

"I apologize for my hearing," Tibbets said.

In this low-ceilinged room he was having trouble making out words, so the pilot of the *Enola Gay* was saying he was sorry to his Japan-born host—sorry for not being able to understand him.

A photographer from the theater staff said that he would like to take a picture of the three crewmen with Tabuchi. As he prepared his camera, he said, "I need for you all to turn around."

Van Kirk, joking with him, said: "The proper word is 'About face.'"

As the four men posed, Van Kirk said to Tabuchi, "You put on a great show."

"Thank you," Tabuchi said, and began to discuss with the crew the traditional foods of Louisiana.

When the photographer was finished, Tabuchi and Tibbets went to a part of the room where Tibbets might be able to hear a little better. Tabuchi spoke of war—of how countries down through history have always fought, and how sometimes the fighting even breaks out within.

"Inside the country," Tabuchi said, referring to the Civil War, "the United States, North and South, fight . . ."

"I understand, " Tibbets said. "We know that."

"My mom and dad," Tabuchi said, "they are from—where they were born—was the prefecture right next to Hiroshima. And my mom, after the bomb, they were told to move. Because of the cloud. They did not know what kind of bomb . . ."

This, Tibbets was hearing. He was staring straight into Tabuchi's eyes.

"Actually," Tabuchi said, talking of the days after the bomb fell, "my mom carried me on her shoulder, and my brother in a . . ."

He stopped, not able to come up with the right English word.

"In a . . ." he said.

"Carriage?" Tibbets said.

"Yes," Tabuchi said. "Carriage."

"OK," Tibbets said.

". . . to go into the mountainside, to get away," Tabuchi said.

He told Tibbets his father had said that had the war continued, "all would have died"; that his father had said the end of the war spared the lives of "men, women, children" all over Japan.

Tibbets said, "In 1959, I was fortunate enough to have as a guest in my house the man who led the airplanes on the attack on Pearl Harbor. Mitsuo Fuchida."

Tabuchi nodded.

"He was a fine man," Tibbets said. "As warriors, we understood each other."

"I am very, very honored to have you here," Tabuchi said.

"I've enjoyed every moment of it, and to make your acquaintance was very nice," Tibbets said. "I hope our paths will cross again."

It was late when we got back to where we were staying. Mrs. Van Kirk was not feeling well; the evening had been long, there had been a lot of walking and climbing, and the consequences of her stroke were more distinct than usual. David Bean drove his van close to the unit where the Van Kirks were staying, and Dutch helped his wife inside and told the rest of us that they were just going to turn in.

The Ferebees said that they were tired, too; we all made our goodnights. Paul IV stood and talked to his grandfather in the parking lot for a few minutes, but then they, too, went to their separate rooms.

I had trouble falling asleep, and when I woke up in the middle of the night I realized that Sunday had turned to Monday. I was going to be leaving before the rest of them; a car was supposed to pick me up right after dawn to take me to the airport in Springfield for the first leg of the trip back to Chicago.

When the alarm radio went off I got dressed, and then walked outside. It was still dark. I knew they'd all be sleeping; I knew that I would not be seeing them before I left.

I walked to each of their doors; I just stood there

for a second. No lights inside any of the three places; not a sound to be heard. I was the only person up and about, my footsteps echoed on the little sidewalk that connected the condominiums, and I wasn't sure why I was doing this. But I stood in front of each of the three doors, and on this Memorial Day morning I thought about the men on the other side, and I knew that this would have to serve as my farewell.

The car arrived right on time, and as the sun came up I departed.

TWENTY-NINE

My father's voice, on the tape he gave to us, describing the day of his return from the war:

We disembarked from our troop ship and got on trucks for that glorious ride back to Camp Patrick Henry, where the welcoming flags were waving and the girls were blowing kisses and people were throwing flowers. . . .

We went through a few requirements when we got back there, and they gave us a huge steak dinner, and I had fresh milk for the first time in eighteen months—which made me deathly sick! But I got well enough to get on a troop train for that long, sooty railroad ride to somewhere in Indiana. The name of the camp in Indiana, or the fort, where we were to be mustered out escapes me at this moment, but I had gotten word to your mother to meet me there, where I would be for only twenty-four to forty-eight hours, and then, by God, it was over.

So that train ride was, I think, the longest that I've experienced in my life. Finally we got to this camp and the train slowly wound around until we stopped and got off, and marched to our quarters and started the first of a few hours of being debriefed and demobilized. Phyllis had driven the same blue/gray Pontiac all the way from Columbus to the camp to pick me up, and that reunion was something that happens to a man only once in a lifetime, and I shall never forget it as long as I live. All the months of mud . . .

He and she headed for home; they wanted to stop off and see his parents.

We drove her Pontiac, and I was relishing all the scenery of Ohio, because it had been in my mind for all of those long months. Of course the first thing we did was drive to Akron to see my mother and father. They were ecstatic, and believe me, we all said a lot of prayers.

I think we stayed there a day or so. . . . I tried to make a deal with the Ford people from whom I had bought the flying omelette lo those many five years before, and had had to give it up because there was no way for me to pay for it. And it so happens that I was very hung over and was shaking like a leaf when we went into that Ford agency, and the salesman was kind of rough, and Dad, bless him, came through. He said, "Do you know what this boy has been through? Just look at him."

Of course my hands were shaking and I was shaking but it was not because of what I went through, it was because I had a terrible hangover. But the guy gave me a car—didn't give it to me, but permitted me to buy one—and that's the situation as it was in the early fall of 1945.

He went back to work for the company that had hired him before he entered the Army; he would end up staying with that company for his entire career, becoming its president before his retirement. My brother, my sister and I would be born; he and my mother would remain a couple until the night he died.

All of that would come later, though. Right now, the war had just been won, and he was home.

His voice on the tape:

I think it's about time to wind this up, but before doing so I think that I ought to speak about goals. I really never was goal-oriented, one of my many faults was and is my habit, if you will, to ad lib my way through life, being lucky most of the time to get away with it.

However, as a kid I did have certain dreams, among which were to be happily married to an understanding, tolerant, intelligent, beautiful and loving woman, to be blessed with happy children, to be a good son to my parents, to be as successful as possible in all of my endeavors, to realize my ambitions, some modest, some a little more ambitious, such as being a good provider for my family. . . .

To live a good, long, full life, to be respected by my peers, to keep what sense of humor I had. . . .

And here were his very last words on the tape— in which he recalled what his earliest hopes had been when, as a child, he had looked out the schoolroom window and had wished for the grandest that life could ever offer:

. . . to serve my country, and to realize a little boy's dream of walking up that diagonal path at King School, after a war, in full uniform, with the love of my life, your mother, on my arm.

ACKNOWLEDGMENTS

There were many people who helped me along the way in the writing of this book, and I'd like to thank them here.

At Morrow/Avon, the professionalism under intense deadline pressure of Tom Dupree and his assistant, Kelly Notaras, made my job much easier. My special gratitude goes to Hamilton Cain and Lou Aronica, whose early support and enthusiasm were indispensable to this project.

At Janklow & Nesbit, Eric Simonoff's unfailing advice, counsel and creativity, as well as his friendship, were and are a constant source of value and enjoyment to me. To Mort Janklow, as always, go my thanks, friendship and great appreciation.

At the *Chicago Tribune*, the men and women with whom I work made the dual tasks of writing a daily newspaper column while writing this book possible. My thanks to Howard Tyner, Ann Marie Lipinski, Gerould Kern, Janet Franz, Joe Leonard, Geoff Brown, Tim Bannon, Kaarin Tisue, Jeff Lyon, Linda Bergstrom, Chris Rauser, Marjorie David, Nadia Cowen, Jim Musser, Tom Hinz, Marsha Peters, Stacy Deibler and Ben Estes. Off the newsroom floors, my continuing thanks go to John Madigan, Jack Fuller, Scott Smith, Owen Youngman and

David Williams. My special gratitude goes to two young women who worked with me at the *Tribune* during the period of my writing this book and who, through their diligence and attention to detail, helped me in large ways and small in getting my work done: Kim Miller and Aimee Nieves. Bill Hageman, who worked closely with me during the editing of the newspaper series that resulted from my first conversations with Paul Tibbets, is as fine an editor as any reporter can ever hope for.

At *Life* magazine, Isolde Motley and Marilyn Johnson have been a constant pleasure to work with.

The staff of the United States Air Force Museum, and the officers, enlisted men and women, and staff of Wright-Patterson Air Force Base were courteous and extremely helpful. To the surviving members of the Doolittle Raiders, and to their families, go not only my thanks, but my deepest admiration.

Gerry Newhouse, his wife Judy and their children could not have treated me with any more thoughtfulness and generosity had I been a member of their family. The military career retrospective that General Tibbets had privately printed some thirty years ago, and that Gerry Newhouse, who himself served as a Marine corporal during the Vietnam war, has kept updated and privately in print, was an invaluable source of research material;

for any reader who has enjoyed this book, I highly recommend it. For information on *Flight of the Enola Gay* (later retitled as *Return of the Enola Gay*), as well as information about lithographs and photographs pertaining to the flight, readers may contact Mr. Newhouse in care of his office at 1620 E. Broad Street, Room 106, Columbus, Ohio 43203.

To help me in writing with as much factual precision as possible about events that took place during my father's time in Africa and Italy more than fifty years ago, surviving soldiers from that era were exceedingly generous with their time and recollections. I would like to give special mention and thanks to two men in particular, both members of the 91st Infantry Division during World War II: Roy Livengood, who in 1943, at the age of eighteen, joined the Army out of his hometown of Concordia, Kansas, and who was awarded a Purple Heart for injuries sustained during combat in Italy; and David Hathaway who also joined the Army in 1943 at the age of eighteen out of his hometown of Grantsville, West Virginia, and who, like Mr. Livengood, was awarded a Purple Heart. Any time I had a question about a date, a place or an incident that occurred overseas during the 91st's time there, they were tireless in their willingness to go over their own records and memories in an effort to come up with the answers.

To Paul Tibbets, Dutch Van Kirk, Tom Ferebee and their families, any words I might attempt to use here to express the depth of my thanks would be insufficient. So I will just say that I will never forget a moment of the time I have spent with them, and that I hope this book has conveyed that time in a way they will find fair and accurate.

ABOUT THE AUTHOR

Bob Greene is a syndicated columnist for the *Chicago Tribune* and columnist for *Life* magazine. His reports and commentary appear in more than two hundred newspapers in the United States, Canada and Japan, and can be read daily at www.chicagotribune.com/go/greene. As a broadcast journalist he has served as contributing correspondent for *ABC News Nightline*.

His bestselling books include **Be True to Your School; Hang Time: Days and Dreams with Michael Jordan; Good Morning, Merry Sunshine**; and, with his sister, D. G. Fulford, **To Our Children's Children: Preserving Family Histories for Generations to Come**.

His first novel, **All Summer Long**, was published in a new paperback edition this spring; his latest collection of journalism, **Chevrolet Summers, Dairy Queen Nights**, will be published in paperback by HarperCollins early next year.